Fourth Wave
in Science Fiction

Fourth Wave Feminism
in Science Fiction and Fantasy

*Volume 2. Essays on Television
Representations, 2013–2019*

Edited by VALERIE ESTELLE FRANKEL

McFarland & Company, Inc., Publishers
Jefferson, North Carolina

ISBN (print) 978-1-4766-7767-5
ISBN (ebook) 978-1-4766-3866-9

Library of Congress and British Library
cataloguing data are available

Front cover (from left): Mandip Gill, Tosin Cole, Jodie Whittaker
(in the title role as the Thirteenth Doctor), Bradley Walsh
and Sharon D Clarke in a 2018 episode of *Doctor Who* (BBC/Photofest)

Printed in the United States of America

*McFarland & Company, Inc., Publishers
Box 611, Jefferson, North Carolina 28640
www.mcfarlandpub.com*

Contents

Introduction   1

Section I: Fighting Authority

"Praise Be!" Power and Resistance in Hulu's *The Handmaid's Tale*
    K. JAMIE WOODLIEF   19

Scattered Stories of Embodied Resistance: *Sense8, Orphan Black*
    and Queer Cultural Production
    AUDREY JANE BLACK   30

Section II: Warriors in a Respectful World

Wynonna Earp, Supergirl and the Power of Choosing
    RESA HAILE   49

"The gods will always smile on the brave women": Exploring
    the Heroines of History Channel's *Vikings*
    STEVEN B. FRANKEL   62

Reclaiming Power from the Toxic Male: Support and Recovery
    in *Marvel's Jessica Jones*
    VALERIE ESTELLE FRANKEL   75

Section III: Intersectionality

From Sidekick to Romantic Lead: Rise of the Strong Black
    Woman
    SUMIKO SAULSON   93

Revisionist History and Intersectional Feminism in *DC's Legends
    of Tomorrow*
    KATHERINE MCLOONE   110

The Problematic White Woman in *Black Mirror*'s "Crocodile"
  Spinster Eskie   127

"Bloke Utopia": Bill Potts, Queer Identity and Cyborg Narratives
  in *Doctor Who*
  Sarah Beth Gilbert   135

Section IV: Girl-Centric Kids

Rebelling Heroines: Hera, Sabine and Ahsoka in *Star Wars: Rebels*
  Stephenie McGucken   151

DC, Marvel and *Star Wars* for Girls: The Transmedia Online
  Adventures
  Valerie Estelle Frankel   167

Rose Arisen: How the Children's Animated Show *Steven Universe*
  Invented the "Reverse Fridge"
  Josephine L. McGuire   189

About the Contributors   203

Index   205

Introduction

Alongside the rise of internet culture, a new wave of feminism is beginning. It is striking for its two-way discussion in which fan critics change the content of their favorite shows to be more respectful of women and minorities. Indeed, this wave of feminism is also intersectional, merging with queer studies, disability studies, and the goals of different races and nationalities as well as a new global sensibility.

Feminism is famed for arriving in waves. First wave feminists claimed the right to vote. Still, Megan Seely, in her book *Fight Like a Girl*, observes, "significant criticism of the first and second waves—such as concerns about racism, generational tensions, and relevance of issues—continue to be central to the dialogue about the women's movement" (39). These struggles were imperfect but paved the way for more progress. While the 1920s were outspoken, the 1940s offered great strides for women in the workplace (and also fictionally, as Wonder Woman and other powerful superheroines arrived).

The 1950s sent women back into the home and conventionality, with romance fiction taking over. Television debuted in this era, G-rated and family-focused. Famous shows of the time include *I Love Lucy, Father Knows Best, The Donna Reed Show,* and *Leave It to Beaver,* all starring the clichéd perfect housewife. Behind the cameras, women fared as badly or worse. Still, a few stood out.

> Women were a rare sight in writers' rooms during television's infancy in the 1950s, but [Madelyn] Pugh not only sat at the head of the table during *I Love Lucy* production meetings, she's also partly responsible for Lucy's becoming a star at all. She and collaborator Bob Carroll, Jr.—with whom she worked for five decades—helped Lucille Ball develop her radio show into a vaudeville act and then a TV pilot, and were involved in every episode of her 1951–1957 classic sitcom. The duo brought us Ball stomping grapes, testing chocolates, lighting her nose on fire, and swigging Vitameatavegamin [Armstrong].

A moment of 1950s diversity besides Lucy's Cuban husband was seen in *The Beulah Show,* on the radio from 1945 to 1954, and then moving to television

1

where it ran concurrently on ABC for three seasons. Beulah was a house-keeper and cook with the comedy deriving from her being much more clever and competent than her employers were in scenes of covert empowerment, though the show was often criticized for stereotyping.

Science fiction television came early with happy-go-lucky "rocketmen" 1950s' shows like *Tom Corbett Space Cadet, Rocky Jones Space Ranger, Flash Gordon, Space Patrol,* and *Buck Rogers.* Women were often screaming damsels, keeping traditional roles beside the muscled heroes. Still, these women were also, like Lt. Uhura a generation later, serving as officers beside the men. While women on the sitcoms were laughable when they tried to enter the men's work world, the space show women were all skilled and effective. The early anthology show *Science Fiction Theatre* (1955–1957) also featured women scientists (and indeed, some shows specifically tried appealing to mothers, as they were buying the family cereal and entertainment).

The *Flash Gordon* television show was the first portrayal of Dale Arden as a scientist and adventurer in her own right, while some female viewers instead rooted for the tougher Princess Aura. Rocky Jones's navigator and translator Vena spoke 37 languages. In *Tom Corbet,* Dr. Joan Dale was an esteemed science professor. The women were all proficient specialists, experts in their fields, serving beside the men. Even as forties' factory workers returned to the home, science fiction attested that in the future they'd be professionals. "Rocketmen series encouraged girls to look at the emerging Space Age and see themselves as a part of it because, on their TV screens, they already had seen girls and women as a part of it," notes Amy Foster in her essay on the topic (79). As she adds:

> Even though all the leading characters were male, we consistently see female characters in these shows. Crystal Mace and Dale Arden serve alongside the Space Angel and Flash Gordon, respectively, as active and respected members of the team. Mace serves as the team's electronics and communications expert (perhaps an inspiration for Star Trek 's Lt. Uhura). Arden, although she is Flash's girlfriend, is often seen flying the Sky Flash, facing potential death bravely, and even getting into physical fights with the enemy, climbing on the back of one in episode 5, "Akim the Terrible," subduing him with a stun gun, then joining with Flash in breaking Akim's mind-control device [Foster 68].

Besides these women on spaceships, television introduced massive moments of science fiction—when *Forbidden Planet* was broadcast on television, everyone stayed home to watch it. The 1953 *War of the Worlds* film was broadcast in pieces as producers took movie serials and turned them into television shows by adding commercials. Many other serials arrived, like 1934's *The Phantom Empire.* This one had strong women, with adventurers Betsy (played by champion teen trick rider Betsy King Ross), Frankie, and Gene kidnapped into a super-scientific underground empire ruled by the evil

Queen Tika. Unusually, the sidekicks rescue the hero (Gene Autry) far more often than he rescues them. Miss Kitty as the tough-as-nails saloon owner on the record-breaking *Gunsmoke* (1955–1975) also deserves a salute.

Another particular nod in this conventional era must go to Sheena the Jungle Girl, a Golden Age comics favorite who graduated to television from 1955 to 1956. Her ripped minidress might be considered exploitative, but she also gave television quite a jolt as she reigned as jungle queen without needing a man. Likewise, *The Adventures of Superman* (1952–1958) was beloved and surprisingly feminist. Lois often needs rescue, but she's competent and smart. In fact, she's typically the one who chases the story down and finds the villain (thus leading to her capture) while Clark and Jimmy are more useless.

In children's programming, *Shirley Temple's Storybook* shared classic fairytales. *Walt Disney's Disneyland* (1954–1958), a prelude to *The Wonderful World of Disney* (1969–1979) and similar anthology shows, varied with some quite feminist scenes and other very conventional ones, often with movie clips and behind-the-scenes drama. This first prime-time anthology series for children was known for the Davy Crockett craze of 1955, though its feminist marks on history are murkier.

The heroine of *Bewitched* (1964–1972) had far more (magic!) power than her husband and continued to defy his wishes that she give it up in a subversive take on *The Feminine Mystique*. In likewise subtle yet assertive moments, the gothic mothers on *The Addams Family* and *The Munsters* were commanding matriarchs who enjoyed injecting counterculture hints and individuality into their sitcom families.

This subversion also began appearing in nongenre television. *The Lucy Show* (1962–1968) featured Lucille Ball as a strong female character who did not rely on a husband. *Alice, Maud, One Day at a Time*, and *All in the Family* addressed complex social issues. *Petticoat Junction* (1963–1970) was a comedy with sexy presentation, but all the women had the brains. On *Get Smart*, Barbara Feldman was the clever one and the man was the comic relief. *Julia* (1968–1971) was the first sitcom to revolve around a professional, single-mother, African American lead. Shattering even more barriers, it directly addressed her husband's death in Vietnam. *¿Que Pasa, USA?*, the first bilingual sitcom, arrived on PBS in 1977. Other shows also broke ground. "When *The Mary Tyler Moore Show* presented a single (and happy) workin' urban gal in the early '70s, it was considered a trailblazer—one of the rare television shows that portrayed a modern woman without being patronizing" (Armstrong). Meanwhile, *The Carol Burnett Show* and *The Mary Tyler Moore Show* launched Gail Parent as a rare female screenwriter of the era. "Here was something that really dealt with women," she said of the latter. "Suddenly there are episodes about being a bridesmaid and how funny it can be. No one had done that. I loved it. It was a topic that you could get into, as a woman. Watching it was so relatable" (Armstrong). Ethel Winant (1922–2003) likewise got promoted to head of casting at CBS.

> She worked with budding talents like Paul Newman, James Dean, and Zsa Zsa Gabor on *Playhouse 90* and was the casting director on *The Twilight Zone* and *The Mary Tyler Moore Show*. In 1973, CBS named Winant vice president, making her the first female exec at that network, but also the first female TV executive in history [Armstrong].

Slowly arriving was the second wave era of equal rights in the workplace and marches for equality. "Coining the phrase 'the personal is political, the political is personal,' the second wave of the women's movement championed the fight to bring recognition to women's lives" (Seely 42). Women's new strength became echoed in the television and film arriving, especially boundary-breaking science fiction. "With this recognition came conscious-raising groups, speak-outs, marches, rallies, demonstrations, feminist publishing houses and publications, research, women's studies programs at colleges and universities, court battles, and legislative efforts to bring women closer to parity with men" (Seely 42).

Over the next decade, science fiction shows grew more complex as *Star Trek, The Twilight Zone, The Outer Limits,* and *Doctor Who* tackled ethical issues. Gender roles were imperfect: Gene Roddenberry was told to demote the female first officer from the show's pilot to a nurse in a short dress, while *Doctor Who* kept its 34-year-old teacher companion for the show's first two years, and then devolved to decades of screaming teenage damsels needing rescue. Nonetheless, the show creators tended to believe in equality and push boundaries as much as they could. *Star Trek* in particular celebrated a multiracial world with a crew of black, Japanese, Russian, Scottish, and literally alien characters, with Lieutenant Uhura a showcase of nonsegregation and professional respect. "Female fans of the show identified Nichols as one of their role models. The first female African American astronaut, Mae Jemison, noted that seeing Lt. Uhura on television inspired her to dream big and believe that a career in space was possible" (Foster 79). Of course, other sixties fantasy and science fiction shows like *I Dream of Jeannie* were more traditionally gendered.

One real gamechanger was the British television show *The Avengers* (1961–1969). A spy show, it also incorporated some science fiction with futuristic machines like cybernauts and robots plotting to take over. Emma Peel, played by Diana Rigg, was the simultaneously tough and feminine crime fighter in a slinky black catsuit. She was so popular that many TV characters emulated her: *Doctor Who* companion Zoe Heriot (1968–1969) was a karate-chopping supergenius from the future in her own tight suit. There were also detective Honey West, April Dancer, *The Girl from U.N.C.L.E., Mission Impossible,* and *The Champions.* Many action women starred in seventies cop shows, while Pam Grier headlined Blaxploitation films. As action women took their place on small screens, and corresponding big ones, fictional women made great strides in agency and power.

Catwoman and Batgirl on *Batman* (1966–1968) were also delightfully powerful, with Eartha Kitt later taking Catwoman's role for added diversity. After *Batman, Wonder Woman* arrived in 1975, with *The Bionic Woman* and *Charlie's Angels* following the next year. Lynda Carter, a supermodel who nonetheless approached her role with strength and seriousness, was a big hit, especially with little girls. *Electra Woman and Dyna Girl, Spider-Woman,* and *The Secrets of Isis* (originally just called *Isis,* 1975–1977) also arrived around this time, while cartoon Wonder Woman was part of the *Super Friends,* helping to shape a superheroine genre.

In fantasy, *Sabrina the Teenage Witch* and *Nanny and the Professor* both emphasized heroines having fun with magic that made them more powerful than the surrounding mortals. On *Doctor Who* (now more popular than ever and spread to an American audience) feminist companion Sarah Jane Smith (1973–1976) wrote her own dialogue to give her outspoken companion some personality. In *Space: 1999* (1975–1977), Barbara Bain as the brilliant Doctor Helena Russell was very empowered. All these offered new role models for impressionable girls.

The egalitarian *Sesame Street* launched in 1969, while the Muppets attained celebrity status and international recognition through *The Muppet Show* (1976–1981). By the mid–1970s, *Sesame Street* had become a childhood institution and was emphasizing hiring women crew members and adding minorities to the cast. Most endearing puppet characters in both shows were male, but Miss Piggy stood out as defiant and assertive, while the shows taught respect, kindness, and inclusion.

"Saucy working-class television mom Roseanne and single-mom career woman Murphy Brown blurred the line between off-screen and on-screen confidence and power—particularly when single-mom Murphy mocked Vice President Dan Quayle's old-fashioned disapproval of her status," notes Deborah Siegel in her critical work *Sisterhood, Interrupted* (115). Feminism was clearly flourishing in the eighties. Meanwhile, *Soap* (1977–1981) became the first sitcom to feature an openly gay character, Jodie Dallas played by Billy Crystal. Post–*Star Wars,* science fiction was likewise springing ahead, though the two movements didn't always sync. While *Quantum Leap, The Incredible Hulk,* and others were male-centric, many 1980s science fiction shows offered ensemble casts. *Battlestar Galactica* (1978) and *Star Trek: The Next Generation* (1989) celebrated a new era. On the former, the women chatted, but the show spent little time on their personalities or friendships. On the latter, the women played the caring doctor/captain's special friend/teen genius's mom and the ship's counselor/first officer's ex. As such, gender roles were rather conventional, though some guest stars made pointed feminist impressions. Both shows had black male central characters for more representation (with disabled fans appreciative of blind Geordi LaForge). *Next Generation* also had an episode with a gay metaphor, though it ended with the alien character chillingly brainwashed to conform. On *Doctor Who,* 1980s companion Peri Brown (1984–1986) was bikinied, slapped by the Doctor, mind-wiped, and hastily married offscreen, but she was succeeded by Ace (1987–1989), a punk teen who hit aliens with a baseball bat, delighting fans through the show's cancellation in Season 26.

Post-feminism and a conservative Reagan administration were taking their toll. In children's shows, conventional gendering was heavy with the Teenage Mutant Ninja Turtles rescuing their gal-pal April O'Neil with some regularity. Twin cartoons *He-Man and the Masters of the Universe* and *She-Ra: Princess of Power* featured warriors with massive gender stereotyping, from He-Man's bodybuilder muscles to She-Ra's flowing blonde hair and minidress. Shows like *Welcome to Pooh Corner, Dumbo's Circus, Inspector Gadget, Duck Tales,* and especially *The Smurfs* defined the Smurfette Principle—one female sidekick in the predominantly male cast. So went representation. More famously, *The Simpsons* launched in the late 1980s, with conventional gender roles but plenty of subversion as the women were far smarter than the show's men.

The 1990s were the years of third wave feminism, often conflated with girl power. This movement was inspired by the lyrics of Madonna, Riot Grrrl, and the Spice Girls. "Originally, girlpower or *grrrlpower* was the catchword of an underground young radical feminist movement that advocated for the improvement of girls' lives. Emerging in the early 1990s as a blend of punk and feminist politics, it became the first powerful youth movement or political subculture to be organized entirely around young women's concerns," notes Anita Harris in *Future Girl: Young Women in the Twenty-First Century* (16–17). It stressed different paths to empowerment—some of them quite surprising and contradictory. "Third-wave feminism meant that you could be a champion of the downtrodden, a critic of oppression; a dominatrix, and a wearer of hot pink lip gloss all at once. You could be a feminist without believing in the goddess or in the essential goodness of women's culture. If you wanted to be spanked before sex, get married, own a BMW, or listen to misogynist hip-hop music, third wavers claimed, you weren't automatically a traitor to the cause," Siegel explains (143).

The standout fantasy shows of the era are *Buffy the Vampire Slayer* and *Xena: Warrior Princess*. Both are strong, funny, powerful chosen ones, mighty and rarely defeated. They're also fully formed characters who grow and change, surrounded by beloved friends. At the same time, both are glamour girls, dressed to appeal to a male audience while empowering a female one.

Their very show titles are diminutizing. Many more heroines of this style appeared: "Girlpower celebrities include such diverse subjects as Lara Croft, Tank Girl, Buffy the Vampire Slayer, Courtney Love, and the Spice Girls (whose own girlpower heroine was, famously, Margaret Thatcher). They are deemed to embody girlpower because they are outspoken, not afraid to take power, believe in themselves, and run their own lives" (Harris 17). A popular cartoon was *The Powerpuff Girls* with its kindergartener heroines "made of sugar, spice and everything nice." Like Buffy and Xena, they were sweet and pretty with compromised images of strength. "The conflation of empowerment, consumption, and personal appearance suggests that because girls can be both feminine and strong, they can wear whatever they want—frilly pink lace or fishnet stockings—without negating their power," explains Rebecca C. Hains in "Power(Puff) Feminism: The Powerpuff Girls as a Site of Strength and Collective Action in the Third Wave" (217).

Around this time, the Japanese anime series *Sailor Moon* reached an American fandom, launching teens' love for magical girl anime and *shōjo* manga. The action heroines in clever plots inspired similar series, including *Magic Knight Rayearth, Nurse Angel Ririka SOS, Wedding Peach, Saint Tail* and *Pretty Cure*. *Sailor Moon* has been called "the biggest breakthrough" in English-dubbed anime until 1995, when it premiered (Drazen 10–11). With this, American teens were reaching out and exploring programming from other cultures. Multiculturalism, taking center stage in Disney films like *Aladdin* and *Mulan*, was a buzzword.

> Looking to women of color writing in the 1970s and early 1980s as their guides, third wavers wrote prolifically about their multiple and multiplied selves. Race, class, and sexuality in all their updated and "outed" permutations—bisexuality, queerness, biraciality, transgenderism—figured prominently in their musings, but this time, multiculturalism became a jumping-off point for exploring modern multiplicities in all their myriad forms [Siegel 142].

In this spirit, cartoons tried to be less sexist and more educational. Other shows were celebrating the new era with more enlightened diversity. *Looney Tunes* (1930–1969) with male characters being massively violent to one other was reimagined as *Tiny Tunes Adventures*—a 50–50 gender split teaching about recycling and cooperation. Similarly, HBO's *Happily Ever After: Fairy Tales for Every Child* (1995–2000) specifically race- and gender-flipped many bedtime stories to emphasize that a popular one like *Cinderella* should belong to everyone.

Pushing barriers, sitcoms like *Spin City* had gay protagonists, while *L.A. Law* had television's first lesbian kiss, and *Friends* the first lesbian wedding. *Will & Grace* (1998–2006) was credited with helping to get gay marriage legalized in real life. In adult science fiction, more shows of this era blended competent women and minorities into the team (*Star Trek: Deep Space Nine*,

Firefly, Farscape, Babylon 5, Stargate). They were fully nuanced and admirable, sometimes even funny, but somehow a white male generally remained in the lead. Gay characters went almost unseen (*Babylon 5*'s relationship of this type had one lover's personality completely destroyed after a single romantic encounter). Still, the female second-in-commands were powerful and competent, with plots and costumes that didn't drag them through romances or weaken their strength. *Voyager*, the fourth *Star Trek* show, finally put a woman at the helm in 1995.

Other genre shows starred central heroines who came to define the nineties. *The X-Files* with tough Mulder and Scully was particularly beloved. *Charmed* and *Birds of Prey* offered female trios of power. *Lois & Clark: The New Adventures of Superman* (1993–1997) cast her as a hard-bitten reporter happy to trample Clark on her way to a Pulitzer, though she falls for Superman and Lex Luthor in rapid succession. *Witchblade*, also a comics adaptation, stars detective chosen one Sara Pezzini, who bonds with a supernatural glove and a long heritage of feminist power. However, after the 1990s came a backlash that removed the strong heroines, or at least underdressed them. John Kenneth Muir concludes in *The Encyclopedia of Superheroes on Film and Television*, "The premature end of *Witchblade*, along with *Birds of Prey* in the winter of 2002, indicated to some that the 'Dawn of the Woman' era in the superhero genre had entered its twilight, leaving only Buffy, in her seventh and final season, to carry the torch" (544).

The 2000s were full of contradictions, as the previous decade's girl power had gone over well, but some shows instead decided to sideline the heroines. *Star Wars: The Clone Wars* offered Anakin as male hero with Ahsoka, his teen girl sidekick in a tube top. New *Doctor Who* returned in 2006, starring an actual blonde teen pop star as companion. Girl power, it seemed, was still prevalent. Still, spinoffs *Torchwood* and *The Sarah Jane Adventures* offered more multiculturalism along with 50–50 gender splits. *Torchwood* was led by Captain Jack Harkness, a pansexual character from the future who had loving relationships with several men on the show, while Sarah Jane starred as a 60-year-old action heroine. The other stand-out show was the dark, gritty remake of *Battlestar Galactica*. Splitting the power, men and women were all edgy, corrupt, and compelling. Some women were weak or manipulative, but the full spectrum was presented, with several women taking over men's roles from the previous incarnation. *Dark Angel* (2000–2002) and *Terminator: The Sarah Connor Chronicles* (2008–2009) both followed strong superheroines on their quests, while *Stargate: Atlantis* (2004–2009) put a woman in charge of the alien base. For younger viewers, *Wizards of Waverly Place* and *Kim Possible* offered empowerment on the Disney Channel.

Some shows of the era were much more compromised. *Star Trek: Enterprise* (2001–2005) put the Vulcan first officer in a catsuit, weakening her. Joss

Whedon's *Dollhouse* explored consent and AI boundaries through science fictional sex slaves but didn't quite make its point. *Heroes* often presented traditional gender roles with women manipulating the powerful men. The *Buffy* spinoff *Angel* sacrificed its women repeatedly; Olivia of *Fringe* was an unwitting test subject. *True Blood* adapted women's paranormal romance but had too many women stripping for the camera. *Lost* had very strong women but turned Kate (originally conceived as island leader) into the prize in a love triangle while the men became basically godlike. *Legend of the Seeker* (2008–2010), created by the *Xena* staff, spent too much time on the fantasy women's salacious torture. All too often, otherwise strong women made stupid romantic decisions that threw their lives into chaos.

The 2010s, however, began offering something markedly different, something so striking many named it the fourth wave. Suddenly, shows like *Orange Is the New Black* and *How to Get Away with Murder* were appearing, in which all the characters were minorities and celebrated for their backgrounds. In contrast with black sitcoms of the 1970s and 1980s, they emphasized a blended America of shared issues. This began to echo a new consciousness of inequality, spurred especially by internet-created international communities. "Fourth-wave feminism is queer, sex-positive, trans-inclusive, body-positive, and digitally driven," explains Constance Grady of *Vox Magazine*.

> The emerging fourth wavers are not just reincarnations of their second wave grandmothers; they bring to the discussion important perspectives taught by third wave feminism. They speak in terms of intersectionality whereby women's suppression can only fully be understood in a context of the marginalization of other groups and genders—feminism is part of a larger consciousness of oppression along with racism, ageism, classism, abelism, and sexual orientation (no "ism" to go with that). Among the third wave's bequests is the importance of inclusion, an acceptance of the sexualized human body as non-threatening, and the role the internet can play in genderbending and leveling hierarchies [Rampton].

Likewise, the science fiction and superhero genres were welcoming minorities, not as a few team members, but making up the full cast. *Babylon 5* had had strong women, but a generation later, the same showrunner produced *Sense8* with every character a minority—living around the world in India, Nairobi, Mexico, and Korea as well as the U.S. and Europe, expanding global consciousness even as they discover how they're deeply connected. *Orphan Black* followed a set of clones who embodied every possible female archetype, with men making up their allies as they battled the patriarchy. They too finally spread around the world, seeking and curing their hidden sisters. *Runaways* had just one straight white male character, who spent his time trying to win the heart of the purple-haired Jewish feminist. *Black Lightning* starred an entire black superhero family. *Agents of S.H.I.E.L.D.* offered a spectrum of multiracial action women. *Doctor Who* broke 55 years of tradition to flip its protagonist into a female. *Once Upon a Time* (2011–2018), Disney's live action adaptation, strove for diversity and agency beyond the cartoons. Seely insists, "Perhaps the largest change we must make is to begin to raise girls to believe in themselves regardless of the images on television, in the movies, and on the pages of magazines" (140). This philosophy, begun by shows like *Maud* and *Buffy,* was reaching new levels of empowerment.

As Seely adds, "We need to promote the message that women and girls' value lies in themselves, in their capabilities, in their thoughts, in their health, and in their strength" (141). While *Star Trek: The Next Generation* had women as doctor and counselor, *Star Trek: Discovery* (2017–present) launched episode one with an Asian female captain and her black female first officer. American girls hoping to see themselves onscreen had dazzling new representation. Still, some find the stories not going far enough. True, this show also offered a *Star Trek* show's first gay couple. However, Michael Burnham's race is treated as invisible, and, after the striking first episode, she serves under several white male captains, focusing on their issues as much as her own, before the plot entangles her with saving Spock. Echoing history, her own priorities are sidelined.

Orange Is the New Black, meanwhile, has basically left white protagonist Piper Chapman behind to focus on the stories of everyone else in the prison— Latina and black women whose cultural experiences are forefront to their plots. Likewise, older, queer heroine Annalise Keating, star of *How to Get Away with Murder*, spends a season defending a black man destroyed by the system, even as she fights to change the law. In its latest "Where We Are on TV" report, the LGBTQIA+ media advocacy group GLAAD found the percentage of lesbian, gay, bisexual, transgender and queer characters on broadcast primetime television had reached a record high in the 2018–19 TV season. In fact, one in eleven characters identified as LGBTQIA+. Shows were also more sensitive to killing them off without reason. Sarah Kate Ellis, President and CEO of GLAAD, writes:

> GLAAD and Harris Poll's Accelerating Acceptance study shows that 20 percent of Americans 18- 34 identify as LGBTQ, a key demo for networks. They now have enough options for inclusive TV programming that they can actually pick and choose what to support in a way that we've not been able to do in the past. It is no longer enough just to have an LGBTQ character present to win LGBTQ audience's attention, there needs to be nuance and depth to their story and they should reflect the full diversity of our community ["Where We Are on TV"].

Will & Grace and *Murphy Brown* have returned, specifically to battle the racism, homophobia, and sexism of the Trump era with liberal voices. Outside television, of course, feminism has also been growing louder. "Over the past few years, as #MeToo and Time's Up pick up momentum, the Women's March floods Washington with pussy hats every year, and a record number of women prepare to run for office, it's beginning to seem that the long-heralded fourth wave might actually be here," Grady quips. Science fiction, it seems, may not be pushing the boundaries of cultural commentary as much as real life.

One exception, the dystopian drama *The Handmaid's Tale,* was ironically created with a feminist Hillary Clinton presidency in mind. Still, as one of the first shows of the Trump era, with increasing state legislation threatening *Roe vs. Wade,* Americans saw themselves in this all-too-believable misogynist theocracy. Women began publicly protesting anti-abortion laws in the iconic red gowns and white hoods, emphasizing the horrors of a society that considered them nothing more than incubators. In "'Praise Be!' Power and Resistance in Hulu's *The Handmaid's Tale,*" K. Jamie Woodlief considers the content as well as the larger message of this history-changing series.

The internet, of course, is the key to fourth wave. "Online is where activists meet and plan their activism, and it's where feminist discourse and debate takes place. Sometimes fourth-wave activism can even take place on the internet (the '#MeToo' tweets), and sometimes it takes place on the streets (the Women's March), but it's conceived and propagated online," Grady adds. Another aspect of fourth wave is the way fan protests are getting more directed, and even changing the content. "As such, the fourth wave's beginnings are often loosely pegged to around 2008, when Facebook, Twitter, and YouTube were firmly entrenched in the cultural fabric and feminist blogs like Jezebel and Feministing were spreading across the web," Grady says. Fan campaigns saved a few rare shows, as Netflix dove in to buy *Lucifer* in its fourth season and promised unhappy fans a closing episode to *Sense8.* "Scattered Stories of Embodied Resistance: *Sense8, Orphan Black* and Queer Cultural Production" by Audrey Jane Black explores the production decisions behind series of this era, from their concepts to cancelations. In fact, the internet is having effects beyond a two-way conversation as it also facilitates a multinational one:

> The Internet has broken barriers down in ways our foremothers never imagined; as governments, we export and import products among nations and involve ourselves in the governing of others; in the name of business we establish multinational corporations that employ host-country citizens, use (and abuse) host-country natural resources, and dictate local and global markets; we share medical knowledge and resources worldwide; we travel extensively; we forge personal relationships; and in many other ways we break the boundaries between nations. The contradiction lies in our quest to be independent and separate while also being an integral part of the global community. The reality is that what one does in one area of the world does affect another area—we are all interrelated on both the personal and the political levels. Nowhere is this truer than in relation to the issues of political and social justice. As we become a more globalized community, our feminism has moved to a greater recognition of women around the world [Seely 51].

With this global awareness comes sensitivity to other fan groups. When *Marvel's Iron Fist* and *The Defenders* on Netflix kept a blond, entitled young man as superhero instead of casting their first Asian central character, fandom anger filled the Net. Other critics began posting how much screentime the women of *Star Wars* received or how many women had been killed to motivate male characters. Some tracked how many *Doctor Who* episodes had female writers and directors and clamored for more women behind the scenes, not just driving the time machine. As these lists and social media campaigns appeared, producers became more sensitive to issues like the constant killing off of lesbian characters. Sumiko Saulson explores these tropes in *The Walking Dead* and other shows in "From Sidekick to Romantic Lead: Rise of the Strong Black Woman." How many women of color, she inquires, are allowed to survive on science fiction shows and how many are still getting brutally killed? She ends her essay with a thorough list of shows starring these breakout black heroines. Spinster Eskie tackles similar tropes with more of a close reading, considering how the anthology show *Black Mirror,* particularly its episodes "Crocodile" and "Black Museum," address race and what this says about this era's television.

Intersectionality is also key. With more queer, trans, and characters of color, the stories reached out to care about plights beyond those of the middle-class white woman—something the earlier waves had been known to neglect. Bill, a black lesbian *Doctor Who* companion, proudly sports an Afro and takes no interest in dating the Doctor. In creating her, showrunners clearly considered the fan protests of how black medical doctor Martha Jones was problematically lovelorn and mistreated. Bill fares much better, with the Doctor actively supporting her and even punching out a racist on her behalf … though her end has fascinatingly poignant metaphors that encapsulate her conflict. Sarah Beth Gilbert considers this young woman's particular struggle across categories in "'Bloke Utopia': Bill Potts, Queer Identity and Cyborg Narratives in *Doctor Who*."

Katherine McLoone considers the statement that a rare onscreen Muslim superheroine, a bisexual captain, and a few self-aware historical heroines make in "Revisionist History and Intersectional Feminism in *DC's Legends of Tomorrow*." This series, launching as a spinoff of DC's *Arrow, The Flash,* and *Supergirl* (with a diverse team but originally lacking much direction beyond that), improved drastically when the queer Sara Lance became captain instead of the entitled futuristic ship owner. A few seasons in, it found its voice as the silliest of the shows, celebrating the absurdities of time travel along with the contradictions in its multifaceted characters.

Many stories like *Marvel's Jessica Jones, Supergirl, Ghostbusters,* or the relaunched *Star Wars* franchise pitted the heroine against the patriarchy in the form of sadistic incels—the misogynistic trolls of the internet. In fact, as the fourth wave gained momentum, Grady explains, "Internet trolls actually tried to launch their own fourth wave in 2014, planning to create a 'pro-sexualization, pro-skinny, anti-fat' feminist movement that the third wave would revile, ultimately miring the entire feminist community in bloody civil war. (It didn't work out.)" Social media speeds meant that this era's backlash was simultaneous, with angry Marvel fans protesting the existence of films like *Captain Marvel* since a story in their franchise had been written to glorify and speak to someone other than themselves. My own "Reclaiming Power from the Toxic Male: Support and Recovery in *Marvel's Jessica Jones*" considers the realistic depiction of trauma in the force of such male entitlement.

Even as online bullying grew, children's shows took a shining new stand for inclusion. Succeeding *Clone Wars* was *Star Wars: Rebels* with a far mightier adult Ahsoka and two central female characters—one in sloppy overalls, the other in full armor. Clearly, the gender messages had shifted with these three women, as Stephenie McGucken reveals in her thoughtful essay in this collection. Other shows joined in on inclusion and positivity. *My Little Pony: Friendship Is Magic* (2010–2019) offers a spectrum of diverse female characters more interested in supporting one another than giggling and crying to solve their problems. A more diverse She-Ra was rebooted for Netflix as well. *Adventure Time* wrapped its 10-season run with a kiss between fan favorite characters Princess Bubblegum and Marceline the Vampire Queen. The beloved *Steven Universe* went further—raising the hero with three (literally) colorful alien superheroic moms. On the show, the symbolism for gay relationships and trans status are quite recognizable and empowering. Josephine L. McGuire looks at these, as well as how Steven's birth signifies a "reverse-fridging"—giving his mother agency instead of removing it in a series of innovative metaphors. Sarah Kate Ellis writes: "Inclusion is not just the right thing to do, but these examples prove that it is good for the bottom line. Audiences are clearly hungry for new stories and perspectives, and fans are showing up to support the content that is telling stories they recognize and can relate to" ("Where We Are on TV").

Other shows, like *Game of Thrones,* started off patriarchally with naked women as set dressing (failing comics author Kelly Sue DeConnick's "sexy lamp test," which is what it sounds like). However, by series end, most of the men had killed one another off and two queens were left to epically battle for the throne, backed by other stand-out heroines like Brienne, Yara, Sansa, and Arya. The show ends with women all participating in the Great Council to choose the new ruler, deciding on egalitarianism over primogeniture. Further, Sansa the new Queen in the North, Yara the ruler of the Iron Islands, Arya discoverer of western lands, and Brienne—an anointed knight and Commander of the Kingsguard—claim positions in their fantasy world never held by women, rewriting pseudo-medieval England to head toward equality. In fact, History Channel's *Vikings* coasted on *Game of Thrones'* popularity but was arguably more feminist from the start, based as it was in Norse culture with its property rights and physical autonomy for women. Steven B. Frankel considers *Vikings* through its historical context, revealing how non–Western models can provide better patterns for female empowerment and male respect.

Shows like *Wynonna Earp* and *Revenge* gender-flipped classic characters or appointed women to inherit male heroes' legacies. Taking this to a higher level, several rebooted franchises welcomed women into central positions, or all the positions, like *Miss Sherlock* and *Ghostbusters*. Resa Haile explores this trend as well as a modern definition of heroism in her "Wynonna Earp, Supergirl and the Power of Choosing." Race flipping and queering have also been popular to create more diverse casts. Following these trends, DC, Marvel, and *Star Wars* allowed more diversity into their giant movie franchises with Rey, Finn, Poe, Rose, Aquaman, Black Panther, Wonder Woman and Captain Marvel, but also girl-centric cartoon spinoffs. In my own essay, I examine the online shows *DC Super Hero Girls*, *Marvel Rising*, and *Star Wars: Forces of Destiny* as stories of inclusion and possibility.

Is this where we're ending up in this wave, or is there further to go? Will next season release a television show more culturally relevant than *The Handmaid's Tale*? More gender-positive than *Steven Universe*? More assertive than *Wynonna Earp*? More choice-affirming than *Orphan Black*? More critical than *Black Mirror*? More inclusive than *Sense8*? Who can say? Of course, current science fiction and fantasy shows are shattering boundaries and, if not being perfect, at least breaking down barriers in pursuit of a new feminist truth.

WORKS CITED

Armstrong, Jennifer. "The Secret History of Women in Television." *Bust,* Feb/Mar 2012. https://bust.com/feminism/14511-the-secret-history-of-women-in-television.html.

Drazen, Patrick. *Anime Explosion! The What? Why? & Wow! of Japanese Animation.* Stone Bridge Press, 2003.

Foster, Amy. "Girls and Space Fever." *1950s "Rocketman" TV Series and Their Fans: Cadets, Rangers, and Junior Space Men,* edited by Cynthia J. Miller, A. Bowdoin Van Riper. Palgrave Macmillan, 2012, pp. 67–82.

Grady, Constance. "The Waves of Feminism, and Why People Keep Fighting Over Them, Explained." *Vox Magazine,* 20 July 2018. https://www.vox.com/2018/3/20/16955588/feminism-waves-explained-first-second-third-fourth.

Haines, Rebecca C. "Power(Puff) Feminism: The Powerpuff Girls as a Site of Strength and Collective Action in the Third Wave." *Women in Popular Culture: Representation, Meaning, and Media,* edited by Marian Meyers. Hampton Press, 2008, pp. 211–235.

Harris, Anita. *Future Girl: Young Women in the Twenty-First Century.* Routledge, 2004.

Muir, John Kenneth. *The Encyclopedia of Superheroes on Film and Television.* McFarland, 2004.

Rampton, Martha. "Four Waves of Feminism." Pacific University, Fall 2008. https://www.pacificu.edu/about/media/four-waves-feminism.

Seely, Megan. *Fight Like a Girl.* New York University Press, 2007.

Siegel, Deborah. *Sisterhood, Interrupted.* Palgrave Macmillan, 2007.

"2018–2019 Where We Are on TV: GLAAD's Annual Report on LGBTQ Inclusion." *GLAAD Media Institute*, Nov 2018. https://glaad.org/files/WWAT/WWAT_GLAAD_2018–2019.pdf.

SECTION I

Fighting Authority

"Praise Be!"

Power and Resistance in Hulu's The Handmaid's Tale

K. Jamie Woodlief

The Handmaid's Tale, written by Margaret Atwood and published in 1984, is a familiar read to high school and college students alike. The novel tells the first-person narrative of Offred, a handmaid in the dystopian country of Gilead, formerly known as America. In this dystopic society, most women still able to reproduce have been forced into reproductive slavery by an extreme religious regime, The Sons of Gilead, following a dangerous drop in fertility. Women in Gilead have had most of their rights revoked: they cannot own property, have money, read books, or dress the way they want (just to name a few). They are valued only for their moral virtue and, in the case of the Handmaids, their ability to bear children. The Tale is currently experiencing a resurgence in popularity in the form of an original Hulu adaptation of the novel created by Bruce Miller. Atwood serves as a consultant on the show and has even made an appearance or two as an Aunt, whose purpose is to train and oversee the Handmaids in Gilead. Perhaps her counsel is one reason why Season 1 followed the book faithfully with only a few, although prominent, differences. Season 2 of the series was released in the Spring of 2018 and began the journey into uncharted territory beyond the words of the original novel. Season 3 is currently on the horizon as this essay is being written, so obviously this tale resonates with audiences of all genders. Once the Hulu series was released, reactions were swift and varied. Many reactions see the series as scarily relevant to our current situation under a new administration. The main character, Offred, at one point warns, "When they slaughtered Congress, we didn't wake up. When they blamed terrorists and suspended the Constitution, we didn't wake up then either. They said it would be temporary. Nothing changes instantaneously. In a gradually heating bath-tub, you'd be boiled to death before you knew it" (Atwood, *The Handmaid's Tale*). The quote has come up again and again in media stories as a warning that should be heeded. The less drastic responses look at the more nuanced and subtle scenes of each episode, depicting instances of sexism women face every day in our current society. The novel, and now the series, raise many questions about representations of feminism and female agency.

Women in the dystopian world of Gilead are placed into a hierarchy after a drop-in fertility due to environmental pollution causes an intense fear of extinction, leaving the door open for a cruel fundamentalist theocracy to overtake the government and revoke women's rights. Handmaids occupy the lowest position on the hierarchy (if we are not counting the un-women forced to labor in polluted wastelands). Women who are fertile are placed in the houses of high-ranking officials and forced into a sadistic ceremonial rape once a month with the hope pregnancy will result. They must relinquish their true names and take on the name of their Commander. Therefore, Offred's Commander's name is Fred (she is "of" him). The Wives of these officials are also forced to take part in the ceremony, and although they experience more freedom than Handmaids (they get to keep their names), they have no power or agency over their own lives; they must defer to their husbands in all deci-sions. The Aunts, perhaps hold the most unclear status in all of Gilead. They exert the most power and influence as they are trusted to train (indoctrinate) the Handmaids and advise them of their duties. They continue to "counsel" the Handmaids after they are placed with a couple, and the Hulu series depicts a power struggle between them and the wives, so it is unclear who holds the higher rank. It is also unclear how the Aunts were chosen for this position. The Marthas, most likely also infertile women or those past the childbearing age, serve as nannies and domestic servants to high-ranking families. They answer to the wives, but keep their names and give orders to the Handmaids. These rankings are important because they lead to abuse, distrust, violence, and betrayal among women struggling to come to terms with being stripped of their rights, and therefore, their agency. They are literally silenced.

Sylvia Walby in *Theorising Patriarchy* identifies six sites of patriarchy for analyzing different forms of gender inequality which include the follow-ing: household (where women's household labor is exploited by husbands and male partners); paid work (where women are excluded from high status jobs, receive less pay and are often employed in segregated sections of the labor force); the state (where there is a systematic bias in favor of men's inter-ests); male violence (which is legitimated by the state); sexuality (where com-pulsory heterosexuality and sexual double standards reign) and cultural institutions (which represent women in negative ways in the media, religion and education). *The Handmaid's Tale* displays all of these pillars of patriarchy through the hierarchy explained above. The first site, household, can be seen in the Marthas and the Handmaids. The Handmaids do the shopping and Marthas cook the food and clean for the high-ranking households. As for the second pillar, paid work, women have no status or power outside of the home, except for maybe the Aunts who only have power over the Handmaids. The Hulu series depicts Serena Joy, the wife of Commander Waterford, as a college educated, well-spoken former professional. In fact, she helped Gilead, and therefore her husband, gain power just to be forced into submission once the Sons of Jacob took over the government. Only men can serve in governmental positions, and therefore they make all of the decisions regarding society, pertaining to pillar number three. There is plenty of cringeworthy violence in the series. Women suffer abuse and torture, including government sanctioned rape and female genital mutilation. These last two acts of violence also pertain to pillar number five, along with the consideration that homosexuality is forbidden in Gilead as sex is for reproductive purposes only and devoid of emotion, with the exception of the illicit Jezebels, where unruly women are placed for the sole pleasure of the high-ranking men who hypocritically proclaim chastity during the day. In Gilead there are no negative representations of women in the media; all such representations of women have been banned in Gilead. In fact, it is this last pillar that is used to justify the subjugation of women in this dystopic society. Second wave feminists in 1970s America coined the phrase "take back the night" referring to the right of women to be able to safely walk the streets. Ironically, the characters of *Handmaid's Tale* have achieved this right, as the handmaids, now property, are more forcefully protected from assault. Aunt Lydia uses this feeling of safety to indoctrinate the Handmaids in the detention center. She claims, "Now we walk along the same street, in red pairs, and no man shouts obscenities at us, speaks to us, touches us. No one whistles. There is more than one kind of freedom. Freedom to and freedom from. In the days of anarchy, it was freedom to. Now you are being given freedom from. Don't underrate it" (Atwood, *The Handmaid's Tale*). Critics of Margaret Atwood have used this quote as evidence the author is a bad feminist and that much of her novel was actually a critique of the second wave of feminism.

That criticism is currently echoed and expanded to the show's actresses with the release of the series on Hulu. Atwood has often expressed in articles and interviews her lack of desire to align herself or her work with the feminist movement. In fact, she has been mildly critical of the second wave of feminism in the '70s, saying, "I didn't want to become a megaphone for any one particular set of beliefs. Having gone through that initial phase of feminism when you weren't supposed to wear frocks and lipstick—I never had any use for that. You should be able to wear them without people saying you are a traitor to your sex" (Loofbourow). Indeed, Offred, dressed sexlessly in the novel, finds herself missing the bathing suits and negligees of the past. Despite the fact that many lauded her novel as a feminist treatise, Atwood denies that was her intent, "I was not in New York, where all of that kicked off, in 1969. I was in Edmonton, Alberta, where there was no feminist movement, and would not be for quite some time" (Loofbourow).

Recently, Atwood responded to the controversy surrounding her thoughts on feminism in an opinion piece published in *The Globe and Mail*. In the article she wonders how she "got into such hot water with the Good Feminists" and clarifies her stance, "My fundamental position is that women are human beings, with the full range of saintly and demonic behaviours this entails, including criminal ones.... Nor do I believe that women are children, incapable of agency or of making moral decisions" (Atwood "Am I"). This same attitude appears to have spread to the cast of the series. After an initial screening of the first episode at the Tribeca film festival in 2017, the cast sat down to answer questions and their collective response to one in particular, whether they consider this show a "feminist work," caused some controversy among many fourth wave feminists who initially saw the show as a relevant warning to our current government's alarming policy decisions regarding women and other disenfranchised groups. Madeline Brewer, who plays hand-maid Janine in the series, preferred to generalize, "I think that any story, if it is a story being told by a strong, powerful woman ... any story that's just a powerful woman owning herself in any way is automatically deemed 'feminist.' But it's just a story about a woman. I don't think that this is any sort of feminist propaganda. I think that it's a story about women and about humans.... This story affects all people" (Bradley). Elisabeth Moss, who plays main character Offred, takes a more direct approach, "For me, [*The Hand-maid's Tale*] is not a feminist story. It's a human story because women's rights are human rights. So, for me it's, I never intended to play Peggy as a feminist. I never intended to play Offred as a feminist. They're women, and they're humans" (Bradley). Considering the obvious feminist plot of both the novel and TV series, these responses are baffling to say the least. Why might there be a need to create distance from feminist movements? Surely the reason is not financial, although making a feminist series could be considered more dangerous than writing a feminist novel from the standpoint of viewership:

> Aside from ideological differences between the mediums, there are also structural, technological, and economic differences between visual media and literature. Novels and short stories are usually the product of an individual, whereas films and televi-sion shows are the work of teams of people, each working on an aspect of the final product ... film production companies need to aim for the large, often young-to-middle aged male, audiences-not the small niche audiences that many feminist presses cater to [Rose 72].

It is clear, however, that *The Handmaid's Tale* is more speculative fiction (a term Atwood prefers) than science fiction, and the intended audience for the series are not young white males. Furthermore, the series resonates with many women of all ages and as *New Yorker* author, Alexandra Schwartz, rightly points out, "In our age of pussy-grabbing Presidents and pussyhats, the word [feminism] has been rehabilitated from its commercially toxic status and spun into marketing gold." Regardless most scholars and critics are not buying that this Tale is not feminist: "The ways in which women are deprived of those rights—in Atwood's fiction, and in the reality, past and present, that she bases it on—are unique.... It is a story about the ways in which women are oppressed in a society run by men for their own benefit (no one involved seems to have a problem with the word 'patriarchy') and about how certain women take advantage of the situation to ally themselves with male power for personal gain" (Schwartz). The question of female agency and the struggle for power through small forms of pushback coupled with the strategic changes made to the book align the Hulu series quite visibly with the fourth wave.

Although the first season of the series closely follows the plot and much of the inner monologue of Atwood's novel, there are a few key differences, mainly in characterization and setting, to consider when weighing theories of gender and cultural constructs. The series brings the setting into our more recognizable modern world, rather than the 1980s, by updating fashions and adding technology. During flashbacks to a pre–Gilead society, smartphones and electronic banking are common as in our present day, and June (Offred's real name) even references Uber. These small changes make the world more relatable for modern audiences. In the book, both the Commander and his wife are described as a much older couple than depicted in the series. This could of course, be for the sake of Hollywood's appeal to the audience, raising questions about ageism, but it also affects the way the audience perceives the traditional concepts of masculinity in the stoic image of the Commander. Other changes are larger and more deliberate, mostly for the sake of diversifying the characters. For one, both Moira, Offred's best friend, and Luke, her husband before the regime takes over, are played by African Americans. This adds the fourth wave issue of intersectionality, less present in the novel. In Atwood's version, men and women of color, labeled "Children of Ham," have been carted off to some unknown location possibly in the Midwest, known as "the National Homeland." History tells us that when minorities get taken away en masse, nothing good has come of it. The society of Gilead in the television series does not seem as racially discriminatory as they are misogynistic. Luke and June have a biracial daughter and several of the handmaids are also women of color, indicating Gilead does accepts children of all colors as their own. Creator of the series Bruce Miller said the change felt "necessary in this day and age." As he adds, "That was a very big discussion with Margaret about what the difference was between reading the words, 'There are no people of color in this world' and seeing an all-white world on your television, which has a very different impact," Miller said of the change. "What's the difference between making a TV show about racists and making a racist TV show where you don't hire any actors of color?" (Dockterman). In addition, Ofglen does not reveal her sexuality or the fact that she has a wife and child in the novel as she does in the series, although Moira does identify as a lesbian in the book. However, in the novel, June has a bit of trouble accepting Moira's sexuality, a conflict which there is no mention of in the TV series. It should be noted that in both versions of Gilead, homosexuality is unacceptable as it goes against the "laws of nature" and procreation that the dystopian society is founded on. Ofglen, in the series, is harshly punished for "gender treachery" when she is found to be having an affair with a Martha. The Martha is hanged, but because Ofglen is still fertile, she undergoes female circumcision as punishment. It seems that most homosexual men who refuse to submit are also executed. While this Bible-based culture condemns male homosexuals beside the females, the straight men's privilege rises to an unheard-of extreme, even as the series condemns them for their cruelty. This emphasis on diversity and acceptance of each individual's experience no matter race, age, sexuality, etc., is consistent with the most current wave of feminism. Also consistent are the major changes made to the heroine of the story, Offred.

In the novel, Offred is not nearly as rebellious as Elizabeth Moss' depiction in the Hulu series. Atwood's Offred does not rock the boat or attempt to exercise rhetorical agency at any point in the book. She refuses to help Ofglen and the resistance; she does not even protest when the Gilead regime revokes women's rights during their rise to power. Creator Bruce Miller explains it is more interesting to create a dichotomy of external obedience and internal rebellion, while the character is also more likable as someone who has not completely given up on the fight. Additionally, in our current climate of feminism, strong female characters who exhibit agency, power and grit have come to be expected. There are several ways Offred and her fellow female characters exert influence and practice rhetorical agency, despite being controlled by a violent patriarchal regime.

Pushback can be seen as a small act of rebellion to the status quo, a take back of agency, a way of reflecting on intention, if the contemplative silence is not interrupted and the receiver is willing to consider the message. Several instances of pushback, both in action and verbal rhetoric, are presented in the Hulu adaptation. In Season 1 Episode 5, Offred pushes back against her Commander as they converse in his office, a forbidden space to handmaids. "Rhetorical spaces are domains held by cultural orthodoxies (Mountford 2003): accepted views, attitudes, and practices that have been, through invariable repetition, calcified so flawlessly that they express as commonsense, as natural—normal" (Ore 13). The Commander is in his domain and thus holds all of the power; he controls the conversation and sets the boundaries, or in some cases, pushes the boundaries, putting Offred in a dangerous position. In this episode, Offred courageously pushes back, in "a purposefully disruptive act of brazen defiance aimed at bringing attention to the interlocking forces of oppression through the deliberate and open transgression of gendered, racial and classed norms" (21). Offred poses a series of questions to the Commander starting with an admonishment of his behavior during the last ceremony, a frigid act of attempted fertilization, in which the Commander's wife is present. The Commander explains his intimate behavior by complaining he finds the act "so impersonal." Offred fires back, "You think?" prompting the Commander to consider the validity of the ceremony and its purpose. The Commander defends himself and the other men in power by claiming women are now better off, "Now you have respect, you have protection, you can fulfill your biological destinies in peace. Children—what else is there to live for?" Offred's response, love, is an example of pushback but does not have much effect on the receiver, who is ready with a defense of patriarchy and oppression. However, the conversation ends with perhaps the best example of pushback in the form of one word. When the Commander asserts his pathetic defense, his "good" intentions, "We only wanted to make the world a better place," Offred asks, "Better?" With this, she calls for the Commander's reflection and a deeper understanding of his actions based on his patriarchal position of privilege. The Commander now must explain what he considers "better" and for whom he applies the term. In the end, his response is weak, but telling, "Better never means better for everyone. It always means worse for some." With this, he acknowledges that those in his class are aware they are oppressing others, casting them as deliberate villains. Resistance is also a form of claiming rhetorical agency, and the series seems determined to show that this fighting spirit is still alive and well within the women of Gilead.

Offred struggles to maintain resiliency in a dystopian patriarchal society, where "moments of rhetorical agency are scarce" (Wolford 5). Given that such cultural structures and socialization processes determine the possibilities of agency, any theory of women's agency "must problematize the relationship between culturally imbedded structures of patriarchy and corresponding practices that enable and constrain the realm of possibilities for women" (Ryan-Kelly 211). Offred finds agency in small rhetorical acts of defiance such as playing Scrabble with her commander and sharing whispered conversations with her walking partner, Ofglen. These acts are made possible through the synchronic kinetic energy of those around her, "Resilience is actually relational instead of individual, and exists within a network of relationships, rather than as one lone person struggling and succeeding against the odds" (Wolford 3). Offred needs the cooperation of Ofglen or else her message of resistance will not be received. Effective agency for a speaker needs an audience to receive the message. She takes a risk, trusting Ofglen is not an "eye" trying to catch her breaking the law and thus learns of a secret network of resistance, setting her on the path to agency and empowerment. It may seem odd to propose that her oppressor, the Commander, aids in giving June a voice, considering his goal and that of the regime he is a part of is to silence women; however, by breaking the rules and giving June magazines to read and the opportunity to form words through a game of Scrabble, he allows her to practice agency at least in what he believes to be a controlled setting. "Rhetorical agents are linked to both culture and collectivities in ways that require negotiation within and against institutional power structures" (Ryan-Kelly 211). June seizes the opportunity to play Scrabble and practice an activity that is forbidden to Handmaids. The opportunity allows her some happiness and relief as her brain remembers how to form words. These opportune moments can also be seen as instances of kairos. Kairotic moments present synchronic aspects of agency, leading to deliberative discourse to initiate acts of resistance. Additionally, although the handmaid Offred replaces was unable to maintain her own resiliency, she leaves a rhetorical message of resistance scratched in a closet, "Don't let the bastards get you down" written in Latin. Offred internalizes and interacts with this scrawled message of forbidden literacy and sisterhood, creating an emergent agency that reinforces her resilience. She lies in the closet tracing the words with her fingers and determines she will continue to fight for her former life rather than succumb as did the Handmaid before her (her suicide is implied in both the book and the series). Although these words impart agency, resolve and power to Offred "...language is not the only way that women gain agency" (Wolford 3).

This assertion is seen in the Handmaid's small acts of solidarity such as silently and swiftly forming a human shield to block a fellow handmaid from having to see her baby being given to another woman to raise. Handmaids must immediately give up the child they have carried to the wife of the household they have been forced to serve. The series depicts how difficult it can be to have their babies ripped from their arms. Working together, the Handmaids rebel by protecting one another and forming an alliance in their misery. As the series progresses, viewers begin to see Offred's acts of clear resistance, most notably in the final episode of Season 1, "Night." In the beginning of the episode, Offred's voiceover states, "They should have never given us uniforms if they didn't want us to be an army," referencing the modest red dresses and white winged headpieces of the handmaids. She is clearly appropriating her oppression to work to her advantage, an expression of resistance. The progression from small acts of diachronic resilience leads to the final act of synchronic resistance and deliberate discourse. "The power of resistance is often unpredictable," (Wolford 4) and certainly those in power seem surprised by the act of rebellion in the final episode. In an act of solidarity absent in the book, all of the Handmaids refuse to stone to death one of their own. One by one each handmaid drops her stone, despite the shouted orders from the terrifying Aunt Lydia, with the knowledge that punishment will be forthcoming. In this act, they display an intentional and transformative act of resistance. They march away from the scene with their heads up, defiant, in possession of rhetorical agency, at least for the moment.

Another source of June's agency, and one major way she can affect change, is through her narration. June is at an impasse, which generally means one is stuck in a certain place, and physically she *is* powerless to change her situation. However, Ann Cvetkovich, in her work *In Depression: A Public Feeling*, claims this stasis does not mean that all hope of becoming unstuck and progressing is lost. Creativity is one way to conquer the hurdle of an impasse, and telling a personal narrative is a creative step in the right direction. Offred drops several clues to the viewer that indicate she is self-consciously telling her story, and recording it in some way, presumably with the hope that a listener at a future date will find comfort and inspiration in her words. Offred's memoir tells of her past life in America, depicted as our current modern world, contrasting with her present situation in the Republic of Gilead. Since writing down her narrative is forbidden, her doing so is an act of rebellion as well as one of bearing witness to atrocities and sharing with posterity a past she must fear will never return. Offred alludes to her impending depression and loss of sanity as she contemplates the window in her room with its shatterproof glass and limited opening: "Maybe the life I think I'm living is a paranoid delusion…. Sanity is a valuable possession; I hoard it the way people once hoarded money. I save it, so I will have enough, when the time comes." Her depression is certainly created by the political constraints placed on her gender. Cvetkovich asserts, "Political depression is pervasive within recent histories of decolonization, civil rights, socialism, and labor politics, and attention to affective politics is a way of trying to come to terms with disappointment, failure, and the slowness of change" (7). Offred must come to terms with the loss of many freedoms that were once afforded to her a few short years before, and she does so by patiently enduring her loss while simultaneously coping through the narrative she weaves of both her past and present life. Cvetkovich's "utopian dreaming" also appears in *The Handmaid's Tale* in the form of Offred's frequent but short-lived flashbacks to life with her husband, child, and best friend before the oppressive regime took power. The images of this past appear in almost every episode and stand in stark contrast to June's current life. "Offred's memories allow her to envision the other, and so provide a form of rebellion against the totalitarian system" (Tolan 166). In one episode, her voiceover speaks directly to her unknown audience, "I would like to believe this is a story I'm telling. I need to believe it. I must believe it. If it's a story I'm telling then I have control over the ending. Then there will be an ending, to the story, and real life will come after it." To control the ending of the story is to gain agency and possibly even social change, though she may not live to see it. Although Offred is at an impasse with seemingly no power to change her current situation, she relies on creativity through the form of narrative to make her voice heard and keep her sanity, while in the larger sphere attempting to initiate political change through personal experience (that is, if anyone receives the message).

Hulu's adaptation of this classic novel makes mostly subtle changes in its first season in order to appeal to a more diverse and inclusive audience. Identifying Offred's real name as June, which is not revealed in the novel, and making her a stronger and more rebellious protagonist is a strategic move by the creators of this series. Would empowered women, and those who identify with the fourth wave of feminism, watch a heroine completely defeated by oppressive patriarchy? A complacent heroine who is content to simply survive without trying to change her situation? A woman with no agency or power? One would assume, as the creators most likely did, that the answer is no. The fear produced in *The Handmaid's Tale* is particularly relevant in America as state and national governments wage war on women's rights. The Handmaids' highly recognizable red dresses and white winged bonnets inspire resistance in the women who donned these uniforms to protest America's current administration on both the national and state levels. The series is certainly anxiety-producing, but that anxiety has led to a whole new generation of activists, with similar aims to the second wave of feminism. Movements such as #metoo and #timesup coupled with women's marches, pink hats, and most notably a midterm election that saw an unprecedented number of women elected to Congress show women are prepared to resist and fight back. They are not content to be "under his eye" and "praise be" for that.

WORKS CITED

Atwood, Margaret. "Am I a Bad Feminist?" *The Globe and Mail.* 13 Jan. 2018.
_____. *The Handmaid's Tale.* Anchor Books, 1986.
Bradley, Laura. "Why Won't *The Handmaid's Tale* Cast Call it Feminist?" *Vanity Fair.* 22 April 2017.
Cvetkovich, Ann. *Depression: A Public Feeling.* Duke University Press, 2012.
Dockterman, Eliana. "The Differences Between *The Handmaid's Tale* Show and Book Explained." *Time.* 1 May 2017.
Falk Jones, Libby. "Breaking Silences in Feminist Dystopias." *Utopian Studies,* no. 3, 1991, pp. 7–11.
Horbury, Alison. "Post-Feminist Impasses in Popular Heroine Television." *Continuum: Journal of Media and Cultural Studies,* vol. 28, no. 2, 2014, pp. 213–225.
Loofbourow, Lili. "How Hulu's *The Handmaid's Tale* Succumbed to the Feminist Curse." *The Week.* 27 Apr. 2017.

Mead, Rebecca. "Margaret Atwood, The Prophet of Dystopia." *The New Yorker.* 17 April 2017.

Ore, Ersula. "Pushback: A Pedagogy of Care." *Pedagogy*, vol. 17, no. 1, 2016, pp. 9–33.

Rose, Maria. "Redefining Women's Power Through Feminist Science Fiction." *Extrapolation*, vol. 46, no. 1, 2005.

Ryan-Kelly, Casey. "Women's Rhetorical Agency in the American West: The New Penelope." *Women's Studies in Communication*, vol. 32, no. 2, Spring 2009.

Schwartz, Alexandra. "Yes, *The Handmaid's Tale* Is Feminist." *The New Yorker.* 27 April 2017.

Stillman, Peter, and Anne Johnson. "Identity, Complicity, and Resistance in the Handmaid's Tale." *Utopian Studies*, vol. 5, no. 2, 1994, pp. 70–86.

Tolan, Fiona. *Margaret Atwood: Feminism and Fiction.* Chapter VI. Editions Rodopi, 2007.

Walby, Sylvia. "Theorising Patriarchy." *Sociology*, vol. 23, no. 2, May 1989, pp. 213–234.

Wolford, Rachel. "When a Woman Owns the Farm: A Case for Diachronic and Synchronic Rhetorical Agency." *enculturation: a journal of rhetoric, writing, and culture*, June 2016.

Scattered Stories of Embodied Resistance

Sense8, Orphan Black
and Queer Cultural Production

AUDREY JANE BLACK

> Biology is always marshaled into the service of political power and social control. There's nothing [it doesn't] impact. So, who gets to control it?—Cosima Herter

> I'm interested in identity and the construction of identity and the way that mainstream genre supplies language for the construction of identity.—Lana Wachowski

Introduction: A New Biopunk

The official poster for *Orphan Black* Season 3 is all too simple: a black-and-white, shoulders-up image of series protagonist Sarah Manning, superimposed with the phrase "I am not your property." *Sense8* (Netflix, 2015–2018), and *Orphan Black* (BBC America, 2013–2017) are original scripted dramatic series revolving around feminist themes and textually saturated in queer subculture and/or political determination.

These shows visualize and theorize stigmatization, persecution, captivity, and resistance in timely contexts of sex, gender, and sexuality, each taking its own angle at connectivity as a mode of resistance. The series recover "biopunk" from its roots in an androcentric cyberpunk subgenre of science fiction, providing the necessary conditions for further stories about somatechnic refusal and an anti-fascist bio-politics. Biopunk typically "revise[s], update[s], and rationalize[s] Gothic-horror motifs of bodily invasion and disruption"

(McHale 255); however, *Sense8* and *Orphan Black* represent something more specific—an always feminist and often queer biopunk ethic, residing not in deep futures, off-World, or alternate dimensions, but here and now, with real and familiar stakes. The queer-feminist biopunk is terminally skeptical of, and unabashedly militant toward "enhancement" and the heroine's enemies are those who seek to alter or control any*body*. Both series' conflicts revolve around a paramilitary biotechnical syndicate—the Biologic Preservation Organization (BPO), led by the nefarious "Whispers" in *Sense8*, and the Dyad Institute/Neolution, led by P.T. Westmoreland in *Orphan Black*.

Both series ended in 2017. *Orphan Black* ran a natural course of five seasons, while *Sense8* was cancelled after only two. Thus, *Sense8* becomes a case study, questioning which stories get to live on when radical queer ones are sent to the gallows. *Sense8* and *Orphan Black* reveal much through the lens of production studies, focusing both on their respective homes in science fiction and their queer and feminist possibilities and interventions in the medium of television more largely.

What made these shows possible, and what have been their limits? What makes something a "queer production" and how is this distinction used? Further, how might new rules for cultural production/distribution in streaming television enable more intersectional identities to complicate hetero/cis-normative scripts (and other discursive hierarchies), and perhaps even alter the very economy of storytelling?

Storytelling Priorities

Sense8 and *Orphan Black* have differential feminist and queer leanings. *Orphan Black* is a show about women and for women, that happens to be queer, while *Sense8* is a show about queers and for queers, that happens to be feminist. Both exhibit queer orientation in their production, but they do not share the same *symbolic capital*. In Pierre Bourdieu's terms, as described in his essay "The Forms of Capital," this capital is both *social* (based on identity and affiliation) and *cultural* (based on resources and inheritance). *Sense8* converts social capital to cultural capital through its queer producers and cast, while *Orphan Black* cannot.

Further, *Orphan Black*'s characters happen to be queer, while *Sense8*'s characters experience queer turmoil. They are endangered by their queerness, and it is recognizable as a daily struggle, while *Orphan Black*'s narrative turmoil is only ever directed for the category "woman." Both series have several diegetic LGBTQIA+ representations and are favorites among queer audiences, but both also suffer from a lack of female representation about-the-line in production, despite a strong onscreen presence.

Participation in television production, or access to means of storytelling production, has always been bound by a cultural politics of representation that essentializes and commoditizes race, gender, and sexuality. If a group of cisgender, straight, white men make a TV show, it isn't considered political, but when women, LGBT people, people of color—and especially combinations thereof— produce culture, locating its value is fraught with alienation (Christian).

Exploring the relationship between financing, casting, production, and distribution—along with the stratified nature of production assets—helps provide a complete picture of relative autonomy (Bourdieu, *Field of Cultural Production*), or the negotiated conditions in which hierarchical tensions play out. Henderson calls the queer solution to this "relay" or a fragmentation of telos that asks us to negotiate and re-negotiate the many places in the lifecycle of a cultural product, whose many ambitions mean that some are more autonomous than others.

Queer Capital

While the Wachowskis, two Chicago-raised siblings, had been making blockbuster films for 20 years, *Sense8* was their first foray into TV. They began developing the series in 2012 with J. Michael Straczynski, creator/producer of *Babylon 5* (Syndicated/TNT, 1994–1999). An original scripted series, *Sense8* was announced in October 2012, only days before the premiere of the Wachowskis' adaptation of bestselling novel *Cloud Atlas* (David Mitchell, 2012). In March of 2013, Netflix, as distributor but not producer, ordered a ten-episode first season.

Sense8 embraces abstract *and* concrete queer intimacy, while focusing on survival and the willingness, literally, to fight back. In *Sense8*, eight people in disparate corners of the globe become telepathically, telekinetically, and televisually linked through an inexplicable evolutionary leap. These "Sensates" slowly awaken to one another within a web of shared experience and action, forming a "Cluster" that must unite against BPO and its plan to weaponize sensate biology before eradicating all sensates. Women and queers continue to struggle to be represented, and especially to produce *their own* representations on screen, as evidenced in the annual reports "The Celluloid Ceiling" by Martha Lauzen and GLAAD's "Where We Are on TV" (Townsend and Deerwater). Queer representations, like others, fall into what Bourdieusian field theory calls a "repertoire of possibilities" determined by a "balance of forces between social agents" (Bourdieu 34). For complex LGBTQIA+ representations that are meaningful to the communities they represent to become produced in culture, some of those agents need to *be* queer, or to *facilitate* queer cultural production.

The Wachowskis are *both* transgender women. Lana, who began transitioning in 2009, and also identifies as lesbian, earned a Human Rights Campaign Visibility Award in 2012. Lilly came out in 2016, taking a hiatus from *Sense8* Season 2 to focus on her transition. For *Sense8*, the Wachowskis demonstrate a clear investment in credentialing their *cast* as queer allies, given that, setting aside on-screen genders and sexualities, seven of the eight series leads have easily discernable queer projects on their resumé.

Sense8 was the first U.S. TV series to feature a transgender character (San Francisco hacker Nomi Marks), played by a trans performer (Jamie Clayton), also written/directed by a trans person (Lana Wachowski). Jamie Clayton has been an out transwoman working in Hollywood since 2010, but she had no existing relationship with the Wachowskis. Tuppence Middleton (playing London-based Icelandic D.J. Riley Blue) was a supporting character in *The Imitation Game* (2014), a biopic of gay crypto-grapher/war hero Alan Turing, while Bae Doona (playing banker/martial artist Sun Bak from Seoul) starred in *A Girl at My Door* (Korea, 2014), in which she plays a rural police officer in a lesbian relationship. Bae and Middleton had existing relationships with the Wachowskis, in that Bae appeared in *Cloud Atlas* (2012), and both Bae and Middleton appeared in *Jupiter Ascending* (2015), the latter of which had premiered in theatres only three months before the release of *Sense8* Season 1.

Max Riemelt (playing German safecracker Wolfgang Bognanow) starred in *Free Fall* (Germany, 2013), in which he plays a gay police officer in an affair with a hetero-domesticated male co-worker. Tina Desai (playing Kala Dandekar, a pharmaceutical tech in Mumbai) is known for her role in *The Best Exotic Marigold Hotel* (U.K., 2011), which features a subplot about a gay affair. In Desai's debut Hindi feature film *Yeh Faasley* (India, 2011), she starred opposite Anupam Kher, the first actor to depict a gay man in a Bollywood film. Miguel Ángel Silvestre (playing actor Lito Rodriguez in Mexico City) is a protégé of out gay writer/director Pedro Almodóvar and starred in his raunchy queer/kinky comedy *I'm So Excited!* (Spain, 2013). Finally, Brian J. Smith (playing Chicago police officer Will Gorski) starred in *Hate Crime* (2005), in which he plays an openly gay man living with his partner in suburban Texas, when the former is murdered by a homophobic Christian fanatic and the latter, failed by law enforcement, must seek justice by other means (lending heavily to the *sensate* ethos). This only leaves Aml Ameen in the first season and Toby Onwumere in the second, playing Capheus Onyango, a van driver in Nairobi, Kenya, without such projects to their names.

Sense8 is unique in that "sensate" is not merely a euphemism for queerness. Several of the characters are *also* diegetically LGBT. Of the eight leads, one (Lito) is gay, and another (Nomi) is a transwoman/lesbian, but of the other seven regular non-leads, one (Lito's boyfriend, Hernan) is gay, and another (Nomi's partner, Amanita) is a cisgender lesbian. The other trademark of the series is its ethno-geographical diversity, as the series' leads consist of eight people, in seven countries, on four continents, as described above.

Keegan calls the cluster "a unified symbiosis—an eightfold composite character" (109), while Lana Wachowski clarifies it as a "*supra* or *meta* character—something both singular and specific while also something universal" (Keegan 148).The rhetoric of *Sense8* comes to the fore as characters revolve around a particular sentiment, sometimes delivering a collective diatribe that represents what the Wachowskis have to say to/about the World. When Mexican actor Lito is harassed by a reporter about his sexuality, the entire cluster responds, cascading ("Who am I?" 202):

> You're not trying to understand *anything*, because labels are the *opposite* of understanding. And who is standing here? Who am I? Do you mean where I'm from? Do you mean what I one day might become? Do you mean what I do? What I've done? Do you mean what *you* see. What *I've* seen? Do you mean what I fear, or what I dream? Do you mean who I love? Do you mean what I've lost? Who am I? I guess who I am is exactly the same as who you are.

Feminist Capital

Like *Sense8, Orphan Black* is about radical connectivity, in this case specifically sisterhood. It focuses on a group of adult female clones who, through a series of improbable events, discover one another and band together to trace and confront their origins and makers. The core group of clones (all played by the exceptionally talented Canadian actress Tatiana Maslany, reacting off the performances of stunt-double Kathryn Alexandre) consists of con artist Sarah Manning, who lives in an unidentified Toronto, along with uptight homemaker and community organizer Alison Hendrix. Cosima Niehaus, completing her Ph.D. in Experimental Evolutionary Developmental Biology at the University of Minnesota, soon joins them. With Cosima a lesbian and Sarah exhibiting bisexual traits, there's additional representation. Cast as the early villainess is Rachel Duncan, a unique self-aware clone and smooth businesswoman from Cambridge who works in Toronto for the company that created them all. Most volatile is Helena, a Ukranian true believer and assassin seeking to murder the unholy copies, as she believes. While the actress plays nine other clones onscreen, these are the central characters.

Together they investigate the nefarious Dyad Institute, whose program created them (and keeps them under tight surveillance). *Orphan Black* has a distinct queer *and* feminist orientation, especially given the genetic source of the clones is a female-identifying intersex person with both male and female DNA. While a male scientist orchestrated their births, they have no actual biological father—a brilliant inversion of the misogynistic denial of a woman's role in reproduction (a trope of cyberpunk, no doubt) that famed feminist Judith Butler calls "autogenesis." A further counter to this is that protagonist Sarah Manning has a daughter, despite her DNA being edited specifically to prevent reproduction.

Most of the lead-character-clones were raised, or live, in Canada or the U.S., though there are many others from Europe and elsewhere. The original core group of Sarah, Allison, and Cosima dub themselves the "Clone Club," and begin counter-surveilling and disrupting Dyad's activities. The members of Clone Club fight for their independence, their bodies, and their lives, frequently rescuing one another just in the nick of time. They also have a growing circle of allies in their friends, families, and partners, and even among Dyad personnel. Of the three performers who appear in all 50 episodes, two are women—Manning (Tatiana Maslany) and her adoptive mother, Siobhan Sadler (Maria Doyle Kennedy), while the other is Manning's decidedly gay foster brother Felix Dawkins (Jordan Gavaris).

Regarding the envisioners of this nearly all-women project, *Orphan Black* co-creators Graeme Manson and John Fawcett graduated film school together in 1997, when Manson's final project was writing what would amount to the Kafkaesque thriller *Cube* (1997). The two filmmakers collaborated on a number of smaller projects leading up to *Orphan Black*. The show was launched with four male executive producers—its two male co-creators, plus then co-presidents at Temple Street Productions, David Fortier and Ivan Schoenberg. Maslany already had a relationship with Temple Street from playing a recurring character (heroin-addict and therapy patient of the title character) in *Being Erica* (CBC, 2009–2011). This likely qualified her for the central role of Manning, a scrappy streetwise hustler. Of the seven people all credited with producing the full fifty episodes of the series, five are men and only two are women (Kerry Appleyard and Claire Welland), while of six people credited with producing twenty to thirty episodes (episodes have multiple producers), three are men and three are women (Karen Walton, Mackenzie Donaldson, and series star Tatiana Maslany). Walton departed after Season 2, while Donaldson and Maslany produced for Seasons 3 through 5.

Of the twelve people to direct *Orphan Black*, a staggering eleven are men. The lone female director, Helen Shaver—best known for her work on *Law & Order: Special Victims Unit* (NBC, 1999–)—worked on only three of fifty episodes. Fawcett directed seventeen episodes, while another male crew member directed eight. Various other male directors helmed between one and four episodes. As for cinematography, Aaron Morton, male, is credited for forty-seven of fifty episodes. The writing process for *Orphan Black* speaks of budgetary constraints but possibly also of egalitarian values as, while the series cut expenses by hiring nine film students as writers, all of whom were also credited for the full fifty episodes, Kim Coghill, Elize Morgan, and Rebecca Sernasie were the only three women among the nine.

Miranda J. Banks, author of "Gender below-the-line: Defining Feminist Production Studies," notes that "gender disparity is a critical issue ... but in order to understand the nature of the professional landscape, it is crucial to look not just at the overall numbers, but to examine the gendering of individual professions within the industry" (95). Historically (in both the U.S. and Canada) there has been tight space for female directors and cinematographers—something feminist Netflix series *Jessica Jones* recently highlighted and combatted when its second season, consisting of thirteen hour-long episodes (2017) were *all* directed by female-identifying filmmakers.

One might have a healthy level of skepticism toward two men creating/running a series about sisterhood-against-patriarchy. However, *Orphan Black* does not suffer from ambivalence toward female empowerment. *Orphan Black*'s development was heavily influenced by Cosima Herter, Ph.D., a "science consultant" (script advisor) and longtime friend of series co-creator Graeme Manson. As an interviewer describes Herter, "listening to her describe her workload, you might as well call her a co-creator of the series" (Maloney). Herter's doctorate in the History and Philosophy of Science, Technology and Medicine makes her very knowledgeable about genetics and cloning, but her feminist politics are what really make the difference for the show.

Herter, who is deeply troubled by Eugenics-minded Darwinian ethics, says that "biology is always marshaled into the service of political power and social control. There's literally nothing you can talk about, in the biological sciences ... that doesn't have a social or political impact." Herter sees gendered violence in the "splice" aesthetics of androcentric cyberpunk, asking, "So who gets to control it? [And why] do they decide which bodies are better than others?" (Maloney). Clearly, women and queers need to tell their own stories, offering competing and overriding narratives to their poor representations of the past, while also simply participating in culture.

Industry Viability Case Study:
Sense8's *Cancellation*

On June 1, 2017, only weeks after the Season 2 premiere, Netflix announced that they would not renew the series. The cancellation prompted an outcry on social media, along with petitions and letter-writing campaigns, and ultimately, Netflix agreed that the Wachowskis could wrap up the series in a special finale episode, which aired June 8, 2018. Netflix executive Cindy Holland published a statement, claiming of *Sense8*:

It is everything we and the fans dreamed it would be: bold, emotional, stunning, kick ass, and out-right unforgettable. Never has there been a more truly global show with an equally diverse and international cast and crew … mirrored by [a] connected community of deeply passionate fans around the world.

The message offered no hint toward motive, although critics and trade press have broken it into three sets of concerns around (1) production, (2) reception, and (3) "network" aspirations, summarized as such: Production cost per episode was too expensive, the season cycle was too long, and marketing did not achieve mainstream traction (Bianco). In terms of reception, viewership was too low and dwindled too fast, reviews were mixed, and awards capital was queer-specific only. As for aspirations, Netflix's long-term programming plan relies on canceling less profitable shows to invest in other new flagship series—which, ironically, is what *Sense8* was supposed to become.

Production Concerns

Season 1 (2015) cost about $4.5 million per episode, but Season 2 (2017) costs soared to $9 million per episode ("Sense8 Producer"), making the series about as expensive as *Game of Thrones* Season 6 (HBO, 2016) (Cuccinello). After wrapping production, but before releasing Season 2, Netflix reportedly opted to not pay talent-holding fees for the fifteen series regulars, including the eight leads, meaning that the cast may not have been available for a Season 3 (Andreeva). If showrunning expenses ran up against cast options, Netflix would have had to either reduce the number of shooting locations or simply cancel the show—and its on-location shooting was the industrial trademark of the series.

Netflix does not own copyrights to Season 1, which was financed by London-based Motion Picture Capital (MPC), ultimately a subsidiary of Reliance Group, the Mumbai conglomerate controlled by Anil Ambani, younger brother of Mukesh Ambani, India's wealthiest person. It seems that, on some level, the Wachowskis wrote the story around its financial support. Netflix *does* have copyrights for Season 2 (both production *and* distribution credits).

The Wachowskis may have traded relative financial autonomy for uninterrupted creative freedom, which may have also affected negotiating power when it came to a renewal decision.

In a rare interview, Lana Wachowski claimed that "my wife, Karin [is] the reason there was a season two of Sense8." Whatever Wachowski means, Season 2 added a new Chicago-based, show-specific production card, "Venus Castina," attributed to both Wachowski and spouse Karin Winslow, who is also a transgender woman and produced a 2014 documentary film about legendary transgender playwright Kate Bornstein, as well as being a professional dominatrix to high-profile Hollywood clients for many years ("Buck Angel"). If kink capital helped build *Sense8*, that only adds to its queerness.

Reception Concerns/"Network" Aspirations

In a note alerting fans that the series would be revived for a proper conclusion, Lana Wachowski told fans, regarding Netflix, "Believe me, they love the show as much as we do but the numbers have always been challenging" (Watchowski, "Death"). Holland told trade press nearly a year after cancellation that "at some point if you don't have the viewership showing up to justify the expense of the series, you're going to want to end it" (Harp). Indeed, *Sense8* with its many plots and characters as well as nebulous science fiction, was difficult to explain—even to people employed in media criticism or production. While queer subcultures gulped up the series, key demographics like action-adventure or science-fiction enthusiasts often struggled to find a foothold and lacked endurance as viewers, let alone fans.

From a Netflix perspective, ground floor originals like *House of Cards* and *Orange Is the New Black*, carrying queer capital of their own (albeit lopsidedly), each earned a Peabody in 2013, and collectively won 8 Primetime Emmys across five seasons. *Sense8*'s biggest accolade has been a GLAAD Media Award for Outstanding Drama Series in 2016. Netflix projects itself as having a budget that seems infinite, yet its appetites are not.

CEO Reed Hastings told reporters, shortly before the cancellation, that he was "always pushing the content team: 'We have to take more risk, you have to try more crazy things. Because we should have a higher cancel rate overall'" (Miller). *Sense8* was a managed risk, not a commitment to diversity, as Holland's lip service would make it seem. As one critic responded to the show's demise, "Suddenly, Netflix is like every other network: a place where series are not guaranteed to come back" (Greve). Netflix took on the Wachowskis' passion project, but it sees the most benefit in scaling up, which is why Hastings has said of hated-by-feminists teen drama *13 Reasons Why*, "You get some just unbelievable winners…. It's a great show, but we didn't realize just how it would catch on" (Davies). Netflix's most shameless bulwark at present is *The Crown*, which costs $130 million per season (Regalado) and has a privileged trajectory, being renewed two seasons ahead with a six-year overall intent (VanArendonk). The streaming giant also paid $100 million just for the rights to *Friends* (NBC, 1994–2004), even for a single year. Netflix began by distinguishing itself as serving marginal audiences, but once faced with real competition, they snap back to pure industry orientation.

Orphan Black's *Precarity/Hybridity*

While it lasted five seasons, *Orphan Black* faced "the customary challenges of most Canadian productions: piecemeal financing and risk-averse network executives" (Tinic 6). Space Network passed on *Orphan Black* in an original offer, and only after Temple Street Productions secured U.S. distribution through BBC America, was Bell Media, Space's parent company, quick to purchase domestic rights, in what Tinic calls a "reverse flow" variety of international joint venture (Dillon). Temple Street then had to secure production capital through public-private partnership endowments, via the Program Development Fund (CPDF), Independent Production Fund (IPF), and Cable Network Fund (CNF). Tinic notes that North American audiences tend to see any kind of European sensibility as "quality TV," and that the BBC acquisition played well in this respect. BBC Worldwide distributed the series in the U.K., while Netflix secured distribution in Spain, Belgium, and the Netherlands. In the U.S., Amazon has an exclusive license for streaming full seasons.

Engineered Globalism

Returning to network level decision making, let us revisit Holland's claim when canceling *Sense8*. What does it mean to be "truly global" or truly "diverse"? Building audience publics is at the heart of the narrative and character projects of these two series. Both have gone to great lengths to engineer participation in both international and intercontinental markets, while at the same time cultivating heavily interactive fandoms. Keegan notes that "*Sense8* mobilizes race, gender, and nationality as stereotypic forms of personhood even as it metanarratively comments on them as constructs—a bimodal strategy the series forces both its characters and audience to straddle" (116). This interpellates extranational audiences through "racial nationalism" as "shorthand to build quickly toward the global shape of its cluster formation" (Keegan 116).

While *Sense8*'s diversity is blaring, *Orphan Black* constructs global audiences far more Eurocentrically, using subtle appeals—often either short-lived, purely symbolic, or ironically removed. Of course, the core group of clones originate from both Anglophone and Francophone Canada, from the United States and the United Kingdom, and (an outlier) Ukraine—the feral, convent-raised assassin, Helena, is conveniently of the same ethno-national origin as Maslany. Technically, all of the clones are biologically Irish, as their DNA has a single source in their intersex parent, Kendall Malone. Other clones hail from Western Europe and beyond. Beth Childs, a police officer in Toronto, dies in the first episode, but has a long life in flashbacks. The American Jennifer Fitzsimmons (already deceased) and Tony Sawicki each have one episode—Tony is an interesting case as he has transitioned into a man. The fluffy, frivlolous Krystal Goderitch, also American, has a longer arc and pops in throughout the final three seasons. Janika Zingler from Austria, Danielle Fournier from France, and Aryanna Giordano of Italy appear only in pictures with decidedly origin-based names. They suggest representation but barely exist. The survivor of their group, Katja Obinger from Germany, dies in episode two. The Helsinki flashback comic books introduce another set of specifically European clones: Niki Lintula from Finland, Ania Kaminska from Poland, Justyna Buzek from the Czech Republic, Danish Sofia Jensen and Dutch twins Fay and Famke (Kennedy et al.). (Ania may be the unnamed European clone killed by Helena in the penultimate episode's flashback.) Once again, all are deceased, though the comic gives them a limited storyline. These are all friends of the Finnish character Veera Suominen, also known as M.K. or Mika, who stars in Seasons 4 and 5. It's the Helsinki girls who arguably begin Clone Club, though they must pass the torch to their New World sisters.

Only in the final episode does the show start playing with clones being from Latin America, native Spanish speakers, and on some level crypto-trans-racial—which doesn't feel great when of a dozen essential performers in the show, there is only one person of color, Kevin Hanchard as African American detective Arthur Bell, who aids Manning from time to time. Bit parts of color go to Sarah's South African birth mother Amelia, a later surrogate named Kendra Dupree, and police IT-guy Raj Singh. There are also Alison's adopted children, Arthur's daughter, and the minor villainess (already deceased) Maggie Chen. Another Asian woman in a larger role is villainess Evie Cho, who dominates Season 4. Despite these hints of diversity, basically everyone else is white, with the clones taking center stage.

Sense8's hailing of audiences through globally diverse, though stereotypical characters is, by comparison, in better faith. Claire Light in "*Sense8* and the Failure of Global Imagination" calls the Wachowskis "aesthetic internationalists [whose] worldview [is] refracted through international pop culture artifacts." Light is troubled by the show's choice to use only English, claiming that the senstates "can use each other's languages, knowledge, and skills, and experience each other's experiences firsthand [which is] incredibly attractive to Americans [from a] monolingual imperialist center." One imagines Netflix wanted the series this way. On considering other Netflix series like *Altered Carbon* (2018–present) or HBO's *Westworld* (2017–present), a broader trend emerges of courting audiences on a global scale by blurring ethnic affinities through cloning, body swaps, consciousness casting, and other devices. While both series dabble in decolonial narratives, and push back against monolingualism, they also take place centuries into the future, and rely on cyber-conceits that often undermine their feminism even while queering racialization and other neocolonial operations.

Authenticity, Identity, Efficacy

Sense8 depicts *organic* queer spectacle. Each season contains an episode with a scene at a pride parade, and both are shot at the events they depict ("I Am Also a We" 102, "Isolated Above, Connected Below" 206). The first frame shot for the series was at San Francisco Pride 2014, where Clayton and Agyeman (Nomi and Amanita) rode with "Dykes on Bikes" (Keppel). In 2016, for Season 2, the leads traveled to Brazil for São Paulo Pride, joining two million spectators (Soldani). The scene in São Paulo depicts closeted Mexican actor Lito coming out as gay to the world on a larger-than-life "kiss cam" with partner Hernan. Keegan argues that "sensate sex is a potent metaphor [of] two sometimes-utopian fantasies: the queer world of public sex … and the science fiction of intimate technological connectivity" (164–165).

Still, what does this "outness" say about closetedness? The *Sense8* "Who am I?" speech aims to make a point about identity that echoes Stuart Hall's *Questions of Cultural Identity*:

Identities are about questions of using the resources of history, language and culture in the process of becoming … not "who we are" or "where we came from," so much as what we might become, how we have been represented and how that bears on how we might represent ourselves. Identities are therefore constituted within, not outside representation.

Recalling Lana Wachowski's statement about the capacity to form identity, as well as concerns about trans alienation from representational protocols, "how we might represent ourselves" is a cerntral concern that also drives Muñoz (away from the here and now), as he theorizes "queerness as horizon."

From a trans* perspective, the storytelling has been revolutionary, according to Keegan, who calls *Sense8* "perhaps the most distinctly 'trans' text in the history of popular cinematic art" (Keegan 109). This exceeds the explicit, Keegan argues, "achieving a unique televisual language that aestheticizes the trans* sensorium as both a narrative and pedagogic form" (Keegan 110). While the asterisk works in trans studies more generally to declare the difference between gender and sex as arbitrary (and one's genital arrangement as nobody's business), here it extends into the more implicit boundary violations the series promotes.

The same is true of "Clone Club." *Orphan Black* and *Sense8* both exude a stigmaphilic lens, as per Henderson (and really Erving Goffman)—even perhaps entering a *traumaphilic* one, in that audiences are interpolated through a traumatic bond (inflected by gender and sexuality). Both series do this well. With reproductive rights and protections for LGBT people on the chopping block in the U.S., discourses that fuel resistance around women's bodily autonomy, especially those that are queer-inflected, are priceless.

Timeliness

Exactly two weeks after the São Paulo filming, 49 people were killed and 58 others wounded at LGBT nightclub Pulse in Orlando, Florida—on Latin night. Media scholar and gay person of color Aymar Jean Christian recalls, of the tragedy, "As I processed what happened.... I thought not only of whether the shooter had representations of #TwoMenKissing to alleviate his fear of difference but also of what representations of queer black and brown people Americans could see to imagine their lives and the loss" (254).

Christian's comment suggests Michael Warner's *The Trouble with Normal: Sex, Politics, and the Ethics of Queer Life*, which warned that "queers do not have the institutions for common memory and general transmission around which straight culture is built. Every new wave of queer youth picks up something from its predecessors but also invents itself from scratch." In her interview with Keegan, Lana Wachowski explains, "The relationship between survival and the imagination is a constant in the landscape of our work. You cannot survive without imagination" (144). *Sense8* displays queer black and brown skin in the throes of passion as a matter of course. Christian's longing illustrates the duty with which queer cultural producers like the Wachowskis are charged—to show the TV industry and Netflix that queer cultural capital is not disposable. If taking cash out of circulation is a crime in the United States, then so should be any such atomization.

Sense8 is saturated in combat, often involving firearms, which prompts Light to call violence its "universal language." However, *Lost* alumnus and series regular Naveen Andrews makes an excellent point that that the show's queer militancy is "anti-fascist in the best sense" (Robinson). Maintaining hope while bullets are flying takes substantial imagination, which is why Keegan says *Sense8* is "the optimistic queer/trans* science fiction that in 2015 we didn't yet sense we would need" (108).

Temporality

Three months after *Sense8* was cancelled, Maslany's *Orphan Black* performance won the 2017 Primetime Emmy Award for Outstanding Lead Actress in a Drama Series—possibly for the sheer technicality of her omni-characterization, but one hopes for the feminism and queerness of the series as well. While it feels deliberate that Cosima, the lesbian core clone on *Orphan Black*, is named after the series' science consultant, there seems to be no extradiegetic queerness to the series otherwise. Maslany has told reporters, "We offer good representation in terms of complex characters that aren't defined necessarily just by their sexuality but by every facet of what it is to be a person" (Kennedy). Cosima, her partner Delphine, and Felix indeed follow this pattern of "happen-to-be-gay." *Sense8*'s queers live parallel struggles as LGBT people and as sensates, which offers a further push into queer production orientation—one to be expected of these producers.

Orphan Black had already aired its second season by the time *Sense8* began production of its first, and it's hard not to read the latter as in conversation with the former, whose bio-punk influence on the zeitgeist of feminist and queer TV cannot be overstated. Nothing could be more illustrative than the fact that *Matrix* "auteurs" the Wachowskis' new series is decidedly *bio-punk*—a firm departure from the supposed *cyber*-pinnacle of their oeuvre. Keegan argues, drawing on Mittell, that "the Wachowskis' recent comings-out provide an unavoidably 'reorienting paratext'" (110). Bourdieu offered the notion of a "divided habitus" to account for class identity and how people depart from their class origins throughout life, often in extreme ways. Bourdieu typically discussed habitus as the class dimensions of developing taste as a consumer, but a divided habitus begs to be retheorized through gender transition. Who the Wachowskis know and trust is a product of historically material endemic gender discrimination in their industry. Having ascended through the ranks in a cis-het-male-dominated field—and, no less, by making action-adventure and sci-fi texts, the Wachowskis are a conundrum. They are both female-identifying, yet their closest collaborators are exclusively male.

For Bourdieu, divided habitus is defined by reconciliation. In the *Sense8* series finale ("Amor Vincit Omnia" 212), the Wachowskis reconfigure their *Matrix* mythscape, where "The Architect," a male creator figure, is supplanted by a female one, "The Mother." Halberstam denounces imperatives for a coherent retroactive narrative of trans lives, but this is easier said than done. In *Sense8*, transwoman Nomi makes a deal with more powerful computer hackers to erase her online past. This longing for "e–Death," or total erasure of former identity, should resonate with any incoherent mind-body life timeline.

Conclusion: Autonomy, Reloaded

Women and queers continue to struggle to be represented, and especially to produce *their own* representations on screen, as evidenced in annual reports like "The Celluloid Ceiling" (Lauzen) and "Where We Are on TV"

(GLAAD). How, then, can queers, women, and queer women tell their own stories? For complex LGBTQIA+ representations that are meaningful to the communities they represent to become produced in culture, some producers need to either *be* queer, or to *facilitate* queer cultural production wholeheartedly. Under what conditions these paradigms that Henderson calls "queer orientation" and "industry orientation" can be reconciled—while still achieving audience scale and series longevity—is a riddle for the Wachowskis, Netflix, and every queer fed up with being a pawn in the Game of Eyeballs.

Orphan Black's Clone Club spilled off the screen, stimulating fans who identified with the ideology of the series, and the Wachowskis' broader audience cluster did the same, spurring a revival, however limited, of the series—an exception, not the rule, to be clear. Like Nomi's e–Death and Neo's waking up to *The Matrix*, we can imagine commitment to genuine diversity, at the level of industry, medium, genre, or individual producer, also an omega point—a doorway into more meaningful, less censored representation, combined with broader scale and visibility. Lana Wachowski tells a story of visiting the Tate Britain museum, where Pre-Raphaelite and Romantic paintings line the walls of a very mainstream "Gallery 57." Wachowski laments the confining of work by queer painters Tino Rodriguez and Virgo Paraiso in an obscure wing of the museum, saying, "I wanted those queer paintings to be in Gallery 57" (Keegan 136).

Netflix is the most LGBTQIA+-inclusive of the three main U.S. streaming services, holding a 65.7 percent share of queer roles, versus 18.6 percent for Amazon and 15.7 percent for Hulu (Townsend and Rainwater 10). Netflix also has the highest percentage of people of color among queer roles, with 26.1 percent, versus 23.1 percent for Hulu and 18.2 percent for Amazon (Townsend and Rainwater 10). However, Farr is correct in saying, "Calls for 'better' representation no longer have the same potential to effect systemic change…. Because capitalism is adaptive, it has incorporated calls for more diverse, fairer, representations into its logic" (160).

While both women and queers too often don't get to tell their own stories, once they do, we have to ask tough questions about which women, which queers, and whether or not "better representation" is a measure of anything but symbolic progress. *Sense8* and *Orphan Black* represent queer-oriented cultural productions designed to interface with popular genre and build communities of resistance through its grammar—all while using the same frameworks of capital and identity and location that continue to trouble production studies, fourth wave feminism, queer politics, and yours truly.

WORKS CITED

Andreeva, Nellie. "*Sense8*: Netflix Reassembling Cast After Options Had Expired, Raising Prospects for Season 3." *Deadline Hollywood*, 2 Mar 2017. http://deadline.com/2017/03/sense8-netflix-cast-new-deals-options-had-expired-season-3-renewal-1201955448.

Banks, Miranda J. "Gender Below-the-line: Defining Feminist Production Studies." *Production Studies: Cultural Studies of Media Industries,* edited by Vicki Mayer, Miranda J. Banks, and John T. Caldwell. Routledge, 2009, pp. 87–98.

Bianco, Julia. "The Real Reason Sense8 Was Canceled." *Looper,* 5 Jun 2017. http://www.looper.com/68464/real-reason-sense8-canceled.

Bourdieu, Pierre. *The Field of Cultural Production: Essays on Art and Literature.* Columbia University Press, 1993.

_____. "The Forms of Capital." *Handbook of Theory and Research for the Sociology of Education,* edited by John G. Richardson. Greenwood Press, 1986, pp. 241–258.

Butler, Judith. *Bodies That Matter: On the Discursive Limits of "Sex."* Psychology Press, 1993.

Christian, Aymar Jean. *Open TV: Innovation beyond Hollywood and the Rise of Web Television.* NYU Press, 2018.

Cuccinello, Hayley. "*Game of Thrones* Season 6 Costs $10 Million Per Episode, Has Biggest Battle Scene Ever." *Forbes,* 22 Apr 2016. https://www.forbes.com/sites/hayleycuccinello/2016/04/22/game-of-thrones-season-6-costs-10-million-per-episode-has-biggest-battle-scene-ever/#30df905e11bb.

Davies, Madeline. "Teens Deserved More Than *13 Reasons Why* Gave Them." *Jezebel,* 8 May 2017. https://themuse.jezebel.com/teens-deserved-more-than-13-reasons-why-gave-them-1795016822.

Dillon, Mark. "Space: Boldly Going Where No Channel Had Gone Before at 15." *Playback,* 5 Sep 2012. http://playbackonline.ca/content/pdf/51557.pdf.

Farr, Brittany. "Seeing Blackness in Prison: Understanding Prison Diversity on Netflix's *Orange Is the New Black.*" *The Netflix Effect: Technology and Entertainment in the 21st Century,* edited by Kevin McDonald and Daniel Smith-Rowsey. Bloomsbury, 2016, pp. 155–169.

Greve, Max. "*Sense8* Is Canceled and That's Why It's Now Netflix's Most Important Show." *Seeking Alpha,* 14 Jul 2017. https://seekingalpha.com/article/4087786-sense8-canceled-now-netflixs-important-show.

Halberstam, J. Jack. *The Queer Art of Failure.* Duke University Press, 2011.

Hall, Stuart. "Introduction: Who Needs 'Identity'?" *Questions of Cultural Identity,* edited by Stuart Hall and Paul Du Gay. Sage, 1996, pp. 1–17.

Harp, Justin. "Netflix Comes Clean about why it Cancelled Sense8." *Digital Spy,* 21 Apr 2018. http://www.digitalspy.com/tv/ustv/news/a855291/why-netflix-cancelled-sense8.

Henderson, Lisa. *Love and Money: Queers, Class, and Cultural Production.* NYU Press, 2013.

Holland, Cindy. "*Sense8* Canceled at Netflix." *Netflix,* 1 Jun 2017. Press Release. https://media.netflix.com/en/press-releases/sense8-will-not-return-for-another-season.

Keegan, Cáel M. *Lana and Lilly Wachowski.* University of Illinois Press, 2018.

Kennedy, Heli, John Fawcett, and Graeme Manson (w) and Alan Quah, Wayne Nichols and Fico Ossio (a). *Orphan Black: Helsinki.* IDW Publishing, 2016.

Kennedy, John R. "*Orphan Black* Star Tatiana Maslany Tears up Talking about LGBT Support." *Global News,* 30 May 2015. https://globalnews.ca/news/2023021/orphan-black-star-tatiana-maslany-tears-up-explaining-support-for-lgbt-people.

Keppel, Josh. "The Wachowskis Begin Filming of New Netflix Series, *Sense8,* in San Francisco." *NBC Bay Area,* 19 June 2014. https://www.nbcbayarea.com/news/local/The-Wachowskis-Sense8-Netflix-Series-San-Francisco-263721841.html.

Lauzen, Martha M. "The Celluloid Ceiling: Behind-the-Scenes Employment of Women on the Top 100, 250, and 500 Films of 2017." *Women in TV Film,* 2018. http://womenintvfilm.sdsu.edu/wp-content/uploads/2018/01/2017_Celluloid_Ceiling_Report.pdf.

Light, Claire. "*Sense8* and the Failure of Global Imagination." *The Nerds of Color* 10, 2015. https://thenerdsofcolor.org/2015/06/10/sense8-and-the-failure-of-global-imagination.

Maloney, Devin. "*Orphan Black* Science Consultant Cosima Herter Breaks Down the Series Finale." *Vanity Fair,* 12 Aug 2017. https://www.vanityfair.com/hollywood/2017/08/orphan-black-series-finale-season-5-cosima-herter-interview.

Manson, Graeme, and John Fawcett, creators. *Orphan Black.* BBC America, 2013–2017.

McHale, Brian. *Constructing Postmodernism.* Routledge, 1992.

Miller, Julie. "Why Netflix Is Actually Aiming for More Cancellations." *Vanity Fair*, 31 May 2017. https://www.vanityfair.com/hollywood/2017/05/netflix-cancel.

Mittell, Jason. *Complex TV: The Poetics of Contemporary Television Storytelling*. NYU Press, 2015.

Muñoz, José Esteban. *Cruising Utopia: The Then and There of Queer Futurity*. NYU Press, 2009.

Regalado, Michelle. "The Most Expensive Netflix Original TV Shows." *TV CheatSheet*, 4 Apr 2018. https://www.cheatsheet.com/entertainment/expensive-netflix-original-tv-shows.html/?a=viewall.

Robinson, Tasha. "Naveen Andrews Considers Sense8 'A direct fuck you' to Global Fascism." *The Verge*, 4 May 2017. https://www.theverge.com/2017/5/4/15458946/naveen-andrews-sense8-netflix-lana-wachowski-lilly.

"*Sense8* Producer: 'If renewed, season 3 of *Sense8* likely to be its last.'" *Newsflix*, 11 May 2017. http://newsflix.altervista.org/sense8-producer-if-renewed-season-3-of-sense8-likely-to-be-its-last.

Soldani, Bianca. "São Paulo Explodes in Colour for Gay Pride Parade's 20th Birthday." *Australia*, 31 May 2016. https://www.sbs.com.au/topics/sexuality/article/2016/05/30/sao-paulo-explodes-colour-gay-pride-parades-20th-birthday.

Tinic, Serra. "Where in the World Is *Orphan Black*? Change and Continuity in Global TV Production and Distribution." *Media Industries Journal*, vol. 1, no. 3, 2015.

Tompkins, Avery. "Asterisk." *Transgender Studies Quarterly*, vol. 1, no. 1–2, 2014.

Townsend, Megan, and Raina Deerwater. "2017–2018 Where We Are on TV: GLAAD's Annual Report on LGBTQ Inclusion." *GLAAD Media Institute*, Nov 2017. http://glaad.org/files/WWAT/WWAT_GLAAD_2017–2018.pdf.

VanArendonk, Kathryn. "Why Should I Care about Queen Elizabeth II, Star of Netflix's *The Crown*?" *Vulture*, 1 Nov 2016. http://www.vulture.com/2016/11/queen-elizabeth-ii-netflix-the-crown.html.

Wachowski, Lana. "Death doesn't let you say goodbye. 2 hour finale episode in the works. Tell your cluster." Twitter, *Sense8*. https://twitter.com/sense8/status/880495946370568194.

Wachowski, Lana, and Lilly and J. Michael Straczynski, creators. *Sense8*. Netflix, 2015–2018.

Warner, Michael. *The Trouble with Normal: Sex, Politics, and the Ethics of Queer Life*. Free Press, 1999.

Warriors
in a Respectful World

Wynonna Earp, Supergirl and the Power of Choosing

Resa Haile

Superman's cousin. Wyatt Earp's great-great-granddaughter. When considering them both, one thing becomes quite clear: One time-honored (although much-derided of late) method of creating powerful female characters is to use a template from male characters. Perhaps she is a genderbent version, like Lucy Liu's Joan Watson on *Elementary* or both Holmes and Watson on Japan's *Miss Sherlock*. Still, this is nothing new: "The practice goes back at least as far as 1940's gender-swapped cinematic take on the stage play *The Front Page* as *His Girl Friday* or the 1943 stage musical (and later, film) *Carmen Jones*, which added a black cast and a contemporaneous flavor to the 1875 opera *Carmen*" (Hassenger). Many classic shows and films offered a sequel or spinoff with a female counterpart, like *The Bionic Woman, The Next Karate Kid,* or even, arguably, *Doctor Who.* Sometimes a role is written for a man but co-opted by a woman, like Sigourney Weaver's action heroine in the *Alien* franchise. Recent shows made bold choices in flipping *Battlestar Galactica*'s heroic Starbuck and Boomer and *Lost in Space*'s Dr. Smith. Lately, big-budget films have been gender-flipping the entire cast, to produce *Ocean's 8, What Men Want,* and *Ghostbusters.* The heroine may inherit the male hero's title, as with the female Thor and Wolverine in Marvel comics. Another choice is that she's a descendant or relative, like Kara Danvers on *Supergirl* (CBS and the CW, 2015–present) or the eponymous heroine of *Wynonna Earp* (Syfy, 2016–present).

Gender-flipping as a concept has had successes and failures. As Amanda Hess of *The New York Times* explains:

> The gender-swapped comedy satisfies a couple of-the-moment entertainment industry imperatives: It allows Hollywood to reanimate lucrative old properties (*Ocean's Eleven* was, of course, itself a remake), while recasting them with diverse casts and woke politics. That's resulted in a boom in comedic parts for women, but they come

49

with baggage. These reboots require women to relive men's stories instead of fashioning their own. And they're subtly expected to fix these old films, to neutralize their sexism and infuse them with feminism, to rebuild them into good movies with good politics, too. They have to do everything the men did, except backwards and with ideals.

Certainly, there are advantages. Stories like these show off that women can be action heroes or masterminds. In a world of the Smurfette Principle (coined by *The New York Times'* Katha Pollitt in 1991) in which a hundred male Smurfs and one Smurfette are standard, an all-women team-up shakes up conventions and destroys marginalization. Multiple actresses are allowed to play off one another instead of remaining in the background of an all-male story. "That sounds like a bare minimum for progress, but considering how few movies place women in leading roles (less than half as many as those starring men), movies with four or five female leads, aimed at general audiences looking for a good time start to look revolutionary," explains Jesse Hassenger of *The Verge.*

This casting also gives women much better roles than those of love interests (Julia Roberts in *Ocean's*) or helpmates (Annie Potts as the *Ghostbusters* receptionist). In the latter, casting Chris Hemsworth as the airheaded "pretty assistant" was funny and also allowed the film to criticize gender roles while getting rid of the creepy workplace power dynamic. "When the women of *Ghostbusters* gently sexually harass their ditsy hunk of a receptionist (Chris Hemsworth in glasses), it lacks the malicious edge of Bill Murray effectively stalking Sigourney Weaver under the guise of busting her ghost. Because real women are physically and socially vulnerable to men, granting sexual power to them on film feels harmless and a little cute," Hess adds.

On genre television, many of these flipped roles have been met with delight. Even *Battlestar* purists adored tough-talking, cigar-smoking Starbuck, a hotshot pilot and flying instructor who marries a sports star and cheats on him with her ex-boyfriend's brother. She does what she wants and absolutely pushes the envelope but also has more nuance than the original Starbuck with familial jokes with her captain and angelic visions of her destiny. Watson on *Elementary*, like Starbuck, is empowered by not playing the male character but by making the role her own. Though caring, feminine, and far more of a detective than the man of the short stories, Joan Watson does channel her counterpart's fascination with Sherlock as a person and as a professional—sharing his adoration of puzzles and mysteries. While fans wondered even before the first episode whether she would date Sherlock, to the relief of many, she remained his colleague.

What about Supergirl and Wynonna? While their origins define the characters to some extent, each uses her choices to truly break out and become paragons of the fourth wave.

No Longer Just a Superman: Supergirl

Both Supergirl and Wynonna got their start in comic books. In 1959, a post-war time of waning interest in comic books, Supergirl bursts from her ship in *Action Comics* #252, a pretty blonde in a short skirt. Her name places her as yet another "girl" counterpart to the more powerful male superhero, and the writing stresses this aspect. When Superman introduces her to the world, he comments, "Physically, she's the mightiest female of all time! But at heart, she's as gentle and sweet and as quick to tears—as any ordinary girl!" Superman, delighted to discover a teenage refugee cousin, places her in an orphanage, promising to watch out for her "like a big brother." She in turn, must play the fifties' clichéd little sister:

> Girls of the time were supposed to be sweet and wholesome. They were told to play with dolls and grow up into homemakers who would use their brains and strength to mop kitchen floors in high heels, dress beautifully, and play jacks with their children. They were also meant to support their husbands in everything, making them feel like real men who could protect their little women.... Superman orders Supergirl to fall in line [Frankel, *Superheroines* 62].

He does not adopt her, however, as this would imperil his secret identity. Instead of letting her fight beside him, in fact, he keeps her in reserve, as he insists, "No Supergirl! I have many cunning enemies! If I'm ever in a bad trap, you're the only one who could rescue me!" In fact, Superman bars her from using her powers until he judges that she can use them "properly." As a feminine copy of Superman, she had his powers but was specifically so girlish that she had very little agency—and what she had, she needed to cultivate in secret. As orphan Linda Lee, she pretends to be cooking or ironing, furtively saving the day but forbidden to seek public acclaim.

Her Supergirl side can only emerge in secret, hidden even from her cousin. While superheroes are occasionally thrown out of town and must operate beneath the government radar, some specifically female ones are ordered to reign in their joie de vivre (She-Hulk), burgeoning superstrength (Pepper Potts in *Iron Man 3*), total power (Dark Phoenix), or entire identity (Supergirl). Thus the secret identity can be a prison as much as a tool for societal acceptance (Frankel, *Superheroines* 65).

> Gender-flipping her threw her into the fifties' strict gender conventions and thus demonstrated the misogyny and repression of the time. While she was the only lasting superheroine of the fifties, her era was clearly unprepared to do justice to female heroes. After this, Supergirl had more complicated arcs including her death and erasure, eventually followed by reboots and, in a sense, resurrection [Kistler].

Another relevant piece of history comes with the CW's teen superhero shows, *Smallville* and *Birds of Prey*. *Smallville* (2001–2011) featured young

Clark Kent, starting as a clumsy, marginalized high school freshman. The producers insisted that the character would not be Superboy, but an all-too-human teen struggling with powers. Executive producers Brian Peterson and Kelly Souders spent ten popular seasons keeping the "No Tights, No Flight" philosophy as they called it. "What we wanted to do all along was show hints at where he was going because that is a whole different story that is yet to be told," Peterson explained. As he concluded, "We all wanted it to be the end of Clark Kent's journey because it's a show *about* Clark Kent," he said. "In the days when we saw him in a flannel shirt, the suit was the furthest thing from his mind" (Goldberg). The difference here was that Clark chose for himself to conceal his abilities and even refused to fly, in contrast with the comics' Supergirl, whose older cousin restricted her. The show actually has its own Supergirl (Laura Vandervoort), as Clark's cousin arrives in Season 7. However, even as he tries cooping her up to protect their secret identities, this alluring teen prances around in a bikini and insists on entering the local beauty pageant to Clark's embarrassment. As she points out that she's doing this because she wants to, she's advocating third wave feminism, a movement that sought to keep the equality of the seventies but reclaim makeup and high heels. Melissa Klein writes in *Third Wave Agenda*, "We are interested in creating not models of androgyny so much as models of contradiction. We want not to get rid of the trappings of traditional femininity or sexuality so much as to pair them with demonstrations of strength or power" (222–223). Supergirl certainly combines all this, though she only sticks around for a season.

Birds of Prey, developed by Laeta Kalogridis for the same network, launched in 2002 as a similar show for teens, but starring three women: Oracle (the former Batgirl), Huntress, and Black Canary, all as active superheroines in a Gotham without Batman. Reviews were critical, even misogynist. In his *The Encyclopedia of Superheroes on Film and Television,* critic John Kenneth Muir calls it "the unholy love child of *Buffy the Vampire Slayer* and *Dark Angel*" with bickering straight from *Charmed* (128). This comparison with its famed contemporaries positions it as third wave as well. In fact, Muir criticizes the show for having too much emphasis on fashion and shopping: "Oracle, Huntress, and [Black Canary] all had issues, from physical paralysis and emotional abandonment to a distrust of men … but they also wore great clothes, seemed to want for nothing materially, and were gorgeous." While the first episode brought in 7.6 million viewers and attracted the network's largest audience ever in the 18–34 demographic, ratings fell quickly and the show wasn't renewed ("Birds of Prey"). Between this and a failed Wonder Woman pilot in 2011, the lore of superheroines failing onscreen continued.

As soon as *Smallville* ended, with the superhero craze growing, The CW searched for a successor or spinoff. This they found with *Arrow* (2012–present) and its own two sibling shows, *The Flash* (The CW, 2014–present) and *Legends of Tomorrow* (The CW, 2016–present). The first two were white-cis-hetero-male-centric, though *Legends* had a multiracial, multigendered ensemble cast. In contrast to these, *Supergirl* launched on CBS in 2015 and then was picked up by The CW, merging the universes and facilitating crossovers. Thus along with its weighty comics heritage, *Supergirl* is itself the "token girl" flip of *Smallville* and the *Arrowverse* shows.

On the *Supergirl* television show, Kara Zor-El (Melissa Benoist) escapes a dying Krypton alongside Superman. While she is a young teen and he is a baby, she ends up arriving years later, leaving her the younger cousin of the established hero—a plot adapted from the comics. As she explains in the first episode's beginning, "My cousin, he didn't need my protection. I didn't have a mission anymore. But even though I had all the same powers he did.... I decided the best thing I could do is fit in. After all, Earth didn't need another hero." Kara is adopted by the Danvers family, who protectively wants her to hide her powers. As with Wynonna and Buffy, Kara's primary relationship is with her sister (who secretly works for a government agency that deals with aliens, a job she got, as she puts it, because she grew up sharing a bathroom with such an alien). The centrality of the sister relationship is key to the show—instead of being defined by Superman, Kara barely sees him, as he balances career and superheroism in a different city. Unlike in the comics, show-Kara quests in her first episode to split off from Superman and forge her own identity.

She begins as ordinary Kara Danvers, media mogul Cat Grant's assistant in an unglamorous job. However, she complains to her sister Alex (Chyler Leigh), "I feel like I'm not living up to my potential. I went to work for Cat Grant because I thought working in a media company run by a powerful woman who actually shapes the way people think would be the way that I could make a difference. But, instead, I just fetch layouts and coffee."

Alex quips, "You always wanted to be normal, right? So, having a crappy boss and absolutely nothing to wear—This is what normal looks like." However, as Kara protests that she doesn't really want to be normal, her super-powered self is eager to break through. When Alex's plane begins to crash, Kara gets the push she needs and saves everyone. After, she babbles delightedly, "I almost forgot how to fly. Well, not so much how but more, more how it feels, like scared, but good scared. Like, like that moment right before you kiss someone for the first time. And now, now it's like I'm not sure what comes next. Or maybe I am sure and I'm just afraid of what it means." She constructs a costume and secret identity to save others even as she chooses on her own to be heroic.

Despite everyone's discouraging Kara from using her powers as a child, she is anxious to use them as a young woman, to help people, to find her place in the world. She is not so much a chosen one as one who chooses, although the moment she reveals herself to the world is when her sister is in danger, and there isn't much chance she would have watched her die on television to protect her secret. With this, she chooses, as all the chosen must do, to save the good, defeat the bad, sacrifice and become herself.

Another of Kara's central relationships is with Cat Grant (Calista Flockhart), the fifty-year-old head of CatCo. As an empire-building matriarch echoing the star of *The Devil Wears Prada*, she's the powerful woman young Kara seeks to become. Flockhart notes, "At the heart of it she really cares about humanity, she really cares about Kara with this motherly instinct. She's mentoring Kara in her own way, it's subtle but it's very much there and she's very much a feminist" ("Calista Flockhart"). However, Kara hesitates when Cat Grant names the new superhero.

> KARA: It's just, uh I don't want to minimize the importance of this. A female superhero. Shouldn't she be called Superwoman?
> CAT: I'm sorry, darling, I just can't hear you over the loud color of your cheap pants.
> KARA: If we call her Supergirl, something less than what she is, doesn't that make us guilty of being anti-feminist? Didn't you say she was a hero?
> CAT: I'm the hero. I stuck a label on the side of this girl, I branded her. She will forever be linked to Catco, to *The Tribune*, to me. And what do you think is so bad about "girl"? Huh? I'm a girl. And your boss, and powerful, and rich, and hot and smart. So if you perceive Supergirl as anything less than excellent, isn't the real problem you? And if you're so smart, Kerah, could you please give me one reason why I shouldn't fire you?

This scene contrasts a grown nineties third wave icon with a fourth waver—as Cat craves merchandising rights and the power of consumerism while a more self-aware and internet-savvy Kara considers superhero tropes, political correctness, and the power of labels. This is underscored by the fact that Calista Flockhart once played nineties girl power icon Ally McBeal. In an interview the actress notes that both characters mirror and contrast:

> Feminist means something different to everybody: to me it means choice. We are not fighting the battle our grandmothers fought to get the vote or go to college, we are past all that. So there is a second, third, maybe fourth wave coming on. Ally embodies feminism, she decided to go to Harvard, she decided to be a lawyer, she was sexually harassed at work and she decided to quit. Cat decided to be a media mogul. She is at a different stage of her life to Ally and has a lot of regrets. They both examine whether a woman can have it all and at what price ["Calista Flockhart"].

Even as she learns the previous generation's lessons from Cat, Supergirl embraces a modern intersectionality, bringing friends under her cape of protection. There's a race-flipped James Olson, a fully grown professional who makes himself a superhero even without powers. Alex comes out as lesbian and dates the sympathetic Latina cop Maggie Sawyer. Pushing the boundaries further, the fourth season brings in television's first transgender superhero: Nia Nal, Dreamgirl. This season kicks off criticizing the political climate in "American Alien" (401). Supergirl faces a hate group as the Graves siblings attack an outspoken Alien Rights activist—forcefully removing the tusks from his arms to literally rid him of his difference. Shocked, Supergirl hates to believe that humanity is so cruel. "Am I crazy? I feel like the world is better than it's ever been—more diversity, more acceptance.... I finally feel like the world is good, and I so badly want it to stay that way," she protests. Privileged because she resembles humans (as an attractive white blonde woman in particular), she realizes she must protect those under threat. With this call to action, she claims a particularly fourth wave identity.

Being the Chosen One: Wynonna

While Supergirl was created specifically to be a female counterpart to Superman, Wynonna (Melanie Scrofano) is not a (fictitious) distaff version of lawman Wyatt Earp or even the mythic Wyatt Earp character of popular culture. Like Supergirl, she's originally a comic book character, based on the series by Beau Smith. Emily Andras (creator/showrunner) explains:

> When I picked up the comic book it did sort of send a tingle up my spine, and I knew there was something special about it. There was something about taking one of the most iconic and male American heroes, that is Wyatt Earp, with all the kind of patriarchal, Western, gun-slinger mythos that surrounds him and making him this curvy badass woman. You're literally flipping it on its head. I loved the idea of taking a Western, which is traditionally so male, and just replacing all the archetypal characters wherever we could and force it to be female [Jetson].

Beau Smith, meanwhile, finds the show quite different from the stories he wrote. As he notes, "I've done Wynonna Earp for 20 years. What [the show] has done, and this is what Emily does, she turns everything upside down and when you think it's off kilter and could be wrong, it's completely right. She gave me the most gracious gift in that I can do the Wynonna Earp that I've always done and add this new layer to it that's been amazing. She created Doc Holliday, Dolls ... all these characters" (Maloney).

Wynonna Earp is perhaps more closely aligned with a previous female television superhero, Buffy Summers of the beloved fantasy series *Buffy the Vampire Slayer* (1997–2002). The central actress sees the connection too. Melanie Scrofano (Wynonna) explains: "I grew up watching old black and white Westerns on Sundays with my dad, so already it felt like, 'I know this.' And I loved *Buffy*. It just seemed like a really cool story to tell" (Jetson).

Like Buffy, she is the Chosen One or maybe the unlucky one, here known as the "Heir" or the "Earp Heir," whose responsibility is to fight the forces of evil and hold back the darkness. The local authorities blame coyotes instead of the Buffy standbys of "PCP" and "gangs" to cover up supernatural incidents (as the antagonistic high school principal insists in episodes like "School Hard"). On memorable occasions throughout the series, both Buffy and Wynonna are told, "You're just a girl." Buffy, responding to someone she has just rescued in the midst of one of the more stressful periods in a stressful life, notes that's what she keeps saying. With this, she claims a nineties-style third wave girl power. Endeavoring to bury her power beneath glamor and girlishness, Buffy tries out for cheerleading and Homecoming Queen even as she adores fashion and shopping. "This kind of girlpower constructs the current generation of young women as a unique category of girls who are self-assured, living lives lightly inflected but by no means driven by feminism, influenced by the philosophy of DIY, and assuming they can have (or at least buy) it all," notes Anita Harris, author of *Future Girl: Young Women in the Twenty-First Century* (17). Buffy is a fierce, mighty chosen one, but makes excuses and claims the title "just a girl" for herself.

A generation later, Wynonna, replying to a revenant who has called her this, corrects him, "I am *the* girl. With the big gun. And I'm going to blow you all to Hell" ("Purgatory," 101). When she claims the title, it's a fierce badge of honor—fourth wavers don't back down from claiming their power and reveling in it. Wynonna's coded as rougher, eschewing Buffy's tiny stakes and holy water for her family's mystic shotgun. Wynonna, in fact, is all grown up—hard drinking, motorcycle riding, bragging about her sexual prowess. An iconic black leather jacket and matching pants or jeans and a bullet-studded gun belt put her visually in the masculine role, in contrast with the more feminine Buffy.

Wynonna combines aspects of Buffy, the responsible one, with her "evil sister" Faith, the hard-drinking Slayer who has one-night stands.

> Faith tempts Buffy to cut class during a test, to steal, to drop recklessly underground, to dance sexily at a club, to escape police custody (injuring and abandoning the police officers). And that's just during one episode. Douglas Petrie, the writer of "Bad Girls" explains, "She's in many ways Buffy's evil twin. She gets to do all the things that Buffy would like to do but can't" [Frankel, *Buffy* 82].

That the heroine can now be the Faith-like character and not be completely messed up (even though many other characters might still think of her that way) is a major step. Still, even here, Wynonna compares herself unfavorably to her absent older sister, the one who was "supposed to" be the Heir. Wynonna grew up plagued with imposter syndrome because her sister, not her, was born to inherit Wyatt Earp's legacy.

When Wynonna heads back to her hometown, the appropriately named Purgatory (the town welcome sign ironically states: "You'll never want to leave!"), ostensibly for the funeral of her uncle, she is traveling to her destiny, like all the chosen ones of myth: to destroy the bad, save the good, sacrifice or become herself.

Before she even reaches home, her attempt to save a young woman fails, and she survives an acrobatic fight against a monstrous opponent. She is late for the funeral, and, oh, yes, it's her birthday, but no one is throwing a party. Her aunt uses the eulogy to make a dig at her for apparently finding it too boring around there, a comment that seems strange as we discover that Wynonna has endured shock treatments and medications when her only condition is awareness of the true horrors in Purgatory and PTSD from one horrible night when revenants attacked, her older sister was kidnaped, and Wynonna accidentally killed her father with Wyatt Earp's mystical gun.

Wynonna's little sister, Waverly, who somehow missed attending the funeral, greets her with a big gun when she discovers Wynonna with her boyfriend, Champ. She doesn't know he's Waverly's boyfriend, and she's just trying to get info about her uncle's death, while the boyfriend escapes blame for his attempted infidelity. But it's a small town, Waverly later tells Wynonna, and her dating options are limited. Despite coming in with gun blazing, Waverly will soon be revealed to be sweet and nerdy, a holder of online degrees, and a speaker of arcane languages, but still a woman who knows where in an attacker's head is the best place to ram a pair of scissors. We will watch her outgrow her boyfriend, whose idea of a compliment is to marvel at how a girl can be so pretty and so smart (which she swiftly shuts down), and become involved with Nicole Haught, a new police officer in town. The audience is invested in the Waverly Earp and Nicole Haught love story (dubbed "WayHaught" by fans and perhaps named with that possible portmanteau in mind).

> Nicole and Waverly, the lesbian couple of the show, also make for the only two people in stable "traditional" relationship on *Wynonna Earp*. They are not shunned, yet the narrow-mindedness of society is addressed. They are not cursed with horrible deaths (which is the norm in most supernatural shows featuring same sex couples), yet they brush death many times over, only to have their love grew stronger and tougher [Dilip].

Becoming the Earp heir on her twenty-seventh birthday, Wynonna inherits her great-great-grandfather's mystical gun, which will send the revenants—people he killed during his lifetime, who have resurrected—back to Hell. If an Heir can complete the cycle of killing all seventy-seven revenants, this is supposed to break the curse. Older sister Willa was supposed to be the next Heir after their father, but she's gone and maybe dead, taken by revenants years ago, the night that twelve-year-old Wynonna, trying to help, killed their father. (This is dealt with later in the first season of the series.)

Some of the revenants are happy the Heir is back in town, thinking she will lead them to Earp's gun. She does, and uses it against them, and also unknowingly frees Earp's best friend from a well where he has been trapped by the same witch who cured his tuberculosis—which the historical Doc Holliday died of. Things in Purgatory are complicated, and not just for women trying to survive and destroy a bunch of misogynist bad guys from another era.

Deputy Marshal Xavier Dolls, sent from a government agency that deals with supernatural threats, wants Wynonna on his team and she soon has no choice but to join, as the Black Badge Agency curtails her personal agency. This is often the case with tough-talking heroes, but the character being a woman throws this into particularly sharp relief.

Although hints of a Doc-Wynonna-Dolls triangle are sprinkled throughout, it tends to skew toward the morally ambiguous Doc before long and fails to establish any stakes or suspense in the audience, despite having the raw material in the actors and backstories (Doc has his immortality, but Dolls also has secrets) to do so. This, meanwhile, establishes that for this heroine, romance isn't the series priority. In the essay "*Wynonna Earp*'s Secret Weapon: Feminism in a Demon-Haunted World," Kat Jetson explains:

> One of those feminist threads is that, besides familial relationships, no woman is defined by her relationship to a man. And, not to diminish the importance of the men on the show because, #SuperSupportive, but their main role in the lives of these very human female superheroes is to tap into their strength and harness it. Characters like Special Agent Xavier Dolls (Shamier Anderson), Doc Holliday (Tim Rozon) and Sheriff Randy Nedley (Greg Lawson) are champions for the growth and strength of these women and want them to succeed.

Wynonna often says no to Doc when he is making tentative attempts at a relationship, noting that it is better if she travels alone. The weight she carries is on her, and her most intense love at the beginning of the series is reserved for her sister, Waverly, much like Buffy and Dawn in Season 5 of *Buffy the Vampire Slayer*.

In Wynonna's first interaction with Doc, he tells her he is a collector "of poker chips and hearts" ("Purgatory"). They discuss Wyatt Earp, with Wynonna as yet unaware of Doc's identity. "He was good at killing, so they called him a hero," she muses. "What kind of person wants to be a gunslinger?"

He dismisses this. "Wyatt Earp wanted to be a farmer. Thirty seconds in the OK Corral and a gunslinger he was made. Sometimes life chooses for us."

Wynonna could walk away from Purgatory; she thinks about it; she tries to convince Waverly to go with her. But in the end, she stays, like Buffy stays in Sunnydale, choosing to hold back the darkness, to be a firefighter "when the floods roll back" (as Buffy explains in the fourth-season dream episode "Restless," 420), choosing to accept being chosen, and embracing her agency in the process.

Season 2's "Everybody Knows" "effectively serves as a 101 class in feminism," according to Jetson, as Wynonna (whose pregnant actress inspired a pregnancy storyline) reveals that the father might not be Doc but a Revenant. "The episode shines a spotlight on the power and confidence that come from being an unapologetically flawed and emotional woman with all manner of desires and needs. A woman who is able to carry herself with dignity and respect and refuses to allow the judgment that comes with ladies' choice, all while disarming every argument one would have against her by way of a bad-ass, slow-motion strut" (Jetson). She's startlingly sex-positive, as she owns her decisions. "Wynonna, like all the other women on the show, does not blink before saying 'my body, my rules' when questioned about her active sex life. From the very beginning of the show, she has had a number of sexual partners, none of whose names neither her nor us fans bothered learning" (Dilip). The heavily pregnant heroine goes on to do action stunts, battling criminals with a motherly power rarely seen on television. Dominique Provost-Chalkley (Waverly) notes:

> I think Melanie gave all women out there a gift this season, because she showed the world that women are an absolute force. She showed us that being pregnant is not a disability. It's exactly what the female body was made to do, and I can tell you now, Melanie Scrofano was working literally five days before she gave birth. She inspired me as a young actress to start pushing past these frustratingly narrow-minded beliefs. What Mel has shown is that you are absolutely just as much, if not more, beautiful and bad-ass pregnant [Jetson].

She then executes the possible father, reclaiming her power and choosing to make a nonbiological family. Katherine Barrell (Officer Nicole Haught) explains, "Symbolically, I thought it was really empowering to show a woman getting out of this abusive situation and choosing that she didn't need the traditional model to raise a healthy, happy child. This whole show, there are so many themes of families that you choose, not necessarily that you're born with. And Wynonna saying, I don't care if you're biologically the dad; you're no good to me and you're no good to this baby. This baby is going to be better off without you" (Jetson).

Conclusion

Both Wynonna and Supergirl started with a male label and grew beyond their comic book characters to become far more independent and empowered. They each introduced an entourage of fourth wave friends and allies.

Of course, this gender-flipping allows representation for viewers of all types. Provost-Chalkley tells of a young deaf lesbian woman telling her she was always afraid to leave the house. She said, "I am here today because of your show, and because I saw Waverly's bravery and how much she's managed." Provost-Chalkley held her hand and replied, "You're the inspiration. You're the real-life version of Waverly in that case" (Jetson). Barrell adds:

> For me especially, because my character is so closely tied with the LGBT community, I've seen how Nicole has empowered a lot of especially young women to come out, or have open conversations about their sexuality with their family. Or, just feel way more empowered about who they are as a woman and then as a gay woman. I've received beautiful letters from people, and have heard stories face to face. It's so powerful when people say, "I saw myself for the first time." It's a great honor to be a part of that. To be the skin of that character means so much to me [Jetson].

Besides this, both heroines stand out for the paths they take, to build chosen families out of the marginalized and embrace difference, to become superheroes and battle evil, even at the cost of all they are. It is these choices that make them truly striking television heroines.

WORKS CITED

Andras, Emily, creator. *Wynonna Earp*. Syfy, 2016–present.
Berlanti, Greg, Andrew Kreisberg, Allison Adler, creators. *Supergirl*. The WB, 2015–present.
Binder, Otto, and Al Plastino. *Action Comics* #252. 1959. *Showcase Presents: Supergirl 1*. DC Comics, 2007.
"*Birds of Prey* Wings Clipped by WB." *CBR*, 18 Nov. 2002 https://www.cbr.com/birds-of-prey-wings-clipped-by-wb.
"Calista Flockhart Compares Cat Grant to Ally McBeal at Supergirl Celebration." *Irish Examiner*, 14 Mar 2016 https://www.irishexaminer.com/breakingnews/entertainment/calista-flockhart-compares-cat-grant-to-ally-mcbeal-at-supergirl-celebration-725086.html.
Dilip, Mangala. "*Wynonna Earp*: What Makes this Syfy Gem the Most Diverse, Positive, Feminist Show of All Time" *Meaww*, 1 Jan 2019. https://meaww.com/wynonna-earp-season-4-what-makes-syfy-gem-diverse-positive-feminist-show-of-all-time.
Frankel, Valerie Estelle. *Buffy and the Heroine's Journey*. McFarland, 2012.
_____. *Superheroines and the Epic Journey*. McFarland, 2016.
Goldberg, Lesley. "*Smallville*: Why We Didn't See Tom Welling in the Suit." *Hollywood Reporter*, 27 May 2011. https://www.hollywoodreporter.com/live-feed/smallville-why-we-didn-t-192811.
Harris, Anita. *Future Girl: Young Women in the Twenty-First Century*. Routledge, 2004.
Hassenger, Jesse. "Gender-swapped and Race-flipped Remakes Aren't Living Up to Their Potential." *The Verge*, 12 Feb. 2019. https://www.theverge.com/2019/2/12/18220797/what-men-want-ghostbusters-the-hustle-remakes-gender-race-flipped.
Hess, Amanda. "The Trouble with Hollywood's Gender Flips." *New York Times*, 12 June 2018. https://www.nytimes.com/2018/06/12/movies/oceans-8-gender-swap.html.
Jetson, Kat. "*Wynonna Earp*'s Secret Weapon: Feminism in a Demon-Haunted World." *Hollywood Reporter*, 18 Aug 2017. https://www.hollywoodreporter.com/live-feed/wynonna-earps-secret-weapon-feminism-a-demon-haunted-world-1030732.
Kistler, Alan Sizzler. "Supergirl: A Brief History of the Last Daughter of Krypton." *Tor*, 23 Oct 2015. https://www.tor.com/2015/10/23/supergirl-a-brief-history-of-the-last-daughter-of-krypton.
Klein, Melissa. "Duality and Redefinition: Young Feminism and the Alternative Music Com-

munity." *Third Wave Agenda: Being Feminist, Doing Feminism*, ed. Leslie Heywood and Jennifer Drake. University of Minnesota Press, 1997.

Maloney, Michael. "Wynonna Earp Cast Talks the Comics, WayHaught, Jeremy's Past & More at Comic-Con 2018 Panel." *TV Insider,* 22 July 2018 https://www.tvinsider.com/704173/wynonna-earp-season-3-comic-con-panel-2018/.

Muir, John Kenneth. *The Encyclopedia of Superheroes on Film and Television.* McFarland, 2004.

Whedon, Joss, creator. *Buffy the Vampire Slayer.* The WB Network and UPN, 1997–2002.

"The gods will always smile on the brave women"

Exploring the Heroines of History Channel's Vikings

Steven B. Frankel

The Stories Say: Thrown aside and abused by the king of Sweden when he invaded my native Norway, I took up arms beside the great king Ragnar of Denmark when he raided Norway. I fought bravely and caught the eye of the king, who sought my hand but only won it by slaying the fierce bear and hound that guarded my home. When my husband cast me aside for another, I stayed loyal to him and led 100 ships to his rescue in a civil war that threatened his throne. But he proved to not be worthy of me, so I slew him and took the crown for myself.—Lagertha

In the opening scenes of *Vikings* (History Channel, 2013–present), we're transported to a land similar to what we expect and meet our first character, Ragnar Lothbrok, who has just returned from an expedition to the British Isles. We see Ragnar as the clichéd Viking warrior at this point, striding ashore from his longboat boasting of his victories and carrying his looted treasure. Rather than greeting him with welcome, the current jarl (the highest rank below the king), Haraldson, sees Ragnar as competition for leadership of the town of Kattegat, and immediately tells Ragnar that all the treasure he's collected belongs to him as the jarl. We appear to be starting on a normal Hero's Journey … at least until Lagertha arrives and upends all expectations.

While the show is portrayed as the story of Ragnar Lothbrok, played by Travis Fimmel, Lagertha is the character who finishes the main story arcs at the end of Season 5. Lagertha (Katheryn Winnick), a self-proclaimed shield maiden based on a figure from Norse sagas and history, is one of six protagonists that the series uses to highlight the Norse view of women and contrast it with the Anglo-Saxon view derived from Rome. The others are Aslaug, Siggy, Judith, Gisla and Porunn. While not every conversation passes the Bechdel Test, enough do to make it clear that the feminism is intentional and not just pasted on in places. Additionally, *Vikings* provides a number of male role models who demonstrate how men should behave in a society that treats women with respect.

Showrunner Michael Hirst's foreword to the licensed show guide explains: "In order to do justice to these fierce Northern raiders, we need to clear our own minds of the clutter of prejudices and received opinions that have always surrounded them." He continues, "What they didn't mention because they didn't know, was that Viking society was far more open and democratic than their own. And that the Vikings had a deeper respect for women, who could own property, divorce their husbands, fight beside their brothers and sons in the shield wall and even rule" (Pollard 5).

When we meet Lagertha, we get a hint that this show will offer more than warriors with horned helmets rescuing damsels in leather bikinis. We continue to learn Lagertha is anything but a typical action heroine as she represents what we now know of Viking culture with regard to women's rights. Women could inherit property, first of all. "Women had no formal role in public life, nor is there any evidence that they could take part in legal procedures but, as Icelandic saga accounts show, a strong-minded woman could enjoy a great deal of practical influence and authority" (Haywood 210–211). Further, a married woman retained property rights after marriage, including her dowry and bride-price, and she could get a divorce if she wished (Haywood 210). Lagertha does all this and more.

A quick search reveals that while we only know highlights of their histories, Lagertha and Ragnar are based on characters from both history and Norse sagas. Ragnar Lodbrok ("hairy breeches") features in conflicting sagas and has a murky yet unmistakable place in history as father of several great Viking leaders. In Saxo Grammaticus's *Gesta Danorum*, he falls for a mighty warrior and weds her. Saxo recounts: "Ladgerda, a skilled Amazon, who, though a maiden, had the courage of a man, and fought in front among the bravest with her hair loose over her shoulders. All marveled at her matchless deeds, for her lock flying down her back betrayed that she was a woman."

The showrunners stick close to what is known about the two characters and Viking culture in general and the most improbable events are the ones that are based on history and saga. Ben Waggoner, translator of *The Sagas of Ragnar Lodbrok*, notes that the hero is a composite character adapted from "a dimly visible historical core, covered by a mass of folktales and legends" (xxiii). Even when the history is known, events are streamlined. In Season 1, Ragnar and his crew raid the monastery on the coast, reimagining the famous "Sack of Lindisfarne" of AD 793. However, Season 3's "Siege of Paris" plot adapts history from AD 911, keeping some accuracy but massively condensing events. Likewise, Aslaug boasts she is the daughter of Sigurd and Brynhild; "To the extent we can date them at all, Sigurd and Brynhild would have lived about 350 years before Ragnar," Waggoner adds (xxiii). Still, the show comes across as smoothly depicted and filled with lively entertainment. This is how historical fiction should be written, filling in the probable colorful backstories between the known points.

The series complexity starts to be revealed when Ragnar leaves for the capital. Lagertha establishes her character when a group of men arrive to rape her and her daughter while Ragnar is away. She retorts, "You couldn't kill me if you tried for a hundred years," and hits one in the crotch with a red-hot sword ("Rites of Passage," 101). In moments, she drives them all off. As it happens, her actress is an accomplished martial artist who holds a third-degree black belt in Taekwondo and a second-degree black belt in Karate. This is not a woman who needs a man to defend her. As the series progresses, we watch her go from a wife who can take care of her family and farm to a jarl in her own right with her own army and ships.

Women in Viking culture could be warriors. They were expected to take care of the family and its property when the men went raiding if they didn't join the raid. A married woman "would expect her husband to involve her with any major decisions affecting the welfare of the family" (Hudson 211). They owned land and led armies. They could rule as jarls or even queens. A man who touched an uninterested woman could lose a hand under Viking law.

It is also at this point when one might question these characters' historical veracity. In history, Viking women defended the family on many levels. "Women were no less zealous in defending the family honor than men. In Icelandic saga literature, for example, *Njal's Saga,* women were often among the instigators of blood feuds" (Haywood 211). However, it must be added, "Women did fight alongside the men, but recent reports suggesting that 50 percent of Viking warriors were women is slightly overinflated" (Rose). In fact, the shieldmaiden concept was popular in sagas, folklore, and myth but unseen in history. Still even if "shieldmaidens" aren't historically accurate, Dr. Shannon Godlove, the coordinator of Columbus State University's Medieval and Renaissance Studies Certificate Program, agrees that "women had a great deal more political influence and many more legal rights" in this particular society than in any other known medieval cultures (Rose).

After gathering volunteers in the second episode, Ragnar, his brother Rollo, and close friend Floki embark on an unauthorized raid to the west. Showrunner Michael Hirst adds:

Ragnar Lothbrok is a farmer who becomes, by turns, an earl and then a Viking king. He is both driven by desire for immortal fame and an abiding curiosity, which he attributes to his ancestor, the god Odin. Far from the cliched version of a Viking hero, Ragnar is thoughtful, intelligent, and introverted. He loves his sons more than plunder. He wants to pillage other lands, but also wants to settle and farm there and become prosperous [Pollard 17].

He also displays the Norse view of women which treats them as equal members of society whose respect is to be earned. As the series continues, we see this Norse attitude contrasted with the view we inherit from the Roman *pater familias*, which underpins our view of women as inferior or even property to be acquired and exploited. Lagertha violently objects to Ragnar's refusal to take her along. She insists, "How dare you? Am I not good enough for you? Am I not strong enough for you?" However, since Ragnar trusts her to protect their land, they agree that she remains behind. "If a husband was away from home, a wife had full responsibility for running the household and family farm until he returned" (Haywood 211). Nonetheless, she comes on the following expedition, as Viking women often did (Haywood 211).

While the Viking warriors have been instructed not to abuse the local population, Lagertha walks in on Knut, the jarl's chosen warrior and spy, attempting to rape a local woman. She orders him to stop and when he refuses, Lagertha kills him in combat. "He raped a Saxon woman. Then he tried to rape me," she says angrily when Ragnar comes to find her ("Trial," 104). Historically, Vikings appear to have shunned rape as it goes unmentioned in all the *Annals of St. Bertin's* descriptions of Viking pillaging, though the rapes committed by Christian kings are repeatedly mentioned (Sawyer 47). Further, Ragnar protects her by taking the blame, as he knows this was the jarl's spy. Upon their return, the current jarl has Ragnar arrested for disobedience. Ragnar escapes and goes out into the wilderness where Lagertha joins him as they escape.

In councils of war, women warriors and wives are always included on the show. While Ragnar is the one who initiates the battles and takes the brunt of the losses, Lagertha is the more analytical ruler and is always there to tilt the balance in the conflict between two sides by supporting Ragnar at the critical moment. Winnick notes, "Lagertha is strong, but she also has faults ... what I love about Lagertha is that she has conflicts and flaws and she questions things ... she's not just a strong vixen" ("Interview").

With Lagertha's help, Ragnar eventually becomes the jarl after defeating the current jarl in single combat. While she maintains his realm in his absence, Lagertha's skill as a leader in her own right is demonstrated when a man brings his wife with an infant. The man claims that a young man stayed at their house for three days, and nine months later, his wife gave birth to a child when the couple had gone years without conceiving. Upon learning that the visitor's name was Rig, Lagertha showcases her knowledge and tells them that Rig is another name for their Norse god Heimdallr. She then tells the man that he should consider himself blessed that the god chose them and warns him that if any harm comes to the child or his wife, he will have to answer to her. This scene emphasizes her ability to negotiate and yet maintain the proprieties of their society.

After he becomes jarl, Ragnar leads his people to raid Wessex, based on historical raids of 830 to 880 (Sawyer 52–57). Here we meet Judith, a composite of a few historical women eager to embrace Viking egalitarianism. As history relates, "Two high-born Frankish women, one of them a queen, did consider finding refuge with Viking protectors against Frankish husbands they believed would kill them. The princess Judith, fleeing her father's anger, apparently did find refuge with the Northman Rorik" (Sawyer 47). Historically, Judith of Flanders (843–870) was the eldest daughter of the West Frankish King and later Holy Roman Emperor Charles the Bald, and then married two Kings of Wessex, Æthelwulf and Æthelbald (Æthelwulf's son and thus her stepson). West Saxon custom was that the king's wife could not be called queen or sit on the throne with her husband. However, her father insisted, and Æthelwulf was desperate for an alliance against the Vikings, so he agreed (Story 240–242). On the show, she's the daughter of King Aelle and Queen Ealhswith of Northumbria. As the series reveals, Egbert and Ælla, whose kingdoms are separated by Mercia, propose an alliance against the Vikings and Mercians by wedding their children, Æthelwulf and Judith. Played by Sarah Greene (Season 2) and Jennie Jacques (Seasons 3–5), she is the second of the strong women with a series-long arc, as she goes from a victim of politics to their orchestrator. Early in her introduction, she refuses being traded away, asserting, "My lord, battered or not, it would make no difference. You don't own me, Father, nor does any man own me. Though encumbered everywhere; I am free" ("Yol," 404). However, her role in this society is highly constrained, as she is aware.

Here we see the contrast between the two societies highlighted. She lives in a culture derived from Roman rule. Her only power is acting through her brother and the other men in her life. We see this contrasted with Lagertha, who is unequaled as city ruler. She's consulted in all of Ragnar's councils, since he values her advice and her army, which is equal to his own. This comparison between the two women and their cultural roles continues through each season. It's finally resolved in the penultimate episode of Season 5. Judith has put her son on the throne by eliminating all competitors. However, while this is happening, Judith finds Lagertha abandoned alone and for all intents, mad in England. She rescues Lagertha and has her nursed back to health. As the main arc and their stories end, the two women reflect on how far they've followed their original dreams from the story's start. In Judith's case, she sees her family ruling England. In Lagertha's case, she fulfills her and Ragnar's shared dream of seeing the Vikings settled in England with its rich agricultural lands. Lagertha finds herself in a final battle to resolve the plot between two of Ragnar's sons. Meanwhile, Judith, having poisoned her one son to eliminate competition for the other, dies of breast cancer.

While some characters are introduced to support other themes of the series, they all reinforce the demonstration of women's equality. Floki, a boat-builder in episode one (loosely based on the historical Hrafna-Flóki Vilgerðarson), is introduced as Ragnar's lifelong friend and counterfoil in that he and Ragnar both struggle with Christianity versus the Old Ways, a major theme. Ragnar eventually accepts some Christianity while Floki never compromises. True to his upbringing, he demonstrates his respect for women, as Floki develops a love for his mate and must seek her consent. Though Ragnar comes to follow the Christian route, nonetheless, he refuses to give in to Christian traditional misogyny.

One fascinating ally for Lagertha is introduced in the first season. When Ragnar kills Haraldson and becomes jarl, Lagertha advises him to treat the jarl's widow, Siggy, with respect rather than banishing her. Siggy and Lagertha regularly interact when Ragnar is off raiding and leaves Lagertha to rule in his stead. These episodes show the women conversing about topics such as family, security of the home and their relationship with each other now that Siggy has gone from wife of the jarl to Lagertha's servant. Siggy displays a subtle feminism, especially when the men are absent:

SIGGY: Women should stick together more.
ASLAUG: That's true.
SIGGY: And we should rule.
ASLAUG: All things would be better [202].

When Siggy first appears in her role as the wife of Jarl Haraldson, she reveals her skills as a master manipulator; she expertly indulges her husband's vanity while deflecting his burgeoning paranoia away from herself. She is shrewd, resourceful and driven by ambition, though power and status are not the only things she wants out of life. She is cunning and ruthless, but she is not an ice queen. By contrast, she has a hot temper and a strong sex drive; her subsequent tumultuous relationship with Ragnar's brother Rollo seems to be motivated by equal parts lust, calculation and frustration. "You see, Rollo, you need me as much as I need you. That is, if you really want to be something," she tells him ("Sacrifice," 108).

Beneath all the scheming, there is a core of compassion in Siggy. What makes her unusual as a female character is that this compassion predominantly reserved for other women; even those who should by rights be her enemies. Despite all her political canny, she is outraged at the thought of her daughter marrying a fat old man three times her age, even though it's an advantageous match. (She goes on to stab said fat old man at the first opportunity.) After the death of her husband, she offers her service to Lagertha in what seems to be an entirely political move designed to get her into Ragnar's inner circle. However, as she supports Lagertha through a devastating miscarriage, it becomes clear that Siggy is developing sincere affection for the wife of her husband's killer. By the time both women lose their only daughters to a plague that sweeps the village, there is an undeniable bond of friendship between them.

Siggy is also an almost frustratingly ambiguous character. She sulks, "I'm supposed to be eternally grateful to my husband's killer. Everything that I was has been stripped away from me. I want my old position back" ("Unforgiven," 206). She then conspires with King Horik to murder Ragnar's young sons in return for marriage and a return to queenship. By end of Season 2, the audience remains unsure where her allegiances lie. She has apparently cemented her loyalty to Ragnar by double-crossing King Horik, but her ambition has not been dampened and she still craves her old position of power.

During Ragnar's rise to power, we're introduced to Harold Bluetooth (for whom Bluetooth phones are named). He's famed for being the first king to unite all of Norway. On a visit to the king preceding Harold, Ragnar encounters the princess Aslaug (Alyssa Sutherland). During their meeting in the first season finale "All Change" (109), the cliché of the princess swooning over the famous warrior is subverted, in a way viewers are coming to expect. In a scene out of the great sagas, Ragnar gives Aslaug the famous folkloric challenge meant as a cleverness test. As he phrases it, "She has set me a challenge and I am up to task. See, I'm less interested in what you say is her beauty, than what I suspect is her wit. So tell her I invite her here to join us…. Neither dressed nor undressed. What else? Neither hungry nor full, neither in company nor alone." As the forward to *The Sagas of Ragnar Lodbrok* notes, this riddling challenge "is a widespread motif, found in tales ranging from Grimms' 'The Peasant's Wise Daughter' to some versions of the Irish tale of Diarmuid and Grainne, to 'The Chick-Pea Seller's Daughter' in *Arabian Nights*" (Waggoner xxiii). *The Sagas of Ragnar Lodbrok* likewise blends in fairytale tropes of disguised royalty, as Aslaug is brought up in rags to obscure her mythic origin as the daughter of Sigurd and Brynhild (a lineage also mentioned on the show). In the latter, she passes his tests, and Ragnar apologizes for his earlier blunders with her. However, his son senses trouble brewing. As Arne quips, "He's enjoying himself in the company of a beautiful woman…. If Lagertha were here, she'd cut his balls off" (109).

Ragnar is attracted to Aslaug and decides that under Viking law as jarl he can take more than one wife (as the series supports). Ragnar returns to Kattegat, where he greets Lagertha, and after the ritual homecoming, he orders her to welcome his pregnant bride. As he proclaims, "Looking at both of you here, in my home.... I see no reason why you two should not get on together. You two are very different, yet both strong. I have heard that similar arrangements exist all over this country" ("Brother's War," 201). Lagertha initially welcomes her, out of sisterhood rather than obedience to Ragnar. After a short time, however, the equal status of Viking woman is emphasized when Lagertha emphasizes her unhappiness and leaves him. When he asks why, she responds, "You insult and humiliate me. I have no choice but to leave you and divorce you" (201). When Ragnar continues to insist he has the right to two wives, she acknowledges it but adds that since he's shamed her, she is leaving with their son and all her goods. This phase of Lagertha's story ends with her departing for her hometown on a wagon with all she owns. Further, the local seer emphasizes Ragnar's lack of power here when he comments, "You are only fooling yourself, Ragnar Lothbrok, if you think the choice is yours to make" ("Answers in Blood," 205). In fact, Ragnar survives this divorce but none of Lagertha's subsequent husbands manage this feat.

Since Aslaug is the most traditionally feminine character so far, it would have been easy to position her as someone we are expected to dislike. When a girly girl character is presented as a rival to a fan favorite warrior, she rarely fares well. Refreshingly, Aslaug does not fit neatly into the homewrecker role, nor is she presented as an automatic inferior to Lagertha (a choice that would have done a disservice to both characters). Alyssa Sutherland, Aslaug, comments, "I don't necessarily think of Aslaug as being a villainess, I think that waters it down. She's not good and she's not bad" (Hayner). She adds, "I love that Aslaug was never fulfilled by Ragnar. She really loved him, but wasn't ever fulfilled—and that gave her motivation" (Hayner). In fact, the show is unambiguous on the point that Ragnar and Ragnar alone ruined his first marriage. The show does not blame Aslaug for desiring him or for expecting him to step up to his duties as the father of her child. She certainly experiences insecurity around Lagertha (as any normal human would), but it neither consumes her nor defines her character. In time, genuine respect and even mutual admiration start to flourish between the two women. They will perhaps never be fast friends, but they are courteous and dignified in each other's presence. Aslaug even admires her competition:

> ASLAUG: I like her.
> RAGNAR: My former wife?
> ASLAUG: Hmm.... I would rather be her. She is formidable ["Blood Eagle," 207].

Delightfully, on *Vikings*, women support other women by default. Lagertha, Siggy and Aslaug all have plenty of reasons not to like each other, but they keep their relationships aloof from the rows and blunders of their menfolk and find commonalities in their struggles and victories as women in a patriarchal society. Popular media loves to paint women as catty and two-faced, and female friendships as fickle things fraught with jealousy and backstabbing. In a landscape like this, it is invigorating to watch a show full of female characters whose relationships are founded on respect and good faith, if not always on outright friendship or alliance.

Later, Ragnar's wives have a confrontation in Kattegat. Lagertha tells her rival, "I was never the usurper, always the usurped. You took my husband, my world, and my happiness. The fact that you're a woman is neither here nor there" ("In the Uncertain Hour Before the Morning," 414). She agrees to let the other woman leave, but then insists on vengeance and kills her. Her actress explains:

> Yes, there is definitely a big epic scene where Lagertha and Aslaug come face to face and I will say it's pretty epic. It's juicy and it's memorable. I wish I could actually give away more but it was a great scene to shoot. Lagertha felt that she needed to take [...] Kattegat and really try to get control back. Kattegat is being run so badly and there's been a lot of problems with Kattegat, like people have been dying, things are not being run in a proper way as it should be. And she feels that she is doing the right thing by reclaiming it, because nobody would rule it better than she does because she truly cares about her people [Murray].

Alyssa Sutherland, Aslaug, comments that her character has already given up as she believes her beloved son Ivar has died: "I think she knows that she's not going to walk away.... So the last thing she does, she kind of gets the last word, and asks for safe passage in front of all those people, knowing that it's not going to happen. She sort of gets the last word from beyond the realm of the living, saying, 'Ha ha—look what I made you do!'" (Hayner). As she adds, "But I think the interesting thing about Aslaug is, she came in with wit and intelligence. That's what Ragnar was interested in. So I like that she went out with wit and intelligence. That was very fitting to me" (Hayner).

Sometime after Lagertha divorces Ragnar, she is challenged for leadership of her city by the warrior Sigvard, who makes it clear that he believes only he should rule. This relationship continues as he finds ways to humiliate her so he can take over. Eventually, he forces her to marry him, establishing himself as jarl.

Various attempts follow to overthrow Ragnar as jarl in his own realm. Based on a historically documented incident, Lagertha finds out, brings her own army, helps defeat the enemy, and rescues Ragnar. According to Saxo, Lagertha, who still loved him, came to his aid with 120 ships. When in the height of the battle, Ragnar's son Siward was wounded, Lagertha saved the day with a counterattack: "Lagertha, who had a matchless spirit though a delicate frame, covered by her splendid bravery the inclination of the soldiers to waver. For she made a sally about, and flew round to the rear of the enemy, taking them unawares, and thus turned the panic of her friends into the camp of the enemy." Key points of this incident on the show are that Lagertha is seen as undisputed leader of her city, as the warriors there unhesitatingly follow her commands to march on the earl. We also see Ragnar, an alpha leader, perfectly willing to accept her help and unsurprised at the rescue. Katheryn Winnick explains:

> Lagertha has always had a lot of different challenges. Throughout this season it's been evident for her at this stage. Going into four, it's really seeing how Kattegat is run and being extremely disappointed that it's not ruled by the right ruler. With King Ragnar not necessarily being there and present as a king should be, and with Queen Aslaug running the show and not necessarily running it the proper way or the strongest way as a ruler to help the people [Murray].

When Lagertha returns home from taking her army to rescue Ragnar, she finds a displeased Sigvard who sends men to beat her during the night. He tries to humiliate her further the next day, but she chooses a different kind of divorce. He attempts rape, and she stabs him in the eye. In Saxo's version, she quarreled with her husband, and slew him with a spearhead she concealed in her gown. Saxo concludes that she then "usurped the whole of his name and sovereignty; for this most presumptuous dame thought it pleasanter to rule without her husband than to share the throne with him." Again, women's rights of the time take center stage when Lagertha doubts how this will be received by the local rulers, but they all acknowledge her right to kill him because he violated her right to say no. This arc ends with a Viking gathering in which all cry "Long live the new queen" ("Boneless," 208). In the same way as her husband ascended, she is now Jarl of Hedeby in her own right for dispatching the previous one. She then goes on to raid the English kingdom of Wessex with King Horik and Jarl Ragnar as their peer.

Now a ruler in her own right, she rejoins Ragnar. "Yes, we are equal," she tells him, after revealing her new status, "I'm sure this is difficult for you" (207). Winnick notes, "Lagertha has gained more status. She's changed a huge amount. When I signed on, she was just a famous wife. In this season, she emerges as her own person even further" ("Interview"). By the end of Season 2, Lagertha has found her own path, and in many ways, it is far more expansive and exciting than anything she could have achieved had she stayed in Kattegatt in the shadow of her famous husband. Her conversations with other famous heroines reveal her triumphs:

> GUNNHILD: You must be the famous shield-maiden, Lagertha.
> LAGERTHA: Oh, you are more famous, Gunnhild. The poets talk of your exploits. They tell how you killed Sweyn Forkbeard when he invaded Gotaland.
> GUNNHILD: And they say that you are now an Jarl in your own right! How did it happen?
> LAGERTHA: I killed my husband when he invaded me.
> Both laugh ["The Lord's Prayer," 210].

Having failed to learn the lessons of Sigvard, Lagertha tries again two years later by grooming Kalf, her second-in-command, to be her consort. Lagertha reveals to Kalf that she is pregnant, and Kalf asks her to marry him. However, just before their wedding, Lagertha sees Kalf pushing her out as jarl, so he can rule. Lagertha stabs and kills Kalf and reclaims her status as jarl in "Promised" (405). Winnick adds, "At this stage Lagertha truly feels alone, I feel, because of all the betrayal that she had" (Murray). During this time, Lagertha acquires two significant women who are shieldmaidens and act as a personal guard. They are fully capable warriors who are respected by all in the town. No one doubts their ability to win any fight.

Another notable heroine, Pórunn, is originally introduced as a slave in Kattegat and a love interest for Ragnar's son Bjorn (who is effectively crown prince at this point), but it quickly becomes apparent that she won't be an easy conquest. She resists his advances as far as she safely can while she's a slave, because this girl understands that real consent cannot exist in context of such a vast power differential. Later, she expresses her desire to become a shield-maiden and Aslaug makes her a free woman (a supportive gesture toward both Pórunn and Lagertha's son). Once this happens, she makes Bjorn work for her love and prove he respects her by fighting her.

Further, Bjorn insists on getting consent before wedding Pórunn, emphasizing that Lagertha's training has taught him respect for women in a culture that insists upon it. Like the film *Black Panther* (2018), this story emphasizes alternate cultures besides a sexist western one. Later, Pórunn makes her own feminist statement, demanding respect over admiration and insisting, "You don't understand. When I was a slave, I loved you. You were the first to treat me as if I was not a slave. But now, I have choices" ("The Lord's Prayer," 210).

Since Ragnar's son finds his own Lagertha, he continues the pattern. The badass Viking warriors show in each generation they have been raised to respect women and treat them as equals. This includes their bodily auton-omy and their property, but it also includes valuing their advice and fighting skills.

Princess Gisla is the last of the six that we meet. Hirst comments: "Princess Gisla is Charles the Bald's only daughter. She is actually not very impressed by her father's faint heart and lack of courage when faced with the Northmen—and even less impressed when her father forces her to marry Rollo, the great warrior, as a way of persuading him to protect Paris rather than attack it" (Pollard 149). Charles the Bald didn't have a daughter named Gisla, but his grandson Charles the Simple, the King of West Francia, did. Charles the Simple gave his daughter to Rollo in 911 after he converted to Christianity. Their descendants included William the Conqueror and thus the line of British kings. Historically, the real marriage didn't go so well, ending with Gisla dead of unknown causes after Rollo had the knights escorting her killed. Still, the show's retelling takes a more feminist turn.

When we first encounter her, she is trying desperately to convince her father to grow a backbone. We quickly see her as another princess who does not need rescuing, but she lives in the society of the Franks where woman are basically property to be used as seen fit. However, when her father marries her off to Rollo, she goes to her wedding bed with a dagger. She makes it clear that Rollo is an unwashed savage in her view and there is no way this marriage will be consummated. Rather than enforce his rights granted by the king, Rollo shows the Norse view that a woman must be respected and that she must consent. This leads to a fairly lengthy storyline where he does everything including learning the Frankish language and manners to earn her respect. The show remakes the chauvinist history into a reverse *Pygmalion* plot in which Gisla converts Rollo into a Frankish nobleman more to her liking.

So many powerful women, each claiming what she desires in Viking society, provide an alternate model to the misogynist history well-known from Western Europe. Moreover, the men of *Vikings* model consent and respect, showing viewers the egalitarian society our world could become again. Instead, the show presents a historically justifiable world where men and women are equals. "One of the most striking things about the *Vikings* series is the portrayal of women as independent contributors to the culture and the raids. The female characters don't feel subject to their male counterparts, and this is mostly true" (Rose). As spokeswoman of such a striking, yet historically accurate retelling, Katheryn Winnick should have the last say on feminism and her character, Lagertha:

> I think that it's the fact that she is constantly getting challenged in her moral compass and her moral ethics are always getting challenged. I think it is what keeps her honest and it keeps her who she is as Lagertha. She is formidable, she is strong, but she is also a woman. She is allowed to be vulnerable; she is allowed to be feminist. She is allowed not to have her shit together at times and that's what makes this character so real and fantastic. It's not just the strengths of her character as a warrior but her strength, her personality, and her strong sense of will is what I think a lot of people identify with.... I think there are a lot of women who identify with her as a strong person and not necessarily just someone in the Viking era in that time period. But I feel that she is really the modern women that everyone can relate to [Murray].

WORKS CITED

Grammaticus, Saxo, edited by Oliver Elton and Frederick York Powell. "The Danish History, Book IX." *The First Nine Books of the Danish History of Saxo Grammaticus*, David Nutt, 1894. https://archive.org/details/firstninebookso00saxo/page/n6.

Haywood, John. *Encyclopedia of the Viking Age*. Thames & Hudson, 2000.

Hayner, Chris E. "*Vikings* Alyssa Sutherland on Aslaug's Reckoning: 'I didn't think she'd last this long.'" *Screener TV*, 21 Dec 2016. http://screenertv.com/television/vikings-kills-aslaug-alyssa-sutherland-explains-her-exit.

Hirst, Michael, creator, *Vikings*. The History Channel, 2013–present.

"Interview with Katheryn Winnick (Lagertha)." *History.co.uk*. https://www.history.co.uk/shows/vikings/articles/interview-with-katheryn-winnick-Lagertha.

Murray, Rebecca. "*Vikings* Season 4 Part 2: Katheryn Winnick Interview on Lagertha, Ragnar, and Fierce Women." *Show Biz Junkies,* 18 Nov 2016. https://www.showbizjunkies.com/tv/vikings-katheryn-winnick-interview-season-4/.

Pollard, Justin. *The World of Vikings*. Chronicle Books, 2015.

Rose, Sundi. "Is Vikings Historically Accurate? What It Gets Right." *Pop Sugar,* 5 Feb 2016. https://www.popsugar.com/entertainment/Vikings-TV-Show-Historically-Accurate-37531824.

Sawyer, Peter, ed. *The Oxford Illustrated History of the Vikings*. Oxford University Press, 1997.

Story, Joanna. *Carolingian Connections: Anglo-Saxon England and Carolingian Francia, c. 750–870*. Ashgate, 2003.

Waggoner, Ben. "Introduction" *The Sagas of Ragnar Lodbrok*. Translated by Ben Waggoner. Troth Publications, 2009, pp. viii–xxvi.

Reclaiming Power from the Toxic Male

Support and Recovery in Marvel's Jessica Jones

VALERIE ESTELLE FRANKEL

Jessica Jones begins her Netflix show (2015–2019) as a cynical private investigator serving violent lowlifes with subpoenas and tracking cheating spouses. She notes, "People do bad shit. I just avoid getting involved with them in the first place. That works for me. Most of the time" (101). She insists she's coping, though the swirling imagery and descents into flashback suggest all the trauma she's keeping bottled up. Still, she's formidable. "The series slowly reveals that Jessica's surly demeanor, self-destructive behaviors, and her general self-loathing stem from having spent a year of her life under the complete control of the heinous Kilgrave," notes Jeffery A. Brown in *The Modern Superhero in Film and Television* (58).

"Unlike most female heroines, we never get a head-to-toe, camera pan scene of Jones (Krysten Ritter) wiggling towards the camera in a post-makeover, skin-tight dress, ready to seduce an unsuspecting male foe with her feminine wiles" (Forster). Setting aside the sexualized "Strong Female Character," the show gives Jessica clothes and attitude that emphasize how little she cares about pleasing others. "By featuring a superheroine who refuses to don a spandex costume and slink around fighting bank robbers or aliens, Jessica Jones offers a mature character and an intimate story of abuse and its effects that expands not just the Marvel Universe, but the possibilities for female characters within the genre." (Brown 59). Showrunner Melissa Rosenberg acknowledges that changing how women are represented in superhero stories was a top priority:

This has always been my goal across my painfully long career. Just the frustration year in and year out, show after show, of watching these absolutely one-dimensional, uninteresting roles for women that are so unrepresentative of who we are. Apparently the only people who can have dark, flawed, interesting characters are white men. When will it be time for women to play those roles? When can we show women as human beings like anyone else? But that's the history of television: women are wives, or the sassy cop—they're the Madonna or the whore. Pick one, that's all you get. But that's been changing over the last few years [Ehrlich].

Of course, Jessica's prickly exterior conceals a great deal of trauma. Like the world-weary private eyes she emulates, she insists she's given up. However, deep within, she's still a superhero. When a couple come to her with the tale of their own kidnapped daughter, taken by the same man who took her years earlier, Jessica's foster-sister Trish encourages her to intervene. She tells Jessica, "I know one thing, you are far better equipped to deal with that animal than some innocent girl from Omaha. You're still the person who tried to do something."

Jessica rejects this argument. "Tried and failed. That's what started this. I was never the hero that you wanted me to be" (101). Still, despite her fear and trauma, she struggles to save the younger victim, tellingly named Hope. At episode end, she discovers her former rapist Kilgrave has used Hope to set a trap for her. She considers running. However, she repeats the line she said at the episode beginning about cheating spouses: "Knowing it's real means you gotta make a decision.... One, keep denying it. Or two ... do something about it." She returns to the fight, marking herself as a hero far more than a victim. Rosenberg describes Jessica's inspirations:

I think with Tony Soprano, and Dexter ... slowly over the last 10 years with Jenji Kohan's *Weeds* and to some extent *Scandal,* women have been breaking in, but networks have been slow to let women into that circle. And for audiences—not studios, but audiences—to allow for a woman to be morally ambiguous and at times ugly as a person in the same way that Tony Soprano and Walter White were, it wasn't acceptable. So that's one of the things that I wanted to do with a female superhero [Ehrlich].

Certainly, that dark, hardbitten, uncompromising character reflects Jessica Jones of the comics (Marvel's hardcore brand Max, which kicks off with her yelling "Fuck" in its first release—her comic *Alias* by writer Brian Michael Bendis and artist Michael Gaydos). The show is a faithful adaptation, working with the story of her nemesis and tormentor the Purple Man even while linking her series to the related shows that became *The Defenders*. "Though *Alias* could have wallowed in the showcase of a broken woman, it instead highlights real trauma and survival. We get a character who might be currently defined by her past, but who is in the process of recovery and healing. And we are allowed to follow along as she survives day by day until she eventually finds closure," notes Hope Nicholson in her book on superheroines (194). As an incredibly mighty nonfeminine, nonsexualized heroine who dresses as she pleases and refuses to smile (rather like her film parallel Captain Marvel), she represents a new, tougher kind of heroine. Through her battle to save innocents and friendships with those most in danger, Jessica Jones offers intersectionality and compassion, even as she sets herself against the worst of villains—the entitled white male.

Trauma

Describing male gaze, essayist Stefani Forster explains, "It's a way to explain a limited male view, where the rest of the characters exist mainly to serve him, his interests, and his storyline" (Forster). This show offers viewers female gaze—though this is far more than a few scenes of Luke Cage shirtless. This is about using the presence of a female perspective on screen to emphasize the story's emotions and characters. "If the male gaze is all about what men see, then the female gaze is about making the audience feel what *women* see and experience. Crazy, right?" (Forster). "The basic formula at the core of most superhero narratives is an allegory for adolescent puberty and a male wish-fulfilling fantasy of becoming a pinnacle of hegemonic masculinity, but Jessica Jones breaks with genre conventions to construct an allegory for physical and psychological abuse," Brown adds (58). It's a very different story told from the perspective of the tortured girlfriend rather than the masculinized hero. Most of her viewpoint, of course, is demonstrated through trauma. Anita Sarkeesian of *Feminist Frequency* explains:

> To its credit, as one critic observed, Jessica Jones conveys the horror of Jessica's past without ever depicting it. In this way, it avoids sensationalizing sexual assault, acknowledges that trauma leaves a lasting impact on people, and relieves the audience of the burden of having to bear witness to the worst of what Jones has endured. By doing this, it demonstrates that as the audience, we can believe in the horror of what she has suffered without needing to see it. This is significant, considering that we live in a culture that still far too often dismisses the accounts of women who have suffered rape and assault. And as writer Arthur Chu noted, the particular brand of psychological abuse the show's villain Kilgrave employs is also noteworthy for the striking similarities it bears to the online abuse many women suffer; Jones can't trust anyone, can't feel safe anywhere. At times, it feels as if the entire world is out to get her.

Too often, rape is used to titillate, and too rarely are the effects of trauma shown. This perspective means reducing the women to sexualized objects instead of sympathizing with their struggles. Considering the difference between her show and others, Melissa Rosenberg insists:

> Rape has become a go-to for so many storytellers. Some of these shows…. I call them
> "Rapelander" or "Rape of Thrones." It becomes a joke after a while, which is so hor-
> rendous and such an additional violation to anyone who has experienced something
> like that—and so many of us have. So it was of paramount importance to all of us to
> not brush past this, to not be like "Yeah it's another rape story … okay, let's move on."
> These experiences in people's lives shape one's way of being in the world, and they
> can inform everything about one's character. It never goes away. But there comes to
> be a place as a survivor where you can find your strength, and Jessica is a survivor
> [Ehrlich].

Much has been made of the stylized filming of the show. The flashbacks,
non-linear and incoherent images, often tinted, jar the viewers, mirroring
the feelings of the traumatized. The dark surreal imagery in the credits opens
a window to Jessica's mindset. As she repeats street names and shares her
coping techniques, she allows the audience to share in her story. "One of the
things that made Kilgrave so scary in the initial episodes was the way the
memory of him haunted Jessica, always lingering at the edge of her thoughts,
out of sight, but never out of mind. It masterfully depicted the way that rape
trauma is a burden that doesn't go away once the act itself is over. In a year
that's been replete with depictions of rape in television, it was refreshing to
see a show tackle the true emotional weight of sexual assault without using
the violation itself to titillate," notes Cate Young in "Rape, Consent and Race
in Marvel's Jessica Jones." The *TV Guide* article "How Jessica Jones Got Rape
Stories Right" chimes in:

> The trauma Jessica endured from Kilgrave goes far beyond rape. As she explains, he
> "violated every cell in my body and every thought in my goddamn head," even mak-
> ing her kill for him. Though most survivors aren't struggling with the weight of mur-
> der, how Jessica flagellates herself over what happened is powerfully resonant. She
> isolates herself from everyone, convinced that she is hopelessly broken and only bur-
> dens those around her. And that—the shame, the self-loathing, the self-doubt—is
> often the trauma hardest for survivors to overcome ["How Jessica Jones"].

In the comics, Jessica is most horrified, not by bathing the Purple Man
and groveling for him but for the blurring of lines between coercion and
acquiescence: "In your head—it doesn't feel any different than when you
think it yourself, you see? It's almost soothing. In my mind, I can't tell the
difference between what he made me do or say and what I do or say on my
own" (#25). "This particular false consciousness is chemically induced, but
this could easily be a description of the patriarchially imposed ideological
false consciousness, with Killgrave as its smirking representative," explains
Roz Kaveney in *Superheroes! Capes and Crusaders in Comics and Films* (68).

Jessica determinedly digs her way out, doing good day by day. Through
the *Alias* comics, she protects Captain America from the consequences of an
affair and aids a young, drugged-out Spider-Woman. Each time, this means

aiding a young woman in danger—the superhero she once was and hopes to be again. Helping them symbolizes reclaiming herself piece by piece. "All in all, Jessica Jones in *Alias* is a great example of how to create a complex female character with past trauma, in which that trauma isn't her defining trait or used simply as a plot device" (Nicholson 195).

Mike Colter, who plays Luke Cage, explains how the show really digs into this type of suffering. He says, "It's very difficult to understand PTSD. In that regard, it opened doors to be relatable to so many people. It's about being damaged, and then trying to figure out how to go on with your life" (Radish). Focusing on a character undergoing this emphasizes the woman's struggle within the madness of an unjust world. Rachael Taylor (playing Jessica's foster-sister Trish Walker) adds:

> What makes it so unique is that it really is an allegory for many different types of abuse, whether it be sexual abuse, physical abuse, or psychological abuse. That's what makes this such an incredibly bold show. It's such a sharp, potent topic that we really should have discussions about more openly and more often. To do it within the framework of the superhero world and the comic book world is so incredibly brave and unique [Radish].

Toxic Male

David Tennant's character, Kilgrave, is so terrifying because he craves torturing Jessica, without guilt, without empathy. He's a picture of entitlement gone mad. Terrified, Jessica resorts to hiding and fleeing. Still, he demonstrates his control by ordering her to send him a daily picture of her, smiling. He thus turns his toxic gaze into a weapon. She complies, to save her friend's life, with a smile that's chilling because it evokes all the smiles abused women must display for their abusers. "While male viewers no doubt see his actions to control her via the threat of violence as abusive, it's unlikely many would associate his *desire* to have them with the way men casually request similar from women on dating sites as though it were a normal and not potentially dangerous request" (Remington). There are other moments when he enacts obvious American fantasies: having unlimited money, dressing well, having the power to empty out a fine restaurant or buy his girlfriend her dream home. In this, he becomes a sick parody of the wealthy, powerful American ... though this is especially chilling as it can encourage viewers to empathize with him instead of his victims, the protagonists.

> Kilgrave does many things representing male fantasies, such as when he joins a high stakes game of poker and forces all the other men to let him win. He eggs them on with emasculating insults, ("Where are your balls?") and boosts his ego even further by compelling the non-participating women in the room to echo his words at them.

When threatened by a man for leaving without giving them a chance to win their money back, Kilgrave slips out by getting him to pound his head against a pole. It's a twist on the "underdog outwits the bad guys" formula, the masculine idea of triumphing against the odds through brains, not brawn, but given a bad taste when we later learn Kilgrave will use the money to buy Jessica's old house to enact a disturbing parody of a marriage and the American Dream [Remington].

In episode 108, "AKA WWJD" (short for What Would Jessica Do), Kilgrave continues to guilt her with all the innocents he will kill in order to get to her. Despairing, she finally surrenders to Kilgrave to stop him from killing. His deluded strategy of buying her childhood home so they can play happy families (to the point of his calling her Jessie, her childhood name) is twisted. In his new fantasyland, they play at a parody of a happy couple. They have dinner, with Kilgrave's security guard and hostages to keep Jessica in line as she guzzles an entire bottle of wine. Later he complains, "I bought Jessica her bloody childhood home and restored it perfectly. If that's not a grand romantic gesture, I don't know what the bloody hell is" (110). He sees this superficial relationship as real even as he views his coercion as consent.

While staying with him, she tries channeling his powers into a force for good and brings him with her to rescue hostages. When he enjoys saving the day but tells her "I can't do it without you," she actually considers staying with him forever to shape him into a hero. Of course, his mental hold is all about manipulation—even as he controls her with guilt, a ghost of his deadly influence remains, along with the ever-present trauma. When Kilgrave responds to her death threats by insisting he has hostages, he adds, "There would've been a rash of suicides across the neighborhood, and who would've been to blame?" When she says it wouldn't be her, he retorts, "You keep telling yourself that. Maybe you'll actually believe it someday" (110). He has taken her agency, but he leaves her and his other victims fearing that some part of them was willing. "Given the low percent of rape that is actually reported, and the extremely-high percent of PTSD from victims, this a perfect parallel for what a rapist actually does: exert power over someone's body and mind" (Formo). Showrunner Melissa Rosenberg notes:

> For me, villains are only interesting if they're complex; the mustache-twirling guys don't give you very much to work with. What I love about Kilgrave is that he's not out to take over the world—that would be much too bothersome for him. He wants what he wants—he wants *who* he wants—and from a very young age he's very literally gotten *everything* he's ever wanted. How does that shape a human being? Who does that turn you into? He never perceives anything that he takes from people as being evil or bad. He's just: "They wanted it." Well yeah, because you *made* them want it! [Ehrlich].

Stuck in this new dynamic of a relationship, however forced, he complains. Notably, his objection is how annoying it is to ask for consent instead of controlling Jessica: "How do you people live like this? Day after day, just hoping people are gonna do what you want. It's unbearable" (108). Asked whether this makes him an American white man, Rosenberg laughs. "Exactly! 'It wasn't rape because she didn't say 'stop,' she didn't say 'no.' She wanted it.' There's such a twisted logic that happens with rapists and these people who have a need for strength and power to just disregard that there's another human being involved. They just objectify that other person. Kilgrave really is the epitome of that" (Ehrlich). Ideally, this show will make viewers rethink consent as discovering what the other person wants instead of applying many forms of coercion, even subtle things or acts of omission, to succeed.

In the final episode, Kilgrave finally gets to define his viewpoint for himself: "'Evil'? Come on, how reductive. I suppose 'me, evil' means 'you, good.' Bullshit. I mean, it's true that I've never given a second thought to anyone that I've let die, but I take no pleasure in it like a truly evil man would. I'm merely removing nuisances. Public service, really" (113). He insists this means he has morality, but it's that of the worst kind of racist or callous billionaire, who sees people without powers (literally in this case, rather than social power) as insignificant. He also tells Jessica, "I have a conscience. It's just more selective. I care if you die. The rest are fungible" (108). Of course, even as he views her as his ideal mate, he ignores her disgust with him. "The story is powerful showing what one villain can do to a single person, instead of trying to destroy the universe or rule the world" (Nicholson 194). It's his affection for her that is the most toxic:

> KILGRAVE: We used to do a lot more than just touch hands.
> JESSICA: Yeah. It's called rape.
> KILGRAVE: What? Which part of staying in five-star hotels, eating in all the best places, doing whatever the hell you wanted, is rape?
> JESSICA: The part where I didn't want to do any of it! Not only did you physically rape me, but you violated every cell in my body and every thought in my goddamn head.
> KILGRAVE: That is not what I was trying to do.
> JESSICA: It doesn't matter what you were trying to do. You raped me. Again and again and again!
> KILGRAVE: No. [shouts] How am I supposed to know? Huh? I never know if someone is doing what they want or what I tell them to!
> JESSICA: Oh, poor you.
> KILGRAVE: You have no idea, do you? I have to painstakingly choose every word I say [108].

"The fact that Kilgrave is seemingly unclear about whether Jessica did or didn't consent doesn't make him any more sympathetic. It makes him more terrifying, because the notion of a man abusing women without full comprehension of his actions is not fantastical. It's bleakly real" ("How Jessica Jones"). Many people, especially those who lack power in society, must carefully choose every word in order to avoid getting not just fired but lynched or sexually abused. As several critics have pointed out, Kilgrave's complaint of not knowing whether she consented is absurd in that while they were together for a year he never bothered to ask (as many men throughout history have not). He sees her as an object, however beloved, and treats her as one. Sarkeesian adds:

> This is also one of the rare moments in the series that lends some complexity to the character of Kilgrave; as horrifying as his actions are, he's doing what he's doing because in his own deeply twisted way, he believes that he genuinely cares for Jessica. Perhaps the most frightening aspect of Kilgrave is that he actually believes his own sick rationalizations; he believes that on some level, Jessica wanted what he did to her. When Jessica reminds him of the fact that he repeatedly raped her, Kilgrave is shocked and genuinely confused. His delusion that she had consented when in reality she had no ability to do so is frighteningly similar to the tales of rapists who don't believe that their sexual encounters constitute assault and abuse.

He's also completely slimy, twisting his most horrific crimes back on Jessica. He insists her drinking problem is her fault not his. As he adds of the moment that broke her, "I did not tell you to kill Reva.... If you remember, I said, 'Take care of her.' Not kill her. You chose to punch her" (108). In this scene, he can be seen manipulating her by blaming her for his crimes. In other moments, however, his obliviousness to having forced her into sex show off his privilege to the point of never having to deal with consequences:

With his twisted morality there's no way to reform him, no way he can ever be retaught. He spends the first season plotting to regain his control over Jessica and devastate her forever, and no appeal to logic, empathy, or decency will halt him. As he commands his father in the final episode: "Give me everything you've got. Maybe I'll get strong enough to control her again. God. Dear God, I would do anything to see the look on her face when she realizes she's helpless. I'd make her want me. Then reject her. Devastate her over and over and over until she wants to die. No, I won't give her that, either. She'd wither away like someone dying of thirst or starvation. Be a certain ring of hell, designed specially for her. Or maybe I'll just kill her" (113). His vendetta against the woman who escaped him is personal in every way. The only solution, as Jessica finally discovers, is to permanently end the threat.

Other Toxic Males

Kilgrave coerces the ex-military man Simpson into attacking Jessica's beloved sister Trish, persuading his way into her apartment and nearly strangling her. Afterwards, Simpson is overcome with guilt. He pleads for Trish to let him in to explain, and when she refuses, he sits outside her door. Considering that Trish has stated that she wants him to leave, his apologies (in fact, a release of emotion more about absolving himself than comforting her) mean he's ignoring her wishes to pursue his own. His choice is understandable, but it subtly emphasizes how much American male toxicity focuses on the men's own needs instead of those stated by others. "Trish is the victim in the situation, and yet Simpson manages to find a way to center himself in the story of this trauma. As with Kilgrave and Jessica, Simpson's abuse is rooted not in a cartoonish hatred of women as we are often led to believe, but rather in prioritizing his own will and desires over Trish's" (Young).

> Simpson's struggle to overcome his mind control manifests in increasingly dangerous ways, yet overlooks the fact that as a white male in a position of authority his insistence on being "forgiven" by Trish is a function of privilege and abuse and not just personality. When the perspective shifts to actions, viewers are often given an excuse not to identify with the masculinity the character expresses, or else they excuse it by suggesting the characters' actions are "not what I would do" [Remington].

Simpson, though bristling with military training, fails to help much. He interferes more than he helps, while his condescending fits of white machismo repel the women. In one memorable scene, Trish cuts off Simpson early during one of his smug mansplaining rants: "Last night was fun, but that doesn't mean that I want your opinion." Later, Simpson calls when Trish is in the middle of a show, pleading, "Look, Trish, it wasn't me. I ... Christ, even I don't buy that." Even as she tries to make him go away, he keeps pushing. "Maybe I could see you later. Nothing says sorry like a rare steak and some cheesecake. Or, you know, tofu and wheat berries, or..." (111). This is a smaller gesture than buying Jessica's childhood home, but it seems nearly as unwanted. Like Kilgrave, Simpson just won't go away. Later, he locks Trish in as he goes off to be a superhero, insisting, "Trish, this is the only way to keep you safe.... I'll take care of things, Trish. It's what I do" (111). Like Kilgrave, his words and grand gestures echo classic masculinity—the powerful man defending his damsel and keeping her safe. However, thanks to the drugs supplied by his super-secret military group, Simpson is out of control. He bludgeons into situations, as he considers blowing up innocents to take Kilgrave down. As a strung-out soldier on drug-powered adrenaline and super strength, he parodies American machismo. What's more, the show depicts him as fundamentally wrong.

> The contrast between Kilgrave and Simpson is genius, as it helps demonstrate the full scale of abuse that men knowingly and unknowingly enact on the women around them. The two men are flip-sides of the same coin. While Kilgrave simply takes what he feels he is entitled to by means of his powers of enhanced persuasion, Simpson initially takes a less forceful but no less sinister approach, exemplified in his treatment of Trish after he realizes that Kilgrave has compelled him to murder her [Young].

The second season likewise offers toxic males. In episode 202, Trish needs a favor from director Maximilian Tatum. If he refuses, she tells him, she will go public about their affair when he was forty and she was sixteen. As she adds, "Going on fifteen. And my mother pimped me out for the lead in your crappy movie." Much like Kilgrave, the director insists he's innocent here and that she was at fault for wanting to be in the film so badly and being willing to resort to blackmail in the present day. As with Kilgrave's insinuations to Jessica, Max's blame and dismissal devastate Trish while coloring her view of herself. "Trish is continually taken advantage of, from her overbearing stage mother to a predatory director to an oblivious fiancé. It's no wonder then, that she spirals so spectacularly in season two, where a drug addiction and a hunger for power nearly leads her to self-destruction" (Steiner).

Chelsea Steiner of *The Mary Sue* notes that other heroines besides Jessica chafe under the patriarchy's assault on their freedoms. All the people who forced Trish to be a child actor and then failed to take her seriously as an adult radio personality emphasize her restrictions in society. Other women have equally difficult negotiations with society:

> In season two we meet Alisa Jones, Jessica's long-lost mother. Alisa was experimented on against her will, which gave her superpowers and an uncontrollable rage. She develops a Stockholm syndrome-style relationship with her doctor, and while her life was saved, she became a Frankenstein's monster of female anger and emotional instability. She is the perfect foil to Jessica: similarly powered, yet lacking the grounding and moral compass of her daughter.

Still, Jessica finds sympathy and commonality for a woman who's been her boss and mild antagonist through the series: the lawyer Jeri Hogarth. She and her girlfriend become Kilgrave's victims as well. Hogarth tells Jessica afterwards, "I don't know what else I can do to pay for my mistakes. I have bled for them, I have lost everything that I care about. Pam is facing murder charges, and she won't see me, and my partners are forcing me out."

In a reversal from her earlier isolation, Jessica responds that she should fight for her place rather than giving this up too. She gives Hogarth an assignment defending another of Kilgrave's victims and adds, "And this does not make us square. But doing something ... good ... it helps with the self-loathing. Trust me" (113). The source of Jessica's determined heroism is revealed as she tries to strengthen this woman so different from herself.

Further, the cutthroat lawyer becomes far more personally vulnerable in the second season. Diagnosed with ALS, she needs help as a new minority—disabled. In fact, the vicious law firm where she has excelled now pushes her out. This emphasizes the patriarchy's desire to turn on the weak rather than supporting and caring for them. For the first time, Hogarth has an enemy she can't control or defeat, and, despairing, she turns to desperate unconventional paths. At last, Hogarth, like Jessica, finds the strength to resist on her own. "She is brought to her lowest point by a female con artist. Hogarth regains her confidence and exacts bloody revenge on everyone who shunned her when she became ill" (Steiner).

As Steiner concludes: "All of the women in *Jessica Jones* are in pain, but they refuse to be passive. They cry, they rage, they self-destruct, but they are always active, always moving. No one is coming to save them. They can only save themselves and each other." In these circumstances, the women band together with Jessica and Trish supporting each other and Jessica struggling to save her mother and Hogarth both. As she reaches out to the other women whose problems are so different from her own, she strikes a blow for intersectionality—a defining fourth wave trait.

Intersectionality

Jessica begins the story insisting she cares for no one, though it's soon revealed that Trish is the one person she loves and trusts. This emphasizes her slowly reaching out to others through the arc of the story, recognizing their needs as different yet parallel to her own and helping them to save themselves. This lies at the heart of fourth wave feminism—intersectionality. This term coined by black feminist scholar Kimberlé Crenshaw in 1989, is "The view that women experience oppression in varying configurations and in varying degrees of intensity. Cultural patterns of oppression are not only interrelated, but are bound together and influenced by the intersectional systems of society. Examples of this include race, gender, class, ability, and ethnicity" (Vidal). It accepts that there can be many other factors pertaining to one's identity, which lead to inequality, which can act in relation to gender.

> Jessica's relationship with her adoptive sister Trish Walker, for instance, is fascinating because of the contrast between them. Jessica drinks way too much and her apartment (and her life) are a mess; Trish is successful and seemingly has her life together. Jessica is emotionally distant and unreliable as a friend; Trish is loyal and dedicated. This relationship is, in the end, at the heart of Jessica Jones; it's here that we see Jessica growing as a person, slowly learning to express her feelings for the people she loves [Sarkeesian].

Jessica through the course of her story discovers the marginalization and abuse others have suffered from Kilgrave—not the man who keeps harping about his stolen jacket in a parody of trauma, but the characters whom he has treated like objects because society does not protect them.

She comforts many others of Kilgrave's victims. First, she bonds with Hope, an innocent young woman much like she used to be. Next, she must extend this sympathy and support to others who share her torture, like Malcolm her drug-addicted neighbor. "She also desperately implores Malcolm to resist his addiction (thus making her self sacrifice significant), to save her 'for once' by saving himself. In recovering from addiction and processing his traumas, Malcolm appears in his own scenes to wonder who he is now, after surviving" (Weida). After making it through this, Malcolm creates a support group for victims of Kilgrave and encourages Jessica to join. By doing so, he follows her model to save others, becoming the hero that Kilgrave and Simpson only convince themselves they are being. "It is this process that leads [Malcolm] to become a collaborative leader like Trish: a hero on the sidelines whose caring and fortitude about helping others exceeds Jessica's at times" (Weida). The gender-flipping continues as Malcolm also provides emotional support, taking the role of both secretary and helpless dupe—ones generally assigned to female characters. Puppy-eyed, useless Reuben, Jessica's adoring neighbor, falls into the same category.

Still, Jessica resists joining the support group, emphasizing that she is not ready to fully take her place among other people in her situation. She still sees herself as a lone hero.

> Besides Jessica's immediate goal of lending credibility to Hope, the act of bearing witness to these survivors also gives Jessica additional leads to fight Kilgrave and, importantly, reveals stories more tragic than her own. Notably, although the support group of survivors forms from the gathering of witnesses, Jessica does not attend the group regularly. She stresses that part of the reason she doesn't attend the group or talk through her issues elsewhere is because although her story is "shitty," someone else's suffering is always greater [Weida].

In the first season, Jessica's greatest ally comes from a different background to the point of leading his own superhero show, located in Harlem and focusing, not on post-rape trauma but on the black experience in America. This is Luke Cage. "Luke Cage's origins are exploitative and date to the Blaxploitation craze, but his origin story parallels important social concerns that came to light at the time he was introduced" (Packer 146). He has an interesting role as he is a popular comics character, destined for his own series shortly after Jessica Jones's, as viewers were aware.

> Luke Cage has endured the test of time, even though he got off to a shady start through Blaxploitation. His character brings several social, racial, and medical issues to the table. Cage's origin story recollects the Tuskegee syphilis experiments performed on African-American men in Alabama. That study was stopped in 1972, after a 40-year run. It became public knowledge in 1972, when the *Washington Star* published details of the U.S. Public Health Service syphilis study. *The New York Times* soon followed suit. Luke Cage the comic book was born in the very same year: 1972. Quite the coincidence [Packer 146].

Like many comics, his helped bring social awareness of injustice. "Times changed after Tuskegee. Luke Cage may have helped change those times as he reminded readers that not everyone who is sent to prison belongs in prison, and that not everyone who volunteers for medical research studies has other recourses" (Packer 146).

His superpowers are arguably more formidable and impressive than Jessica's. Still, on her show he functions as the confidante and love interest, a role complicated by the eventual revelation that Jessica was coerced into killing his wife. Still, he's treated the way female characters usually are, as he provides emotional support and is objectified for his glistening muscles. He actually reacts without judgment when Jessica tries to buy drugs to knock out Kilgrave in the third episode. "Luke has never bought into most of the stock but unneeded aspects of superheroing—the costume, the mask, the secret identity—and he has always been 'hero for hire'—a mercenary. He is not Captain America, nor does he pretend to be; he is not the embodiment of an ideal, just a working stiff with powers," Kaveney notes (84). His actor, Mike Colter, adds:

> The way that I was able to see how Luke dealt with Jessica, he's a supporter. He could have intervened with Kilgrave, but that was something she had to deal with for herself. He couldn't come to her rescue because that wouldn't change the horror of what she'd been through. In that regard, it defined who he was and how he looked at her, as a person who's a complete individual that can do things for herself, but if she needed him, he was there for her [Radish].

His kindness to her, even as he sets aside his own significant backstory, and the revelation of how much her past has affected him, emphasizes the concept of shared goals between communities. When he is critically injured, Jessica must find him help and doctors who can accommodate his particular needs. She drags him to the hospital, but no one will help her there. "He's one of those," the startled doctor says of unconscious Luke. However, Jessica insists they help. She appeals to Night Nurse: "Look, I know that we scare you, and that you've never seen anything like us, but this is a good man!" (113). Claire, touched by Jessica's appeal, offers to try alternate methods. With innovation and adaptability, they save him.

Luke's wife, like Jessica, was seeking the truth, and only by sharing their knowledge can they defeat their enemy, the entitled white man. At the same time, it must be noted how Luke and his wife Reva are both severely mistreated in the story: "The only significant, named woman of color character is dead before the narrative begins and never speaks a word, while the black male characters are all subjected to incredible violence in service of the white female protagonist" (Young). Reva's death jolts Jessica from her obedience, but this too is a disturbing trope suggesting the white woman can abuse and discard people of color in her quest for self-actualization. Luke becomes her partner, but by hiding this vital murder from him, Jessica is controlling and taking advantage of the invulnerable hero—ironic and problematic in a story so devoted to consent. "It's disappointing that the show, knowingly or not, replicates the same cycles of abuse that routinely play out within the feminist movement, by positioning violence against black women as the justified cost of white women's liberation" (Young).

Triumph

Her final showdown demands the most of Jessica: she walks willingly into Kilgrave's trap, surrenders, and gives herself up to his orders, her worst nightmare from the first episode. She even lets Kilgrave caress her beloved sister. "From your perspective, I'll be raping her every day. My skin will be touching hers. She'll be my plaything. She'll be my slave. And in her mind, she'll be dying, isn't that right?" he asks slimily. The look on Jessica's face of misery and horror, offered up for Kilgrave to see, finally convinces him. When he unleashes his power and she turns passive, he joyfully rushes to her and says: "Oh, God, it's true, isn't it? You would let me take your beloved sister. My God. It's finally over. You're mine now. No more fighting. No more of these ugly displays. You'll be with me now. Look, after a while … however long it takes…. I know…. I know you will feel what I feel. Let's start with a smile." She smiles for him, very artificially, complying with his favorite command, then, throwing the word back at him, she breaks his neck.

This scene does not bring her an instant recovery from her trauma. The purplish street gleams and the music echoes ominously. Jessica is even arrested for murder. Still, she has found some peace and stability by removing the threat. Now she will need a new purpose. Her actress, Kristen Ritter, adds: "For Jessica, that final victorious, triumphant moment when she kills Kilgrave, I found that very conflicting, in terms of her head space. He's the reason why she got up, every day. He's the reason why she went out in the world. It really gave her a purpose. And I don't think that the past trauma just goes away with his death. So, her head space is really complex" (Radish). Nonetheless, there's the triumph of freedom and safety as she finally destroys her tormentor.

The comic has a different ending, finding her happily pregnant and building a life with her boyfriend in an image of growth but also a conventional fairytale ending. "Part of that closure involves having sex with the super-hot superhot Power Man (aka Luke Cage) and getting pregnant by him. So I'm not saying you won't come across a few tropes in the book that aren't disappointing to see," Nicholson admits (194). The Netflix show chooses a different direction, having her and Luke part (as he heads toward his own series and their eventual team-up in *The Defenders*). Meanwhile, Jessica continues at Alias Investigations, training Malcolm as a sidekick in her quest to do good. Their problems aren't all solved. "All the issues that plagued Jessica throughout the season do not magically go away after killing Kilgrave. The world still does not believe his victims, despite the mounting number of those who've come forward. Kilgrave's death has not erased Jessica's PTSD, nor has it helped her recognize her own self-worth, a feat that is now probably made harder by the rising body count for which she blames herself" ("How Jessica Jones"). The show doesn't offer perfect healing, just a path to getting through the day. For Jessica, that's a triumph.

Works Cited

Bendis, Brian Michael, and Michael Gaydos. *Alias Ultimate Collection Book 2 (Alias #16–28)*. Max Comics, 2010.

Brown, Jeffrey A. *The Modern Superhero in Film and Television*. Taylor & Francis, 2017.

Ehrlich, David. "'Jessica Jones' Creator on the 'Tony Soprano' of Female Superheroes." *Rolling Stone*, 19 Nov 2015. https://www.rollingstone.com/tv/tv-news/jessica-jones-creator-on-the-tony-soprano-of-female-superheroes-33676/.

Formo, Brian. "Why *Jessica Jones* and *Spotlight* Are a Step Forward for Victims of Abuse." *Collider*, 9 Dec 2015. http://collider.com/jessica-jones-spotlight-sexual-abuse.

Forster, Stefani. "Yes, There's Such a Thing as a 'Female Gaze.' But It's Not What You Think." *Medium*, 12 June 2018. https://medium.com/truly-social/yes-theres-such-a-thing-as-a-female-gaze-but-it-s-not-what-you-think-d27be6fc2fed.

"How Jessica Jones Got Rape Stories Right." *TV Guide*, Dec. 3. 2015. http://medford.wicked local.com.

Kaveney, Roz. *Superheroes! Capes and Crusaders in Comics and Films*. I.B. Tauris, 2008.

Marvel's Jessica Jones. Netflix. 2015–2018. Web.

Nicholson, Hope. *The Spectacular Sisterhood of Superwomen*. Quirk Books, 2017.

Packer, Sharon. *Superheroes and Superegos: Analyzing the Minds Behind the Masks*. ABC-Clio, 2010.

Radish, Christina. "*Jessica Jones* Cast on Season 2 Possibilities, Sex Scenes, and *Luke Cage*." *Collider*, 28 Jan 2016. http://collider.com/jessica-jones-season-2-sex-scenes-luke-cage.

Remington, Scott. 'Jessica Jones,' The Kilgrave Mirror and the Distancing Effect of Negative Masculinity." *Bitch Flicks*, January 21, 2016. http://www.btchflcks.com/2016/01/the-kilgrave-mirror-and-the-distancing-effect-of-negative-masculinity.html.

Sarkeesian, Anita. "Some Thoughts on Jessica Jones," *Feminist Frequency*, 1 Dec. 2015, http://femfreq.tumblr.com/post/134336278616/some-thoughts-on-jessica-jones.

Steiner, Chelsea. "Jessica Jones and Its Legacy of Female Anger." *The Mary Sue*, 19 Feb. 2019 https://www.themarysue.com/rip-jessica-jones.

Vidal, Ava. "'Intersectional Feminism.' What the Hell Is It? (And Why You Should Care)." *The Telegraph* 15, 2014.

Weida, Courtney Lee. "From the Hellmouth to Hell's Kitchen: Analyzing Aesthetics of Women Survivors and Spaces in Buffy the Vampire Slayer and Jessica Jones." *Jessica Jones, Scarred Superhero: Essays on Gender, Trauma and Addiction in the Netflix Series*, edited by Tim Rayborn and Abigail Keyes, McFarland, 2018, pp. 189–202.

Young, Cate. "Rape, Consent and Race in Marvel's Jessica Jones." *Bitch Flicks*, 11 Dec 2015 http://www.btchflcks.com/2015/12/rape-consent-and-race-in-marvels-jessica-jones.html.

SECTION III

Intersectionality

From Sidekick
to Romantic Lead

Rise of the Strong Black Woman

Sumiko Saulson

On November 4, 2018, on AMC, the unthinkable happened. A show's white leading man went missing, presumed dead. His strong black woman love interest became the new central character.

Eight years into the show, *The Walking Dead* seemingly bumped off Rick Grimes, the central protagonist, in the fifth episode of the ninth season of the critically acclaimed zombie apocalypse soap-opera, *What Comes After*. The main point of view character usually can't just die off without the show ending. Jeff Stone of *IndieWire* protests:

> From the show's opening moments, Rick Grimes has been our eyes as we watched the world slide into zombie hell. [...] through all the years Rick has been the constant; he's the character everyone else orbits around, the one who leads, the one guy you know won't be killed each episode (no matter how much of a drag that becomes) [Stone].

Rick vanishes, and the show leaps forward several years, where a young Judith Grimes has saved a group of travelers, apparently stepping up into her dead brother Carl's shoes. That leaves the enigmatic Michonne in Rick's shoes as the show's primary point of view character, leader, and community builder. This is also the ultimate nail in the coffin to the show's hottest romance since Maggie Greene (Lauren Cohan) and Glenn Rhee (Steven Yeun) got together, Rick and Michonne, aka Richonne.

Still, romances tend to end fatally on *TWD*, and like Rick and Lori (Lori died), Shane and Lori (Shane died), Glenn and Maggie (Glenn died), Andrea and Michonne (Andrea died), Sasha and Bob (Bob died), Sasha and Abraham

(Abraham died), Beth and Daryl (Beth died), Carol and Tyrese (Tyrese died) … well, you get the picture. Love never lasts for long on *TWD*. It also seems there can only be one serious multi-season stable love story at a time. Lori died right around the time Glenn and Maggie got together, and Glenn died right after Michonne and Rick's love for one another was confirmed as romantic. One might speculate that the only reason Carol and Daryl are both still alive is that they keep secretly hooking up and never get serious.

The Walking Dead's Richonne (Harjo) was a big deal because it elevated Michonne from sidekick to romantic female lead. She was no longer a strong black woman trope that didn't need a man. She wasn't a mammy stereotype babysitting Rick's children Carl and Judith. Still, there were problematic things about Richonne from day one. During their courtship, Michonne's dead black son was relegated to a plot device for bonding scenes with Carl. Indeed, the romance trajectory started much later. Michonne's maternal affection for Carl (Chandler Rigg) started with a scene in Season 4, Episode 15, "Us" on the way to Terminus. Noetta Harjo of *Geek Girl Authority* explains:

> Michonne and Carl walk along the tracks to see who can keep balance [...] Rick watches them play. Michonne was always so good with Carl and Judith. Rick noticed it from the beginning. She gave Carl a sort of mother figure to watch over him and a best friend to confide in. I'm pretty sure this was the moment they started to become a family [Harjo].

A 2016 study of Facebook followers for *The Walking Dead* franchise showed that women dominated show interest, with 54.17 percent women and 45.83 percent men among binary identified individuals liking the show's page (Brett). Women also appeared more heavily among older viewers. This showed through when the show attempted to get rid of Carol but had to bring her back due to protesting from this core demographic. This massive female viewership is likely why the show keeps romance front and center. Killing off Glenn Rhee was riskier for the television program because its viewer audience is both more female and strongly minority-centered, with Latino viewers leading the pack. Gary Levin of *USA Today* notes:

> Nielsen data for 2017 to date, analyzed by USA Today, shows that no single program is ranked in the top 5 among whites, blacks, Asian-Americans and Hispanics (Two, AMC's The Walking Dead and NBC's This Is Us, were among the most popular for three of those groups) [Levin].

Asian Americans view *The Walking Dead* at high rates as well but are not core television viewers the way African Americans and Latinos are. "African-Americans watch far more TV than any other group—nearly 44 hours a week last fall, Nielsen says—while Asian-Americans watch the least (less than 15 hours)" (Levin). Furthermore, Michonne was one of the show and comic's most popular characters—arguably the most popular. She had a strong appeal among white male viewers as a romantic and sexual focal point of interest and is older than Maggie so appeals to older female viewers.

Black woman/white man relationships are still controversial, although black men often date interracially. Themes about black women/white men and slavery/colonialism were echoed in plotlines about Sasha, who lost her black boyfriend Bob, only to be wind up first in a voluntary situation with a white man, then a forced ordeal with unwanted advances by evil white plantation lord wannabe Negan, followed by her meaningless self-sacrifice. Like Glenn, Sasha fell to the rising star of Michonne.

There is a complicated relationship between fiction and hyper-violence toward people of color. Although the television show swayed away from the outright racist rant of the villain in the comic book, where he said he didn't want to kill Glenn because he didn't want to seem racist for killing the only Asian and then killed him anyway, the character remained inherently bigoted. Glenn's death was particularly brutal, and the fact that he had married and impregnated a young white girl before Negan killed him makes Negan a symbolic metaphor for angry white men who want revenge against minorities for taking what is theirs (a trope seen in many recent villains in *Star Wars* and *Ghostbusters*, among others). The show underscores this trope by having Negan threaten to force Maggie into his harem and rape her immediately after her husband's death (Murphy). He eventually grooms Sasha as a potential concubine instead.

The placement of Sasha (Sonequa Martin-Green), another black woman, as Michonne's foil is particularly disturbing. As Michonne's fortunes rose with Rick, Sasha's declined. Sasha was the first woman in a black on black relationship in the series, which generally shows only white couples or interracial couples involving at least one white person despite a large black cast. Michonne had a white husband before the zombie apocalypse and ends up with Rick. Sasha goes from Bob to Abraham, and like Maggie, has her man killed by Negan, who tries to replace him. Negan claims to rescue her from a man who tried to rape her but pressures her to join his harem afterward. Instead of Sasha escaping like Maggie, she ends up dying trying to kill Negan rather than submit to being raped by him.

The Walking Dead's handling of black characters and their relationships is often problematic. Still … for a brief shining moment, it is the Michonne show. Michonne, a strong black woman who stole the show the moment she walked on set carrying a katana with two undead walkers on leashes in tow, is played by the charismatic actress Danai Gurira and has an almost super-heroic appeal. Audiences had long complained of the generally lackluster writing and acting associated with Rick Grimes, played as a subtle and thoughtful character by Andrew Lincoln. He gained a bit of heat through his romantic association with the ass-kicker Michonne. Although his broody strong silent type would return to the captain's helm, his temporary absence completed Michonne's assent from a near-stock strong black woman sidekick trope to love interest and then star.

This was all made possible by a recent trend—the rise of the black woman in horror, science-fiction and fantasy. Perhaps this rise could be called a resurgence, for not since the seventies have there been so many black women in leading lady roles. Some of these are straight lead characters, occasionally dazzling in their strength and power as with the heroines of the CW super-hero show *Black Lightning*, but most of them are (a bit more disappointingly) romantic leads in stories with a male protagonist.

The year 2018 was a great one for black women in film, due in no small part to the box office smash *Black Panther,* starring a cavalcade of amazing black talent, including so much sister star-powered wattage that almost every black girl wound up with a *Black Panther* themed cosplay from spry, intelligent teen Shuri (Letitia Wright) right on up to regal matriarch Queen Ramonda (Angela Bassett). There was also glamorous, stubborn spy and love interest Nakia (Lupita Nyong'o) and an entire troop of warrior women led by Danai Gurira's Okoye: In fact, Lupita Nyong'o, Danai Gurira, Angela Bassett and Letitia Wright made a big impression on the audience while the film made a big take at the box office, grossing more than 1.1 billion worldwide and becoming the seventh highest grossing film of all time. However, it wasn't the only showcase for the rising crop of black starlets in science fiction and fantasy. *A Wrinkle in Time* starred Storm Reid, Gugu Mbatha-Raw, and Oprah Winfrey, three black women. Additionally, *Sorry to Bother You* and *Annihilation* featured Tessa Thompson as black female lead.

Sorry to Bother You is a dark comedy sci-fi horror film currently available on Hulu wherein we gradually learn that Oakland, California, resident Cassius "Cash" Green, who seems to be living in the present, is actually in a future dystopia where those in debt sell themselves into slavery by signing up for a lifetime of servitude with a company called WorryFree.

Dark-skinned black women are being cast with both black and white men as love interests these days, and in same-sex pairings as well. Unfortunately, there is still a lot of failure to sustain lesbian relationships in mainstream television and cinema. Michonne on the *Walking Dead* television show was originally romantically involved with Andrea, but they killed her off. Similarly, Stephen King's *Under the Dome* (2013–2015) introduced a black/white lesbian couple in the form of Aisha Hinds as Carolyn Hill and Samantha Mathis as Dr. Alice Calvert, only to quickly wipe out the Calvert character and leave Carolyn Hill as the single, sexless black mammy stereotype raising their white daughter Norrie Calvert-Hill (played by Mackenzie Lintz). Aisha Hinds is another dark-skinned sister who has appeared in a number of sci-fi, horror and fantasy offerings, including the upcoming

Godzilla: King of the Monsters (2019), *Breed* (2015), *Cult* (2013) and *True Blood* (2008–2010). In 2016, GLAAD noted that more than 25 queer, female characters died onscreen—including Lexa on *The 100*, Denise on *The Walking Dead*, and Nora and Mary Louise on *The Vampire Diaries*. Sometimes this occurred "solely to further a straight, cisgender character's plotline—which sends a dangerous message to audiences" (Bradley). This pattern is, unfortunately, famous enough to be called the "Dead Lesbian Syndrome," as Karen Frost notes in "Hollywood Still Doesn't Get its Dead Lesbian Issue":

> In 2016, *Vox* calculated all American primetime network and streaming platform series deaths in the 2015–2016 season (the character killed appeared in at least three episodes). The article found that 56% of deaths were male, and 44% female ... proportionally consistent with the fact that 43% of regular characters on primetime broadcast programming are women, per *GLAAD's 2015–2016 Where We Are on TV*. Minority deaths were even slightly underrepresented: 33% of characters on broadcast are people of color, but they were only 26% of the characters killed. Queer males fared a little worse: they are 2% of characters, but 3% of deaths, meaning their kill rate is 1.5 times higher than one would expect based on their representation. Then there are the lesbian deaths. 10% of deaths this TV season were lesbian or bi women, but they are only 2% of all TV characters. This means that while other minority groups are *relatively* well proportionally represented in character deaths, gay women are killed at five times higher a rate than should be indicated by their appearance. This isn't just coincidence.

True Blood (2008–2014) featured a number of dynamic characters of African heritage, many of them women, but none was as prominent as Rutina Wesley in the role of Tara Thornton. She was the best friend of the lead character Sookie Stackhouse, played by Anna Paquin. Like most of Sookie's young mortal friends, she was hot and always had to evade paranormal romantic come-ons from lecherous ancient immortals. A fiery young lesbian chocolate sister, she had often troubled relationship with white women. However, she remained fiercely independent and powerful until they replaced her bigoted religious black mother (played by Adina Porter) with the ancient white vampire lover and mother figure Pam De Beaufort (played by Kristin Bauer van Straten). Tara was so cowed by Pam that one began to sense the homophobia and fear of supernatural creatures that her mother epitomized, while oppressive, was less soul-crushing than becoming the sex slave of an ancient white plantation lord.

Tara Thornton was perhaps the most liberated and least repressed of the queer women represented in mainstream sci-fi, fantasy and horror. That made her eventual decline even more painful to watch. Still, she was very well written, as was the show's male femme character Lafayette Reynolds, played by Nelsan Ellis who tragically died in 2017 at only 39 years of age.

Adina Porter, who played Tara's mother, Lettie Mae Thornton, is also a heavy hitter in black speculative fiction. She is a regular on *American Horror*

Story now, even though she had only a tiny bit part as Sally Freeman when *Season 1: Murder House* debuted in 2011. She has been a major fixture since 2016's *AHS: Roanoke,* in which she played Lee Harris, a law enforcement officer who got pulled into a bizarre series of events while investigating cult-like murders in Virginia. She also played major characters Beverly Hope on *AHS: Cult,* and Dinah Stevens in *AHS: Apocalypse.* That makes her one of the three major black female presences on the show, along with Angela Bassett as Desiree Dupree, Marie Laveau, Ramona Royale, Lee Harris, and Monet Tumusiime, while Gabourey Sidibe plays Queenie and Regina Ross.

The first major appearances by black characters on *American Horror Story* were in *Season 3: Coven.* The season pitted racist plantation owner Delphine LaLaurie (Kathy Bates) against voodoo priestess Marie Laveau (Bassett). Although it turned out some award-winning performances, it was met with mixed reviews due to its extreme violence and seeming mining of sensationalistic aspects of racism and cruelty toward slaves for ratings (Bolonik).

A sex scene between Gabourey Sidibe as Queenie and a murdered black man who had been a slave to Delphine was particularly disturbing. He'd been magically made a Minotaur after he was tortured, his head removed, and replaced with a bovine head. As he had been murdered for showing sexual interest in Delphine's white daughters, there was more than one cringe-worthy element to Queen's purported lust for and objectification of a black man's decapitated corpse. Was the program making some sort of untoward statement about Delphine's young, thin, white daughters and Delphine (a larger, older white woman) and Queenie (a young, bigger black girl) lusting after a dismembered Mandingo figure? What does that say about the show's attitude toward Queen and black girls in general?

The sexuality of black characters and black women in relationships is also a problematic theme in *Game of Thrones,* where Grey Worm (portrayed by Jacob Anderson) is one of a number of largely African eunuchs serving in the Unsullied army of the white savior mother figure Daenerys Targaryen (Emilia Clarke). While the characters are literally desexualized, having been rendered unthreatening by castration, the show later sexualizes the character by showing him providing oral sex to Daenerys' advisor Missandei (Nathalie Emmanuel), a former slave played by a black actress who (outside this romance) devotes herself entirely to advancing and supporting her mistress. While Daenerys's subjects and the slavish devotion of the Unsullied have been discussed ad infinitum, the scene between Missandei and Grey Worm returned power, sexuality, and independence to the previously disempowered couple. Their courtship occurs over multiple seasons and normalizes disabled sexuality. They choose consensual sex and love despite their previous treatment at the hands of slavers and embrace a plotline about their own desires, not those of Daenerys.

Fan outrage over the death of Missandei in "The Last of the Starks," the fourth episode of Season 8, was redoubled when the fifth episode revealed that she'd essentially been fridged in order to turn Daenerys Targaryen into a villain, pitted against the white male hero Jon Snow. Although Dany's white savior complex has oft been addressed, Missandei and the Unsullied represented the bulk of non-white character interaction on the show. Casting Dany as the Mad Queen destroying without remorse in a bloodthirsty lust for vengeance hardly boded well for her largely black armies or black representation on the show.

Missandei's death—in chains, as when we met her, uttering the same words that convinced Dany to free her—is problematic. Although it works as an analogy for the long-standing scars of the African slave trade, it is painful for a lot of viewers, triggering the trauma of most African Americans by evoking such imagery. This is doubly problematic because Missandei is the only significant woman of color on cast. Nathalie Emmanuel told *Entertainment Weekly:*

> I understand people's outrage, I understand people's heartbreak, because this is the conversation around representation. It's safe to say that *Game of Thrones* has been under criticism for their lack of representation and the truth of it is that Missandei and Grey Worm have represented so many people because there's only two of them. So this is a conversation going forward about when you're casting shows like this, that you are inclusive in your casting. I knew what it meant that she was there, I know what it means that I am existing in the spaces that I am because when I was growing up, I didn't see people like me but it wasn't until she was gone that I really felt what it really, truly meant until I saw the outcry and outpouring of love and outrage and upset about it, I really understood what it meant [Sinha-Roy].

The show sacrifices its most important woman of color and virtually only black woman as a character development ploy. Missandei is fridged twice over—once for her white queen Daenerys and another for her black lover Grey Worm. Liberated from chains, Missandei dies in chains. Furious, Missandei's beloved Grey Worm subsequently leads the Unsullied as they join Daenerys and her dragon Drogon in gleefully burning King's Landing to the ground. Next, Grey Worm and the Unsullied are poised to face off against Jon Snow in the season finale. A large mass of people of color, many of whom are portrayed by actors of African heritage, stand on the verge of yet another massive battle that seems likely to end in massive black carnage and death. As providence has it, Jon Snow puts a quick end to the mad queen Daenerys Targaryen, and in doing so frees the Unsullied from servitude under Daenerys.

Daenerys—with her typical Targaryen power lust—has refused to rest until she sits on the Iron Throne. From the moment she takes up the title Khalessi, she becomes the embodiment of colonialism. First the pseudo-

Mongolian Dothraki, then the pseudo-African Unsullied fight and die to the battle cry of the platinum-blonde white savior figure. However, the bastard Targaryen Jon Snow has no desire to sit on the Iron Throne. His vision isn't clouded by ambition. He sees Daenerys as a false savior and cuts her down.

In an instant, Grey Worm is liberated from the charismatic mass-murderer who purchased him and the Unsullied at auction and then professed to be his savior, despite using him and other slaves to forward her military ambitions. Had Daenerys come to sit on the Iron Throne, Grey Worm would have remained her chief war advisor and never been free. A few episodes previous, Missandei died in chains not only literally, but metaphorically, still enslaved to Daenerys despite pretty words to the contrary. She spoke nineteen languages, but made not one move that wasn't in servitude to her white queen. Her education was only used to help the queen enslave and enthrall others, while promising freedom never truly granted.

Only in death does the martyred Missandei become true queen of the Unsullied and return to them her birthplace, Naath. Freed from servitude to the woman who purchased them, Grey Worm follows the queen of his heart now, keeping his promise to Missandei to travel to Isle of Butterflies in the Summer Sea off the northwestern coast of Sothoryos to the wise and wonderful Peaceful People she was born among. In doing so, he sets aside his sword, declares Missandei's peaceful ways superior to the warlike ways of Daenerys, and leads the Unsullied to the promised land of Missandei's childhood, a paradise he only ever dreamed about.

On *Sleepy Hollow,* which aired 2013 to 2017, some speculated female lead Abbie Mills would become romantically involved with male lead, Ichabod Crane. Instead, in what many viewers saw as a cop out, they killed off Abbie, and reunited Ichabod with his long-dead antifeminist white wife. The show's ratings plummeted, and it soon was cancelled.

Speaking of disturbing white dominance over black female sexuality, in *Valerian and the City of a Thousand Planets,* Rihanna plays the most *Star Trek: The Original Series*–style virtual sex slave imaginable in the character Bubble. The sexually adept pole dancer is rescued from her (literal) pimp by Major Valerian (Dane DeHaan) and Sergeant Laureline (Cara Delevingne). She becomes their Girl Friday, sidekick, and seemingly bisexual unicorn third wheel, ostensibly crushing on them both until she dies defending the white couple she loves so much. It is the most disgusting display of colonialism and fetishizing a person of color since the 1960s.

Still, the fascination with light-skinned, mixed, racially ambiguous black girls remains. Meg Murry, portrayed by Storm Reid in *A Wrinkle in Time*, was a light-skinned biracial protagonist who also had a white boyfriend. While darker skinned actor Michael B. Jordan made the IMDb Break-Out Star List for 2018 (IMDb-Editors) for his amazing performance as Killmonger in *Black Panther,* none of the dark sisters did. No one would expect to see any of the more established actresses there, but what about Letitia Wright, the British-Guyanese actress who plays Shuri? She is not there, and the only two black women are Afrolatina Tessa Thompson (Afro-Panamanian father, British and Mexican mother) and biracial Brit Hannah John-Kamen, of Norwegian and Nigerian ancestry (which is not to say that Tessa Thompson and Hannah John-Kamen, listed third and second respectively, don't belong on the list).

Historically, a limited number of black women have appeared over and over again in sci-fi, horror, and fantasy roles. Angela Bassett, a regular fixture on *American Horror Story,* is one of them. She costarred in *Supernova* (2000) with James Spader, in roles that suggested that she was the star and Spader her love interest. She started in 1995's *Strange Days.* She was a major player in *American Horror Story: Coven* and went on to play major roles on *AHS: Freakshow, Hostel,* and *Roanoke.* Gabourey Sidibe and Adina Porter have also played significant roles on *AHS,* which uses a lot of African American actors (Cuba Gooding, Jr., was also on the program). Still, *AHS* has a sometimes problematic relationship with its black characters.

Halle Berry is another black woman who has historically appeared in numerous speculative fiction films, notably as Storm or Ororo Monroe in *X-Men* (2000). Despite criticism over a light-skinned biracial black woman playing the dark-skinned Marvel character, Berry went on to play Storm in *X2: X-Men United* (2003), *X-Men: The Last Stand* (2006) and *X-Men: Days of Future Past* (2014). Her casting may have influenced the selection of light-skinned black actress Alexandra Shipp in another controversial move for the *X-Men: Apocalypse* (2016) and in the upcoming *Dark Phoenix* (2019) as she was supposed to be a younger version of the Storm from the 2000 cast. There is some speculation that the appearance of Ororo Monroe as a love interest for T'Challa, the Black Panther, later in that comic book series will cause the producers to cast an older, darker skinned actress. The comic book character is the daughter of an African woman and an African American man, both of whom are dark skinned.

Black Panther had many powerful black women as sidekicks, and love interest Lupita Nyong'o as the love interest Nakia got relatively little airtime. Thanks to Dania Gurira and Lupita Nyong'o, dark skinned, undeniably black women of African heritage are back in vogue, along with one of speculative fiction's biggest black stars of the nineties, Angela Bassett, standing right behind them as Wakanda's beautiful, ageless matriarch Queen Ramonda.

Colorism in the United States makes it so that light-skinned and biracial actresses (and quite often, actresses who are both light-skinned and biracial) usually get roles, especially in historically-popular-among-white-audiences vehicles such as superhero movies. Gina Torres, the Afro-Latina actress best known for *Firefly* (2002–2003) and its 2005 follow-up *Serenity* was also Nebula in *Hercules: The Legendary Journeys* (1997–1999), starred in *Cleopatra 2525* (2000–2001), and played the villainess Jasmine on *Angel* (2003). More recently, along with many non-science fiction roles, she's played Lauren on *Westworld* and voiced Ketsu Onyo on *Star Wars: Rebels* and *Star Wars: Forces of Destiny*. Another Afro-Latina actress, Zoe Saldana, is a regular feature in sci-fi, fantasy and horror films. She plays Gamora in the Marvel Cinematic Universe and Lieutenant Uhura in *Star Trek* (2009) and its sequels. She starred in the *Rosemary's Baby* miniseries (2014); *Quantum Is Calling* (2016), and more. Likewise, Rosario Dawson, of Puerto Rican, white, and Afro-Cuban descent, appeared in *Sin City* (2005) and plays Claire Temple in *The Defenders* and its four companion shows on Netflix, where she supports all the central heroes by patching up their injuries.

Controversies over light-skinned casting and the so-called paper bag test (which made it so that black women weren't cast unless they were as light as or lighter than a paper bag), do not take away from the groundbreaking work that Halle Berry has done for black women in sci-fi, fantasy and horror films. She also appeared in *Catwoman* (2004), *Gothika* (2003), *Perfect Stranger* (2007), *Cloud Atlas* (2012), *Dark Tide* (2012), *Extant* (2014–2015), and *Kingsman: The Golden Circle* (2017). She's become a fixture in the genre.

Afro-Latina actresses like Gina Torres, Rosario Dawson, and Zoe Saldana challenge our notions of what blackness is, but due to their lighter complexions, they also reinforce the brown paper bag trope. African American is a term used to describe citizens of the United States who are of African heritage. Many African Americans are unaware that just like people of African heritage in the United States and Afro-Caribbean people (those from nations like Jamaican and Haiti), Afro-Latin people from Central and South America are descended from slaves who arrived here during the Trans-Atlantic Slave Trade. In fact, the largest racial demographic in South America is African and the largest population of African people outside of the United States is in South America. Racial equity is a huge issue in South American countries like Brazil. However, the homogenized racially blended society has an issue with colorism and treats race differently than most of the United States, taking a more Creole type approach that categorizes people by blood quantum.

With all this, we find balance between the overall need for black female representation, the need to keep dark skinned women up front and center, the need to avoid passingness for mixed-race black actresses, and general colorism. Passingness is an issue that comes up often with male actors of African heritage such as the legendary Dwayne Johnson, aka The Rock, and Vin Diesel. Due to the preference for light-skinned actresses and the brown paper bag test, light-skinned women are less likely to try to pass themselves off as other races, especially if they are Americans. That is because passing is less beneficial for them than it is for men like The Rock, who do not claim to be white when they play their parts, yet make little mention of their heritage when playing parts like the Greek God Heracles. Black and Samoan, the actor often plays roles where he is presumed white. Vin Diesel, uncertain of his parentage, believes he is a quarter black, His blackness rarely comes up anymore, even though back in 2001 he was on the cover of *Essence*.

British attitude towards biracial black identity differs from the African American attitude because so many biracial Brits have a black parent who is not from a slave background. That is not to say that the Trans Atlantic Slave Trade didn't affect Britain, but that the UK has many more African immigrants arriving post slavery. Black folks make up 13.4 percent of the United States population, with 2.7 percent of Americans being biracial of any mixture (U.S. Census Bureau). By contrast, black Africans doubled in the UK between the 2001 and 2011 census. black people are 3.4 percent of the UK's population and only 0.12 percent self-reported as mixed race black (Office for National Statistics).

Afro-British actresses are ubiquitous, including biracial black actresses. Some examples are Lenora Crichlow, who started as Annie Sawyer in *Being Human*; Antonia Thomas and Karla Crome from *Misfits*; and Hannah John-Kamen, a British actress of Nigerian and Norwegian parentage. Her credits include *The Killjoys*, Zandor in *Ready Player One*, and Ghost in *Ant-Man and the Wasp*. When it is explicitly made clear that she is biracial, as in *Ant-Man and the Wasp*, she is cast similarly to African American actresses. However, in other roles, she is racially ambiguous.

Conversely, biracial African American actresses who appear black and publicly claim blackness like Halle Berry and Lisa Bonet are rarely thought of or referred to as other than black by the public. Racially ambiguous appearing actresses like Zoë Kravitz do not enjoy the same relationship to blackness and may actually lose roles for declining to pass as other races. The question remains: can black women rise to female lead roles in sci-fi without being overly sexualized and stereotyped? And can we do it without always being with a white man?

In the case of Lupita Nyong'o, undeniably yes. No one is ever going to forget she played T'Challa's girlfriend, even if Storm creeps up later on. Further, no one can imagine T'Challa without a dark-skinned woman at his side—and another dark-skinned woman or twelve having his back. Next, the Kenyan-Mexican actress is staring in the Jordan Peele film *Us* alongside Trinbagonian American actor Winston Duke, best known for his role as M'Baku in *Black Panther*. The critically acclaimed film is already getting Oscar buzz. They are joined by teen Shahadi Wright Joseph and ten-year-old Evan Alex, together playing the dream African American nuclear family. Lupita has risen to a certain spot in the African American consciousness as the poster girl for beautiful chocolate families. Because she is a dark-skinned girl, she triumphantly diverges from the typical brown-skinned black girl casting for Afrocentric or black family-centered films, such as Taraji P. Henson (best known for *Empire* and *Hustle and Flow*). That said, there was a significant controversy around her casting in the *Star Wars* franchise as she voiced a wise CGI alien, Maz Kanata, but did not appear onscreen. The essay "Hyper-tokenism II: Othering the Black Female Body in *Star Wars: The Force Awakens*" emphasizes how much Nyong'o's addition to the cast along with John Boyega and Oscar Isaac's casting announcements made many hopeful of a new level of inclusion and diversity. However, the lovely actress was hidden behind a tiny wrinkled form, thus prohibiting her beauty from competing with Daisy Ridley's while burying Nyong'o behind the CGI caricature "like burying the beauty and talent of Grace Kelly behind the grotesque costume of the creature from the film *The Creature from the Black Lagoon*" (Seewood). As the critique continues:

> Hyper-tokenism is ultimately the effort of any White controlled studio and its White filmmakers to give the appearance of racial diversity in a film franchise or television series but—and this is very important—full dramatic agency is reserved and exercised by the White characters at the ending of an installment of the franchise or the finale of the series or franchise. The accusation is clear and simple: Lupita Nyong'o was cast as Maz Kanata directly after her Oscar win as a direct means of securing Black audience loyalty and feigning racial diversity in the *Star Wars* franchise, but her physical presence was erased to insure spectator identification with the White heroine of this installment of the *Star Wars* franchise.

Outside of Lupita Nyong'o, with few exceptions, dark skinned black actresses in leading lady roles are almost universally paired with white or other non-black leading men. Exceptions like Angela Bassett are also often seen with non-black actors more often than black ones.

Bonnie Bennett, portrayed by Kat Graham on *The Vampire Diaries* (2009–2017), is a fine example of a prominent black female character never seen with a black paramour. One of the three main female cast members, she was first romantically attached to the main character Elena Gilbert's brother, Jeremy, then to vampire Lorenzo St. John. The popular character was often seen with black family members and ancestors, so much so that they spun off a book series on the Bennett Witches. Witches, slaves, and the antebellum south are frequent features in black backstories for horror and supernatural characters. Bonnie Bennett and the Bennett Witches are prime examples. The Bennett Witches, only known survivors of a Salem Witch Trial era coven that migrated to Mystic Falls, often showed up in the series. In addition to Bonnie, they included her ancestor Beatrice Bennett, Bonnie's mother Abbie Bennett and her grandmother Sheila Bennett. The beloved character is likely responsible for the show's large black following and the inclusion of numerous African Americans and other people of color in the show's spin offs *The Originals* and *The Legacies.*

When Claire Holt, the actress who played ancient vampire Rebekah Mikaelson, needed time off *The Originals,* the show producers decided to use it as an opportunity to pair her black boyfriend Marcel with a black actress. Charles Michael Davis, who played Marcel Gerard, was one of the show's major draws. He played the adopted son of werewolf/vampire hybrid and bad boy Klaus Mikaelson (Joseph Morgan). Marcel was a biracial black slave who was rescued by his evil plantation lord father by Klaus, a white rejected half-lupine who identified with him. He killed the plantation lord and adopted the child. However, an angry Marcel resented the new replacement patriarch and started an affair with his sister Rebekah. Klaus and Marcel's tearing up the screen in their battle for dominance over the supernatural communities of New Orleans (witches, werewolves and vampires) was the heart of the show.

Further, Maisie Richardson-Sellers played a witch named Eva Sinclair whose body was possessed by Rebekah. Richardson-Sellers bore resemblance to Claire Holt, which sold the bodily possession plot. However, the "white girl walking around in a black skin dating a black man plot" was problematic. Maisie Richardson-Sellers' three-season run in the two roles (2014–2017) was glorious. The actress is now on the cast of the DC superhero show *Legends of Tomorrow,* where she spent two years dominating the screen as Amaya Jiwe, the Golden Age superhero Vixen. Still, Amaya's plot of falling in love with her white superhero teammate but knowing she was unhappily destined to return to her own time and marry an African to beget her superhero granddaughter, her heir, was quite problematic. Season 3 ended with her accepting this destiny. However, Season 4 saw the actress return as a different main character. Amaya's leaving yet her actress's continuing as Charlie, a magical fugitive and rebel trickster, emphasizes her active fan base and the showrunners' appreciation of her. In fact, as Charlie, Maisie can cut loose and have a more fun, dynamic storyline without the burden of her other character's destiny. Thus far, she's remained romantically unencumbered.

Sexual liberation and sexual power give way to fetishization and once again, the women exist for the white male gaze. This is a trope involving the black woman as hypersexual, primal and primordial. Indeed, all of us are the genetic result of Eve, the first woman, whom science defines as black. This fear of black women as savage, sexual and dangerous is also an after-effect of hundreds of years of scientific racism used to justify colonialism and oppression, as with the well-known Venus De Hottentot, Sarah Baartman. Justin Parkinson of *BBC* comments:

Brought to Europe seemingly on false pretences by a British doctor, stage-named the "Hottentot Venus," she was paraded around "freak shows" in London and Paris, with crowds invited to look at her large buttocks. Today she is seen by many as the epitome of colonial exploitation and racism, of the ridicule and commodification of black people [Parkinson].

The Gina Torres character Jasmine on *Angel* (2004) was another example of this trope: An all-consuming goddess who must control and imbibe all that she sees. Many of Angela Bassett's characters on *American Horror Story* also fall into this tired old trope. Tia Dalma, played by Naomie Harris, from the films *Pirates of the Caribbean: Dead Man's Chest* and *Pirates of the Caribbean: At World's End,* may be the most famous.

Yetide Badaki, the Nigerian actress who plays Bilquis in Neil Gaiman's *American Gods* (2017–present) is a hypersexualized goddess who gains power by devouring men and women with her vagina. Men who are called kings challenge her, and she has to defeat and consume him. However, other men and women are eager supplicants and willing sacrifices. Technical Boy, one of the new gods, encourages her to bring the internet into her devotion rituals and murderous dating. He is a young, white cismale hipster in this incarnation, although he changes appearance. Still, he doesn't rein her in, so she continues to be solo and a force. That doesn't change the overall primal black sex goddess vibe.

These sorts of portrayals of the black woman and other problematic stereotypes, such as the Angry Black Woman trope that informs the upcoming Octavia Spencer vehicle *Ma,* continue to dominate. The horror film features a black woman obsessed with getting revenge on the white man who rejected her in high school and all of the bratty little white kids from her old school by pretending to be a cool-assed chick happy to buy them alcohol and party.

This kind of imagery just shows that no matter how far we have come, we have a long way to go. For every positive portrayal of black women in speculative fiction cinema, there is one with a tired old stereotype rearing its head. For every black woman as a romantic lead, there are three more occupying the same old hateful mammy bag we've been trying to escape since slavery. For every intelligent forward-thinking character like Uhura in *Star Trek,* there is a naïve, grateful self-sacrificing native sex slave trope like Bubble in *Valerian and the City of a Thousand Planets.* Too many are love-interests, or worse, like Thandie Newton as Val on *Solo,* who is quickly sacrificed after only a few lines.

Feminism and racial equity, along with the fourth wave feminist concept of intersectionality, require that we do not ignore, but take on these historical stereotypes head-on. There is hope. More and more, we see thoughtful speculative fiction in cinema, like Jordan Peele's *Us* (2019), which stars Lupita in dual roles as the terrifying Red and kindly Adeline, the black family-centered married mother of four. *Black Lightning* offers an entire family of loving, successful superheroes with two independent daughters and a brilliant though un-superpowered mother. *Star Trek: Discovery* gives its lead Michael Burnham real angst over her allegiance. Children's shows showcase teen genius Riri Williams who built her own Iron Man suit (*Marvel Rising: Heart of Iron*) and *Steven Universe*'s sassy, stoic supermom Garnet, who shows viewers a loving, stable lesbian relationship. These types of roles give some meat to the black woman as romantic lead and heroine, beyond simplification and sexual objectification.

Sci-Fi, Fantasy and Horror Television and Film Within the Past 10 Years Featuring Black Female Leads, Love Interests and Sex Symbols

After Earth (2013)—Zoë Kravitz as Senshi Raige

The Aliens (2016)—Michaela Coel as Lilyhot

Allegiant (2016)—Zoë Kravitz as Christina

Altered Carbon (2018–present)—Renée Elise Goldsberry as Quellcrist Falconer, Simone Missick as Trepp

Always a Witch (2019)—Cristina Warner as Isabel de Aranoa

American Gods (2017–present)—Yetide Badaki as Bilquis

Ant-Man and the Wasp (2018)—Hannah John-Kamen as Ghost.

Beautiful Creatures (2013)—Viola Davis as Amarie Treadeau, "Amma"

Being Human UK (2008–2013)—Lenora Crichlow as Annie Sawyer

Black Lightning (2018–present)—China Anne McClain as Jennifer Pierce, Nafessa Williams as Anissa Pierce, and Christine Adams as Lynn Pierce

Black Mirror (2016–2017)—Michaela Coel as Shania

Charmed (2018–present)—Madeleine Mantock as Macy Vaughn

Class (2016)—Vivian Oparah as Tanya Adeola

Cloud Atlas (2012)—Halle Berry as Jocasta Ayrs/Luisa Rey

Dark Matter (2015–2017)—Melanie Liburd as Nyx Harper

DC Super Hero Girls (2015–present)—Teala Dunn as Bumblebee

Deadpool 2 (2018)—Zazie Beetz as Domino

Divergent (2014)—Zoë Kravitz as Christina

Doctor Who (1963–present)—Freema Agyeman as Martha Jones, Pearl Mackie as Bill Potts

Emerald City (2017)—Jordan Loughran as Ozma / Tip

The Expanse (2015–present)—Dominique Tipper as Naomi Nagata

Fantastic Beasts: The Crimes of Grindelwald (2018)—Zoë Kravitz as Leta Lestrange

The Flash (2014–present)—Candice Patton as Iris West

Game of Thrones (2013–2017)—Nathalie Emmanuel as Missandei

Ghostbusters (2016)—Leslie Jones as Patty Tolan

The Girl with All the Gifts (2016)—Sennia Nanua as Melanie

Gotham (2014–2017)—Jada Pinkett Smith as Fish Mooney

The Hunger Games (2012)—Amandla Stenberg as Rue

Insurgent (2015)—Zoë Kravitz as Christina

Killjoys (2015–present)—Hannah John-Kamen as Dutch

Legends of Tomorrow (2016–present)—Maisie Richardson-Sellers as Vixen/Charlie

Lost (2004–2010)—L. Scott Caldwell as Rose Nadler

Luke Cage/The Defenders (2016–2018)—Simone Missick as Misty Knight, Rosario Dawson as Claire Temple

Ma (2019)—Octavia Spencer as Ma

Mad Max: Fury Road (2015)—Zoë Kravitz as Toast the Knowing

Marvel Rising: Heart of Iron (2019)—Sofia Wylie as Ironheart

The Maze Runner: The Death Cure (2018)—Nathalie Emmanuel as Harriet

Midnight, Texas (2017–present)—Parisa Fitz-Henley as Fiji Cavanaugh

Misfits (2009–2013)—Antonia Thomas as Alisha Daniel, Karla Crome as Jess

Nightflyers (2018)—Jodie Turner-Smith as Melantha Jhirl

Pooka (2018)—Latarsha Rose as Melanie

The Princess and the Frog (2009)—Anika Noni Rose as Tiana

Ready Player One (2018)—Hannah John-Kamen as Zandor

Scary Movie series (2000–2013)—Brenda Meeks as Regina Hall

Solo (2016)—Thandie Newton as Val

Sorry to Bother You (2018)—Tessa Thompson as Detroit

Spider-Man: Far From Home (2019)—Zendaya as Michelle (MJ)

Spider-Man: Homecoming (2017)—Zendaya as Michelle (MJ)

Star Trek (2009)—Zoe Saldana as Uhura

Star Trek: Discovery (2017–present)—Sonequa Martin-Green as Michael Burnham

Steven Universe (2013–2019)—Estelle as Garnet, Shelby Rabara as Peridot

Suicide Squad (2016)—Viola Davis as Amanda Waller

Thor: Ragnarok (2017)—Tessa Thompson as Valkyrie

True Blood (2008–2014)—Rutina Wesley as Tara Thornton

The Umbrella Academy (2019–present)—Mary J. Blige as Cha-Cha, Emmy Raver-Lampman as Allison Hargreeves

Valerian and the City of a Thousand Planets (2017)—Rihanna as Bubble

Vixen (2015–2016)—Megalyn Echikunwoke as Vixen, Anika Noni Rose as Kuasa

The Walking Dead (2010–present)—Danai Gurira as Michonne, Sonequa Martin-Green as Sasha

Westworld (2016–present)—Tessa Thompson as Charlotte Hale

A Wrinkle in Time (2018)—Oprah Winfrey as Mrs. Which, Storm Reid as Meg Murry, and Gugu Mbatha-Raw as Mrs. Murry

X-Men: Apocalypse (2016)—Alexandra Shipp as Storm

X-Men: First Class (2011)—Zoë Kravitz as Angel Salvadore

Works Cited

Bolonik, Kera. "Does *American Horror Story: Coven* Have a Race Problem?" *Medium,* 12 November 2013. https://medium.com/the-t-v-age/does-american-horror-story-coven-have-a-race-problem-630826392a2c.

Bradley, Laura. "TV Is Better for L.G.B.T.Q. Characters than Ever—Unless You're a Lesbian." *Vanity Fair,* 3 Nov 2016. https://www.vanityfair.com/hollywood/2016/11/tv-lgbtq-repre sentation-glaad-report-dead-lesbian-syndrome.

Brett. *Demo-Graphic: The Walking Dead.* 4 Apr 2016. https://graphicpolicy.com/2016/04/04/demo-graphics-the-walking-dead-3.

Chadhuri, Shohini. *Feminist Film Theorists.* Routledge, 2006.

Frost, Karen. "Hollywood Still Doesn't Get Its Dead Lesbian Issue." *After Ellen,* June 4, 2018. https://www.afterellen.com/tv/491943-hollywood-still-doesnt-get-dead-lesbian-issue.

Harjo, Noetta. "Top 8 Richonne Moments on *The Walking Dead* with the Two Dead Chicks Podcast." *Geek Girl Authority,* vol. 1, no. 3, 2018. https://www.geekgirlauthority.com/top-8-richonne-moments-on-the-walking-dead-with-the-two-dead-chicks-podcast.

IMDb Editors. "Top 10 Breakout Stars of 2018." *IMDB,* January 2019. 14 Mar 2019. https://www.imdb.com/best-of/breakout-stars-of-2018/ls045252579.

Kirkman, Robert. *The Walking Dead: Something to Fear.* Vol. 17. 11 July 2012.

Levin, Gary. "Who's Watching What: TV Shows Ranked by Racial and Ethnic Groups." *USA Today,* 28 June 2017.

Murphy, Shaunna. "The Walking Dead Has a Complicated History with Sexual Violence." *TV Guide,* 27 March 2017. https://www.tvguide.com/news/walking-dead-sasha-sexual-assault-scene-negan.

Office for National Statistics. "UK Census." 2011.

Parkinson, Justin. "The Significance of Sarah Baartman." *BBC News Magazine,* 2016. https://www.bbc.com/news/magazine-35240987.

Seewood, Andre. "Hyper-tokenism II: Othering the Black Female Body in *Star Wars: The Force Awakens*" *IndieWire,* 6 Jan 2016. https://www.indiewire.com/2016/01/hyper-token ism-ii-othering-the-black-female-body-in-star-wars-the-force-awakens-162223.

Sinha-Roy, Piya. "Nathalie Emmanuel on why *Game of Thrones*' Lack of Diversity Made Missandei's Death More Painful," *EW,* 12 May 2019. https://ew.com/tv/2019/05/12/nathalie-emmanuel-missandei-game-of-thrones-diversity.

Stone, Jeff. "*The Walking Dead* Review: Rick Grimes Says Goodbye In 'What Comes After.'" *IndieWire,* 2018. https://www.indiewire.com/2018/11/walking-dead-season-9-episode-5-review-what-comes-after-rick-grimes-spoilers-1202018074.

U.S. Census Bureau. "U.S. Census." 2017.

Revisionist History and Intersectional Feminism in *DC's Legends of Tomorrow*

Katherine McLoone

In "Helen Hunt," a third-season episode of *DC's Legends of Tomorrow* (2016–present), Golden Age Hollywood has a problem: Helen of Troy has come unstuck in time and wandered onto a movie set, where she enthralls every man—including producers and casting agents—who sees her. As a result, up-and-coming starlet Hedy Lamarr does not get her breakout role and therefore never invents the frequency-hopping technology that make modern computing possible. Enter the titular time-traveling Legends, the ragtag bunch of "don't call us heroes" who have caused this "anachronism" and now must solve it in order to fix history, get their timeship working again, and practice intersectional feminism.

A mixture of science fiction, mysticism, and silliness, *Legends of Tomorrow* portrays a plucky group of time-travelers who attempt—and often fail—to fix historical flaws and historical villainy. Or, in the words of the show itself: "this team of misfits and outcasts is determined to fix the history which they have broken. Not because they are heroes, but because they are legends" ("Return of the Mack").

After a mediocre first season plagued by a "Women in Refrigerators" trope and too little sense of its own campiness, *Legends* pivoted both in plot and in character: in the second season, Sara Lance, a queer former assassin, became the team's captain; that season also introduced Amaya Jiwe, a native of the fictional African nation of Zambesi whose mystical totem-amulet allows her to wield the power of animals. In the third season, *Legends* made headlines with the introduction of Zari Tomaz, a Muslim American hacker from 2042 with a mystical totem of her own (Evatt). (These totems comprise

110

a five-totem search that fills the season.) Those three women represent diversity of race, religion, orientation, and experiences. The community they participate in and build, as well as the conversations they have about that community's goals, demonstrate a striking though imperfect intersectional feminism.

In *Bitch Doctrine*, Laurie Penny boils fourth wave feminism down to four components: it is "digital, intersectional, globally connected and mad as hell" (124). In doing so, she draws on the notion of intersectionality that dates back to Kimberlé Crenshaw's 1989 call for a new feminism: one which acknowledges that so-called "feminism" is often white feminism, as it fails to take into account the systems of oppression under which women of color—particularly black women—operate (Crenshaw, "Demarginalizing" 140 *et passim*).

Since then, intersectionality has become something of a buzzword as its relevance, parameters, and even meaning have shifted. In a recent interview, Crenshaw responded to the question of whether a broad understanding of intersectionality is a "misunderstanding": in her response, she points out that "intersectionality is a lens through which you can see where power comes and collides, where it interlocks and intersects. It's not simply that there's a race problem here, a gender problem here, and a class or LGBTQ+ problem there. Many times, that framework erases what happens to people who are subject to all of these things" (Crenshaw, "Interview").

The "interlocking" quality of today's fourth wave, intersectional feminism attempts to both identify those frameworks and dismantle them. In *Intersectionality: Origins, Contestations, Horizons*, Anna Carastathis argues that "intersectionality constitutes a profound challenge ... intersectionality-as-challenge urges us to grapple with and overcome our entrenched perceptual-cognitive habits of essentialism, categorical purity, and segregation" (4). In her reading, intersectionality is not "identity politics" ("Demarginalizing" 7 *et passim*). Rather, drawing on Alison Bailey's "On Intersectionality, Empathy, and Feminist Solidarity," Carastathis notes that "intersectionality *reveals* relationships of subordination in homogenizing, falsely universal feminist politics; it does not *produce* this 'fragmentation'" (165, emphasis in original).

Intersectionality, therefore, is both a mode of "critique" and a set of "political and intellectual challenges" (8). It is a gimlet-eyed stance and a set of goals. Or, in the words, of Chandra Talpade Mohanty, "The first project is one of deconstructing and dismantling; the second is one of building and constructing" (Mohanty 17). Hers is a definition of "Third World Feminism" that contains within itself the give-and-take nature of intersectional fourth wave feminism as articulated by Crenshaw, Carastathis, Bailey, and others—to which we can add Penny's emphasis on global connections and digital savvy. This vision of intersectional feminism is, at heart, conversational and adaptable.

Within this framework, *Legends of Tomorrow* articulates an intersectional feminism that is both imperfect and endlessly striving for perfection. *Legends* builds on its flawed start to include a diversity of voices. It portrays how we might spotlight the women that history chose to forget, and it engages present-day political concerns to look toward a better future.

The Past: Clichés and the Male Gaze

Legends of Tomorrow premiered on January 21, 2016, as a spin off from *Arrow* (2012–present), Greg Berlanti's successful adaptation of the Green Arrow character from DC Comics.[1] *Arrow* in itself took on the mantle of young Superman's highly successful *Smallville* (The CW, 2001–2011), and these two male-centric shows were followed by another, *The Flash* (The CW, 2014–present), the female-centric *Supergirl* (CBS then The CW, 2015–present) and finally the mixed hero team of *Legends*. A fifth series should be mentioned: *Vixen,* by executive producers Greg Berlanti, Marc Guggenheim and Andrew Kreisberg, debuted on August 25, 2015, on The CW's online streaming platform, CW Seed, with guest appearances by Arrow and the Flash. A second season followed the next year, tying in heavily to the *Legends* search for the totems. However, this cartoon, totaling twelve four-to-seven-minute episodes, clearly lacked the studio confidence of the other shows' twenty-two-hour-episode full seasons. When this treatment of the franchise's black female superhero show is weighed against the gender balance of the others, a decided bias appears.

In the first season, *Legends* stars some of the more charming villains, rogues, and supporting characters of what is called the Berlantiverse. Sara Lance (White Canary) lived and died—twice—on *Arrow*; Ray Palmer (The Atom) had a multi-episode arc on that show. Leonard Snart (Captain Cold) and Mick Rory (Heat Wave) were captured—and escaped from—the Flash and his team of superheroes. Dr. Martin Stein and Jefferson Jackson, the two people who make up the nuclear-powered Firestorm, got their start on *The Flash*, as did Kendra Saunders (Hawkgirl), whose reincarnated romance with Carter Hall (Hawkman) formed the backbone of the first season's fight against the immortal villain Vandal Savage. Rip Hunter, a disgraced Time Master, brings them all together in the pilot episode with the promise that they will become "legends" if they help save the world (with time-travel) from Vandal Savage. Only later does Rip Hunter explain that he chose the Legends because their "lives have minimal effect on the recorded timeline," which makes them useful for his quest to save his wife and son, who were killed by Savage in 2166 ("Pilot, Part 1").

In other words, the show was off to a rocky start. The premise is a classic example of what comic-book writer Gail Simone termed "Women in Refrigerators": the comic-book cliché in which a woman is killed to motivate a male hero to action. Further, numerous pre-established pairings, such as the Hawkpeople, Captain Cold and Heat Wave, and the Firestorm duo, meshed oddly with the ensemble structure. There was some diversity, as African American actor Franz Drameh played Firestorm and Hispanic/mixed race Ciara Renée played Hawkgirl with black/mixed-race actor Wentworth Miller as Captain Cold. The remaining lineup were white characters, led by a white British man (whose knowledge of the future and ownership of the time ship positioned them all as helpless). Within this group, the two female characters were problematic, to say the least: Sara Lance, a semi-reformed assassin trained by the League of Assassins, needed to learn to contain her "bloodlust" (the unquenchable desire to kill created by her resurrection in the Lazarus Pit of Nanda Parbat); this cast her as barely in control of her own body. Kendra Saunders, as Hawkgirl, was unsure of her fate and uncertain in her powers. She was also quickly stuck in an awkward love triangle between Ray Palmer and the ill-fated Hawkman, who died in the pilot but, thanks to time travel and reincarnation, kept popping up again. For a bonus third character, British actress Amy Louise Pemberton played the voice of their ship, Gideon, as a perpetual obedient secretary with no personal desires.

A fight scene in the pilot episode illustrates the touch-and-go quality of the first season of *Legends*. On a trip to 1975 in search of more information about Savage, most of the team goes on a mission to a local university, but because Rip Hunter "doesn't need anyone killed, maimed, or robbed," Sara Lance, Mick Rory, and Leonard Snart stay behind, as does Jefferson Jackson, who—unsurprisingly—still resents being drugged and forced into a timeship by Martin Stein ("Pilot, Part 1"). In a show that will later celebrate the "outcast" status of many, if not all, of its characters, the pilot's willingness to separate out the socially-acceptable from the surly stands out. That Jackson, who is African American, is not permitted to join Sara, Snart, and Mick for a drink at a local bar only increases the uneasy marginalization.

At the bar, Sara, whose bisexuality was established during her arc on *Arrow*, invites Snart to dance. "You go ahead," he says. "I'll watch." As a Captain and Tennille song plays in the background, Sara walks out of frame. The camera lingers on Snart's face: we watch him smiling as he watches Sara walk to the empty dancefloor. The camera cuts to Sara dancing, alone and in a spotlight, in her superhero costume: a light gray skin-tight jumpsuit with exposed shoulders, shot from the back. The camera pushes in as she turns toward the camera. When a bar patron invites her to the parking lot in a menacing tone, she stops dancing and explains that he is "not [her] type, but [his] lady, on the other hand, well, she looks just [her] speed" ("Pilot, Part I"). When he refuses to acknowledge her rejection and grabs her, Sara breaks his

arm, turns to Snart, and says, "I got this" ("Pilot, Part 1"). As the fight esca-
lates—drawing in those belligerent drinkers who, in television shows, always
seem willing to join a fight—the camera cuts quickly as Sara punches and
kicks her way through an increasingly-larger group of burly men while Snart
and Mick continue to watch. Eventually, she says, "Now I could use a little
help," and they join the melee ("Pilot, Part 1").

The result is uneven at best. The music, drinking, and fighting build
camaraderie among the three most violent Legends; Sara's interactions with
both Snart and the violent bar patron emphasizes her bisexuality and her
fighting ability—both positive moments toward a show in the process of
developing an ethos of communal strength based on diversity. However, the
dancing scene epitomizes John Berger's formulation of Laura Mulvey's idea
of the male gaze: "men look at women…" and the camera frame, like a Renaissance painting, includes a male stand-in in which "the spectator-owner
will in fantasy oust the other man, or else identify with him" (Berger 46, 56).
At this point, *Legends* was a show that wanted to have its feminist cake and
ogle it, too—all while ignoring the problematic racial dynamics of drugging
and isolating an African American man.

The Present: Revisionist History and Intersectional Feminism

Flash forward to Season 3: things have changed. Sara Lance is now the
team's captain. The Hawkpeople and Rip Hunter, along with their trite storylines, are gone. Amaya Jiwe, a former member of the Justice Society in the
1940s, has joined the Legends after her team-leader and boyfriend is killed;
she wears one of the mystical totems of Zambesi and can summon the spirits
of animals to improve her fighting abilities as the superhero Vixen (future
grandmother to the Vixen of the cartoon, Mari McCabe). The second season
also introduced Nate Heywood as a historian with hemophilia, which is cured
by Ray Palmer's technology (with the side effect of allowing Nate to turn into
a man of steel). The third season adds Zari Tomaz, a Muslim American hacker
and wisecracker from the year 2042, in which all religion has been outlawed.

Starting in the second season, *Legends* learned to take itself less seriously
and, in doing so, deal with sensitive subjects more gracefully. Recalling
Mohanty's language discussed above, the show begins to engage in the second
project of global feminism by "building and constructing" a more nuanced
narrative (Mohanty 17). In the second season, after Rip Hunter's departure,
the team was captainless until a 1940s superhero of the Justice League
assumed Dr. Martin Stein, as an older white man, was the "team leader" ("The
Justice Society of America"). That conflict revealed—and Stein realized—

that aged white manliness was not a sufficient qualification; Sara's ability to think quickly in emergencies and watch out for others made her more qualified for the job.

Also in the second season, Amaya's character struggles with her responsibilities to both the Legends and the people of her native country: she knows she must return to 1940s Zambesi to protect her community from colonialism and other negative influences (as well as someday pass on the totem to her granddaughter), but she also wants to continue to protect the world at large. The third season's new character, Zari Tomaz, balances her hacking skills with the superpowers derived from a mystical amulet she inherited from her brother, who was killed both for being superpowered and for being Muslim. Even such characters as Mick Rory, mostly gruff, macho muscle accompanied by occasional foolish comic relief, grapples with the aftereffects of an abusive childhood and self-harm (in the first season's "Last Refuge" and the third season's "Welcome to the Jungle").

The show's new focus moved away from clichés and toward a portrayal of "outcasts" for reasons of gender, orientation, race, religion, and ability. In doing so, it opened up the possibility of using its camera as a "lens through which you can see where power comes and collides, where it interlocks and intersects" (recalling Crenshaw's quote above), as well as showing how those who are subject to power might form a diverse community in a constant process of examining, correcting, and even revising dominant power structures.

The introductory spiels for each episode, which explain the show's overriding concept to a potentially new audience, demonstrate the focus on dismantling entrenched masculinity and highlighting a diversity of voices—especially those voices of those who are "outcast" from a white, heteronormative, able-bodied patriarchy. In the first season, the introduction to each episode was narrated by Rip Hunter. The second season introduces numerous variants, spoken by different characters, for the introductory spiel. No longer is the show's mission determined by one man, but by many people, a "group of outcasts and misfits" ("Shogun").

Against this ensemble background, which highlights the individualities of character and identity, as well as the interplay of culture and self, the team devotes itself to stopping both specific villains bent on world domination and the "anachronisms" (such as a saber-tooth tiger in P.T. Barnum's circus) that can result from their time travel. Captain Sara Lance introduces "Helen Hunt" with the following exposition: "How will we be remembered? Will it be for saving the world twice? Nope. We're the team who broke time. That's right: history has been torn to shreds, which means it's up to us to put it back together, piece by piece, fixing these so-called anachronisms before *we* get torn to shreds. So, please, don't call us heroes. We're legends" ("Helen Hunt").

"Helen Hunt" aired on November 14, 2017, one year after Donald Trump was elected as president with a promise to "Make America Great Again," and three months after white supremacists rallied, rioted, and murdered Heather Heyer in Charlottesville, Virginia, under the auspices of protecting monuments of Confederate heroes from destruction. There's no definitive evidence that "Helen Hunt"—or *Legends of Tomorrow* as a whole—is a direct response to specific events in American politics,[2] but the show undeniably picks up on the question of the moment: how history, as both a collective memory and a fluid narrative, works.

The premise of making America great *again* is one of nostalgia for a non-existent, better past. It is revisionist history made into a campaign slogan. The pretense of the Charlottesville Unite the Right rally was one of reclaiming and protecting a version of history in which Confederate generals were not traitors but heroes and representatives of an idealized past that has been "torn to shreds" (echoing Sara's intro) by what participants would likely call evil liberals (although their language might be stronger). As Julian Maxwell Hayter explains in *The Washington Post*, "Charlottesville … reshaped the conversation about history, exposing the disparity among historical truth, historical interpretation and mythology. The alt-right is clinging to distorted history—one created by segregationists in service to white supremacy—in order to advance their white-nationalist political project" (Hayter).

Legends, on the other hand, has more nuance. Sara's introductory spiel to "Helen Hunt" acknowledges past guilt ("We're the team who broke time"), then identifies the resultant problem ("history has been torn to shreds"), and explains the responsibility and duty to community ("which means it's up to us to put it back together, piece by piece fixing these so-called anachronisms"), while exploring the personal and political consequences of failure ("before *we* get torn to shreds"). In that formulation, a global problem requires on-the-ground personal solutions to prevent further problems. It is activism, with costumes.

Throughout "Helen Hunt," *Legends* toggles between comedy and critique, conversation and action. When Helen of Troy is displaced from the ancient world to 1940s Hollywood, her sexual allure has a ripple effect. She is so beautiful that her powers are almost mystical: no man can resist her, and each one fights over the right to cast her, act as her agent, or sleep with her. At first blush, this a problematic portrayal of female beauty that defines beauty only in relation to the male gaze. Helen's extreme sexualization, a power over which she has no control, also assumes male heteronormativity. No men are seen resisting her appeal (which implies all men on screen are straight), yet bisexual women, such as Sara Lance, are utterly immune.

However, the show allows these issues to arise in conversation among the characters: sexism and objectification are the jumping-off points for a dialogue. Nate, the team's historian, explains that the Trojan War was instigated by Paris's abduction of Helen, "all in the name of her beauty" ("Helen Hunt"). Nonetheless, Zari counters: "You make it sound like it's her fault. Men always find a reason to fight. That's not on her," a statement she later reiterates to Helen herself, who worries she is to blame—"This isn't your fault" ("Helen Hunt"). Mick Rory, whose masculinity is always just shy of toxic, throws in his own hat with, "It depends. How hot is she?" Nate says to the group that Helen is "all right," but mouths "really hot" to Mick ("Helen Hunt").

This complicated exchange demonstrates—and, arguably, implicitly critiques—male banter about female bodies, but spotlights Zari's awareness of how male desire often results in female blame, even as she perpetuates a rather dated perspective that "men always find a reason to fight." This is not, in other words, perfect feminism (whatever that means). Rather, it is a conversation about women, men, power, and sex. *Legends* portrays a variety of viewpoints, some more enlightened than others, that nonetheless lead toward a trajectory of correction.

Men do fight over Helen throughout the story, but all of the Legends, regardless of gender, work together to fight for a common good of restoring history. Misandry as a feminist critique rears its head, as well: when Zari and Sara debate the merits of sneaking into a studio head's estate with a horse trailer (a lovely Trojan War joke), Zari asks, "You really think they'll fall for this stuff?" Sara responds, "Have men gotten smarter in the past few thousand years?" "Nope," says Zari. However, they are proved wrong when a guard demands to check the contents of the trailer, avoiding precisely the mistake that led to the fall of Troy. Nonetheless, upon finding women ready for a fight rather than horses, the guard says, "Oh, prized whores"—a pun on horses, an example of female objectification, and an implicit argument that although men have gotten smarter, patriarchy nonetheless continues to objectify women. Amaya punches him.

Throughout the episode, female characters frequently defend female autonomy, argue against rape-culture misunderstandings of female objectification, and value intellect over sexual desire and sexual appeal, as when Sara describes Helen as "more than just a pretty face" ("Helen Hunt"). Even real-life screen siren and inventor Hedy Lamarr has her say (despite not fully knowing about precisely what is happen with Helen's time-displacement): "Any girl can look glamorous. She just has to stand still and look stupid"— likely a real quote, and at the very least one often attributed to Lamarr (Rhodes).

That quote, which balances an awareness of Lamarr's own beauty with a sense of her scientific acumen, reflects the episode's portrayal of beauty, desirability, and history. Lamarr is Martin Stein's "hall pass"—the one woman, in all of time, that his wife gave him permission to sleep with. Still, Stein's attraction is not exclusively visual: as a scientist, he is also aware of Lamarr's history. As he explains, "Brilliant and beautiful … she is also an inventor. Her patent on frequency hopping revolutionized the world" ("Helen Hunt"). However, because Helen's temporal displacement knocks Lamarr out of the running for a debut starring role, Lamarr never invents the frequency-hopping technology that allows the Legends' timeship to travel, leaving them stranded in history.

Lamarr's role as an inventor is not mere set decoration. Above, we saw Julian Maxwell Hayter's articulation of the problem of Charlottesville: "The alt-right is clinging to distorted history—one created by segregationists in service to white supremacy." We might alter those lines to describe Lamarr's omission from the history of science: "So-called traditionalists cling to distorted history, one created by misogynists in service to patriarchy." Only with books such as Richard Rhodes' 2012 *Hedy's Folly: The Life and Breakthrough Inventions of Hedy Lamarr, the Most Beautiful Woman in the World* has Lamarr's contribution gained wider knowledge. Rhodes explains that Lamarr "believed she could devise [a weapon to use against the Germans during World War II] and help change the course of the war" (Rhodes). Work like Rhodes' book are a form of what is sometimes called "revisionist history"— as though revising for accuracy is a problem rather than a goal, bringing lost information to light. Or, to echo Mohanty's language above, revisionism is a process of deconstructing and constructing. It is an awareness that history is a vibrant conversation, not a closed dictum.

Legends actively participates in that construction and conversation. Whereas historians attempt to create and recreate the dominant historical narrative in the name of accuracy, the Legends attempt to correct mistakes in history, as when Helen of Troy's Hollywood ascendance prevents Hedy Lamarr from inventing frequency-hopping technology. The Legends, as characters, restore history. *Legends*, as a show, draws on the work of historical restoration to tell some of the stories that have been lost.

Lamarr's restoration is not the show's first foray into revisionist history. In the second-season premiere, an "anachronism" leads to the Nazis developing an A-bomb during World War II. The Legends attempt to solve the problem by making sure the Nazis are not able to abduct Albert Einstein. However, their plan goes awry, because they are missing an important piece of the historical puzzle: it turns out the Legends need to protect both the famous Einstein and his first wife, Mileva Maric, who, some historians argue, may have influenced Einstein's work (Banovic). Their solution is for Einstein to publicly announce his (now-former) wife's influence "for over thirty years" ("Out of Time"). Doing so will not only thwart the Nazis and keep Maric safe; it will also fix an error by revising history to be more accurate and inclusive. As macho Mick Rory says to Einstein, "It's the right thing to do. Don't be a jerk" ("Out of Time"). Martin Stein eagerly explains the likely ramifications of Einstein's actions: "People won't say, 'Hey, you're a regular Einstein.' They'll say, 'You're like one of the Einsteins'" ("Out of Time"). Nate processes the ramifications: "I can't believe we just changed history"; Martin Stein responds, "No … we saved it" ("Out of Time").

They didn't save the world, though—not in this case. Although the Nazis never developed the A-bomb, Mileva Maric, "Mrs. Einstein," still remains little more than a footnote (although the show likely did educate a few viewers on her importance). The Legends occupied the stance of fourth wave intersection feminism, rising to its challenges, but were unable to perfectly construct a new reality through that critical engagement. The project of revising history is never easy.

And never simple. How much to revise, construct, or change history is a question that emerges throughout the show, especially in "Helen Hunt." Near the end of that episode, Amaya says, "We are the protectors of history. Not its editors" ("Helen Hunt"). "Editors" here is a vague term: Is Amaya rejecting the idea of changing historical fact, or rejecting the idea of clarifying our understandings of those facts? The answer is never fully teased out, which allows viewers to consider its meaning. More importantly, *Legends* doesn't let that idea speak for the show as a whole. Although Zari and Amaya don't discuss their perspectives with each other in this episode, Amaya's hands-off approach to history contrasts with Zari's hands-on solution to the problem of Helen of Troy.

Fixing anachronisms, like the presence of Helen of Troy in Hollywood, should be easy: the goal is to return the anachronism to their proper time period. However, Helen has no desire to return to Troy. She is aware that her powers of allurement represent a threat. She struggles under the entrenched patriarchy of the ancient Mediterranean, and she is drawn to both the fighting abilities of the female Legends and the ideology underpinning their skills: "It gives me hope," she says, "knowing you come from a time in which women have the same opportunities as men" ("Helen Hunt").

Zari describes her solution: "I think I just hacked history: According to the historical record," she says to Helen, "you disappeared halfway through the war, but it didn't affect the war"; therefore, Helen can disappear from the Trojan War without causing any historical changes ("Helen Hunt"). Producer Phil Klemmer explained this perspective in light of the shifting focus of *Legends*: "Sometimes history is a little bit messed up to begin with—part of [the characters'] process is realizing they aren't just time custodians, that they sort of have the ability to change the world they live in" (Klemmer). For Zari, that means instead of returning Helen to where she belongs, Zari drops her off on the island of Themyscira, home of the Amazons and Wonder Woman, with a nod to Helen's powers of allurement and desire to do righteous violence: "best thing about this place? No boys allowed" ("Helen Hunt"). Sometimes, Zari suggests, the solution is a supportive community and the means to find it.

The Future: Muslim Women on Screen

Zari's focus on unorthodox solutions stems from her backstory. In her birthplace of 2042 Seattle, the quasi-governmental secret agency A.R.G.U.S. has made superheroes, and religion, "illegal" ("Zari"). Because Zari is Muslim, she and her family were on the run; her family was killed and Zari managed to take her brother's totem, which gives her power over air. She is snarky and rebellious, surviving as long as she did due to her superior hacking abilities.

Her character is loosely based on the DC Comics character, Isis, who dates back to the 1970s (fortunately, the show disposed of that codename), but the iteration portrayed on *Legends* is more rooted in recent trends in the global comics industry and present-day politics. As Wajahat Ali explains in the Foreword to Sophia Rose Arjana's *Veiled Superheroes: Islam, Feminism, and Popular Culture*, there are currently numerous female Muslim superheroes in comics and graphic novels: from Ms. Marvel and the X-Man Dust to Burqa Avenger, Bloody Nesrine, and the heroines of *The 99* (Ali xii). Arjana herself explains how characters like this—and like Zari—subvert the trope in which "Muslim girls and women … are often seen as tools of subjugation that makes the pacification of Muslim men necessary" (1)—a trope that is based on what Reina Lewis calls "gendered Orientalism," a binary division of the world into "the brightness of Western freedom amid the despotism of the East" (Lewis 217).

The political context of *Legends of Tomorrow* subverts that binary, and it does so at a difficult time in America's political and religious landscape. Zari's first episode aired on October 24, 2017, just ten months after President Trump's initial "Muslim ban" (ACLU). As Mercedes Yanora explains, "The political climate invariably influences how Muslims and non–Muslims alike view Muslims, both real and fictional" (111). *Legends,* by implicitly responding to recent political events simply by portraying a female Muslim character, resets the East/West juxtaposition of gendered Orientalism, which is no longer predicated on a notion of "Western freedom" but the opposite: religion has been outlawed in the United States of 2042.

Later, the fourth-season premiere explicitly links the tyranny of 2042 to present-day America: Zari and the Legends travel to 2018 Washington, D.C., and Zari briefly observes her young self and her mother. "It would be so easy," she says, "to just walk over there and tell [my mother] to get her family and go to Canada before everything changes; before this country that she worked so hard to become a citizen of betrays her…. How could anyone be afraid of her?" ("The Virgin Gary").

Recalling Carastathis's definition of intersectional as a *challenge*, we can see that *Legends* challenges the two dominant political narrative of Muslims: one in which Muslims are enemies and terrorists, the other in which Muslim women are victims in need of saving from Muslim men and from Islam itself. Rather, *Legends* pushes against the trend described by Martin Lund and A. David Lewis: "Villainous images of Muslims have been normalized over decades to the point where they barely provoke a response" (Lund and Lewis 1). Zari's character is remarkable not just for her heroism but also for her depth, which prevents her from being a token: she loves junk food, video games, and humor. She plays the violin, celebrates Ramadan, and complains about the discomfort of the group's period-appropriate costumes. In Zari, *Legends* both deconstructs racist clichés and construct a new, more nuanced portrayal of being Muslim.

Still, this portrayal, however necessary, is not perfect. In "'And, erm, religious stuff': Islam, Liberalism, and the Limits of Tolerance in the Stories of Faiza Hussain," Kevin Wanner points out that relatability for a Muslim superhero depends on "assumptions about what counts as a 'real' or 'normal' person, what an 'everyday religious person' is like—even what it is to be 'human'" (Wanner 41). Wanner links these assumptions to liberalism's flattening effect on religious practice, the notion that we are all the same under the skin. Drawing on Bruce Lincoln's articulation of minimalist and maximalist religious belief, Wanner delineates the problem of the "minimal Muslim": "What makes [Faiza, the subject of his article] so 'normal' and 'identifiable' to readers who own norms and identities have been shaped within and by liberal orders is that she conceals, reveals, and enacts her religion in ways that liberalism deems legitimate and salutary" (43). A minimal Muslim, in other words, is just like anybody else with minor cultural decoration.

Is Zari a "minimal Muslim"? And is that a bad thing? Zari's spotlight episode, "Here I Go Again," follows a *Groundhog Day*–esque repeated time loop during which Zari does nothing particularly religious. In fact, Zari rarely does anything that denotes religion as a part of her life, worldview, or even practice. The only example of how being Muslim differs from being any other way of being occurs in "I, Ava," when Zari must train Mick in the use of a new mystical totem while she is fasting for Ramadan. Mick, whose macho exterior acts as a foil to anything resembling polite behavior, doesn't understand why Zari won't eat bacon: "What, you Jewish?" ("I, Ava"). Zari's response, which appears to be influenced by hunger-induced anger, is to spin Mick around in a cyclone before asking him, "Ramadan is just a stupid, 1400-year-old tradition to you, right? So why I am I even talking about it?" ("I,

Ava"). Mick, demonstrating a macho version of contrition, offers to help her cook *iftar*. Zari explains to him that she refused to fast when she was younger, but her mother had always said, "Ramadan is not just a time for honoring God, but a time to honor tradition, family, community. So whenever I fast or cook *iftar*, it makes me feel connected to my mom" ("I, Ava"). Zari is a practicing Muslim, in other words, but the relevance of Ramadan is anchored in "tradition, family, community"—not theology, doctrine, or revelation. This version of Islam reflects elements of contemporary practice, yet also flattens the experience of being Muslim to its most "minimal." It is worth noting that "I, Ava" aired in late March 2018; Ramadan did not start until mid–May of that year.

More problematically, Zari also exists in what we might consider a default–Christian universe, one well-represented by Mick's comments about pork and Judaism, as many of the Berlantiverse shows including Christmas episodes. On *The Flash*, multiverse-hopping genius Harrison Wells says, "Some traditions are multi-versal" when referring to his Christmas-decorating habits ("The Present"), which implies that Christianity is located across timelines. In *Legends'* third season, scientist Ray Palmer, giving voice to a stuffed-animal deity named Beebo, tells a group of medieval Vikings who think they are defending Odin that Beebo "is risen from the grave" ("Beebo the God of War"). "Like Christ himself," responds one Viking, prompting Palmer to say (in another possible blow against the rising Fundamentalism in the Trump era), "Yes! Jesus is the one true God, which doesn't mean science or evolution isn't real" ("Beebo the God of War"). Palmer's enthusiastic delivery of that line indicates a belief in liberalism-inflected Christianity. That same episode also portrays Martin Stein shopping for a Hanukkah gift for his daughter: his Jewishness amid a Christmas-shopping frenzy is communicated by a novelty sweater decorated with a menorah and a dreidel that is nonetheless an adaptation of the "ugly Christmas sweater." It is hard, in other words, to distinguish between the minimal Christianity of twenty-first century American culture and the minimal Islam or Judaism of those who exist within that culture.

What matters most about Zari, of course, is simply that she exists. Representation of a woman with technology skills, as well as a hero who is Muslim, matters. As actress Tala Ashe described it at a Comic Con panel:

> Representation is something that has always been important to me. I was very much thrust into this position where suddenly I had this mantle of being the first Muslim-American superhero and, I think, one of the only Middle Eastern superheroes. We have a lot of work to do, and that responsibility has been just as important to me as the actual work. And that manifests—social media is such a wonderful thing in a lot of ways, because it allows our fans to be in touch with us, and I get these incredible messages from young men and women who are either Muslim or they're brown in

some way, and they're like "I never see myself represented." And I never saw myself represented when I was a child. I think you can't underestimate what that does to someone's imagination.... I think this will change the world, especially for young women, it's not—it opens, it broadens their horizons in a way that I think, hopefully, is going to reverberate into our future [@talaashe].

In this extended quotation—a clip of which Ashe has pinned to the top of her Twitter page—we see Ashe's awareness of the power of Zari's presence on screen. She posits her own role—and Zari's—as one that is aware that there is "a lot of work to do." The Legends may revise history and sometimes even "hack" it; *Legends* itself revises the portrayal of Muslim women, doing the activist work of pop-culture intersectionality. Here, Ashe hits upon the formula that transformed *Legends* from a flawed show to a sensitive, albeit imperfect, articulation of precisely the challenges and goals of intersectional feminism.

Conclusion

In Season 4, with history nominally repaired, new main characters arrive. Vixen accepts her destiny in Africa, but her actress continues as the shapeshifting Charlie, an anarchist rebel trickster, stressing the versatility of the superheroine and extending intersectionality to a new woman who refuses to obey the system. Sara finds a steady girlfriend in Ava Sharpe (Jes Macallan), who heads the Time Bureau and also adventures beside Sara as the ultimate power couple ... though she has dark secrets in her own past. Nate joins the Time Bureau for a time, allowing more marginalized heroes to take the spotlight. Matt Ryan as John Constantine and Courtney Ford as Nora Darhk bring magic abilities (and some bisexuality) to the team for more boundary-stretching. Further, Nora uses words like victim and survivor to take back her power for the demon who tormented her, while the team provide support in this allegory of violence against women.

Adam Tsekhman as Agent Gary Green is the "nerd" audience stand-in—a loveable goofball who's the Legends' number-one fan within the Time Bureau, joined by an Asian heroine in Ramona Young's cheerful fangirlish Mona Wu. She soon becomes a full team member with her own superpowers. Keiynan Lonsdale as Wally West/Kid Flash helps out as well. With all this, the show emphasizes a continuing devotion to diversity, even as its team-ups with the Time Bureau make them seem increasingly global (or rather, universal). More silliness emphasizes that the show—in contrast with the much grimmer *Arrow*—has finally found its niche.

The Legends are a "team of misfits and outcasts." They were brought together by Rip Hunter's agenda, chosen not because they were skilled but because they were irrelevant to history. From that rough beginning, they decide to do good and fix history's mistakes (and their own errors). They don't always agree—diversity is never perfect agreement—but each character demonstrates a thoughtfulness about outcasts and a willingness to consider how, recalling Crenshaw, "[a simple] framework erases what happens to people who are subject to all of these [oppressions]" ("Interview"), even as they are subject to those oppressions themselves.

As we saw above, Chandra Talpade Mohanty argues that "the first project is one of deconstructing and dismantling; the second is one of building and constructing" (Mohanty 17). In portraying these difficult, intersectional, and thoughtful characters, *Legends of Tomorrow* deconstructed its own flawed premise and approach. From there, it built a plucky, messy show that mixes comedy and criticism, challenges and goals, diversity of characters and diversity of viewpoints. The result is not perfect—and that may be the point. Intersectional feminism is set of challenges and a set of goals, a give-and-take, just as much as the creation of a television show is. Sara Lance asks, "How will we be remembered?" and *Legends* has begun to do the work of answering that question: maybe not as heroes, possibly as legends, and definitely as feminists.

NOTES

1. Many of the characters on *Legends* have comic-book analogues, but this essay will focus exclusively on the television show.
2. Although it is a possibility. In the second-season episode "Doomworld," in which the villainous Legion of Doom has rewritten reality through the power of the Spear of Destiny, the leader of the group, Eobard Thawne, implies that he knows Donald Trump quite well and had some role in helping him get elected.

WORKS CITED

@talaashe. "#RepresentationMatters." Re-tweet of video clip from Comic Con of Tala Ashe discussing representation. Twitter, 1 November 2018, 7:29 a.m., https://twitter.com/talaashe/status/1058003099753824256.
ACLU Washington. Timeline of the Muslim Ban. https://www.aclu-wa.org/pages/timeline-muslim-ban.
Ali, Wajahat. Foreword. *Veiled Superheroes: Islam, Feminism, and Popular Culture* by Sophia Rose Arjana, Lexington, 2017, pp. ix–xiv.
Arjana, Sophia Rose. "Muslim Women in Western Popular Culture." *Veiled Superheroes: Islam, Feminism, and Popular Culture,* Lexington, 2017, pp. 1–22.
Bailey, Alison. "On Intersectionality, Empathy, and Feminist Solidarity: A Reply to Naomi Jack." *Journal for Peace and Justice Studies* vol. 19, no. 1: 14–36 qtd. in Carastathis, Anna. *Intersectionality: Origins, Contestations, Horizons.* University of Nebraska Press, 2016.
Banovic, Rebecca, "Does Albert Einstein's first wife Mileva Maric deserve credit for some of his work?" *The Independent*, 13 June 2018. https://www.independent.co.uk/news/long_reads/mileva-maric-albert-einsten-physics-science-history-women-a8396411.html.
"Beebo the God of War." *DC's Legends of Tomorrow*, written by Grainne Godfree and James Eagan, directed by Kevin Mock, DC Entertainment, and Warner Bros. Television, 2017.
Berger, John. *Ways of Seeing.* British Broadcasting Company and Penguin Books, 1972.
Carastathis, Anna. *Intersectionality: Origins, Contestations, Horizons.* University of Nebraska Press, 2016.

Crenshaw, Kimberlé. "Demarginalizing the Intersection of Race and Sex: A Black Feminist Critique of Antidiscrimination Doctrine, Feminist Theory and Antiracist Politics." *University of Chicago Legal Forum* 1989, no. 1, pp. 139–167.

_____. Interview, no interviewer given. "Kimberlé Crenshaw on Intersectionality, More than Two Decades Later" Columbia Law School. 8 July 2017, https://www.law.columbia.edu/pt-br/news/2017/06/kimberle-crenshaw-intersectionality.

"Doomworld." *DC's Legends of Tomorrow*, written by Ray Utarnachitt and Sarah Hernandez, directed by Mairzee Almas, DC Entertainment, and Warner Bros. Television, 2017.

Evatt, Nicole. "*Legends* Star Shatters Stereotypes with Muslim Superhero." *U.S. News and World Report*, 10 October 2017, https://www.usnews.com/news/best-states/california/articles/2017–10–10/legends-star-shatters-stereotypes-with-muslim-superhero.

Hayter, Julian Maxwell. "Charlottesville Was about Memory, not Monuments." *Washington Post*, 10 August 2018. https://www.washingtonpost.com/news/made-by-history/wp/2018/08/10/charlottesville-was-about-memory-not-monuments.

"Helen Hunt." *DC's Legends of Tomorrow*, written by Keto Shimizu and Ubah Mohamed, directed by David Geddes, Berlanti Productions, DC Entertainment, and Warner Bros. Television, 2017.

"I, Ava." *DC's Legends of Tomorrow*, written by Ray Utarnachitt and Daphne Miles, directed by Dean Choe, DC Entertainment, and Warner Bros. Television, 2018.

"The Justice Society of America." *DC's Legends of Tomorrow*, written by Chris Fedak and Sarah Nicole Jones, directed by Michael Grossman, DC Entertainment, and Warner Bros. Television, 2016.

Klemmer, Phil. Interview with the cast and crew of *Legends of Tomorrow* by Matt Webb Mitovich. *TVLine*, 22 July 2018. https://tvline.com/2018/07/22/legends-of-tomorrow-season-4-cast-preview-monsters-no-crossover-event.

"Last Refuge." *DC's Legends of Tomorrow*, written by Chris Fedak and Matthew Maala, directed by Rachel Talalay, DC Entertainment, and Warner Bros. Television, 2016.

Lewis, Reina. *Gendered Orientalism: Race, Femininity, and Representation*. Routledge, 2013, p. 213.

Lund, Martin, and A. David Lewis. "Whence the Muslim Superhero?" *Muslim Superheroes: Comics, Islam, and Representation, op. cit.*, pp. 1–19.

Mitovich, Matt Webb. Interview with the cast and crew of *Legends of Tomorrow, TV Line*, 22 July 2018. https://tvline.com/2018/07/22/legends-of-tomorrow-season-4-cast-preview-monsters-no-crossover-event.

Mohanty, Chandra Talpade. "Under Western Eyes: Feminist Scholarship and Colonial Discourses." *Feminism without Borders: Decolonizing Theory, Practicing Solidarity*, Duke University Press, 2003, pp. 17–42.

"Out of Time." *DC's Legends of Tomorrow*, story by Greg Berlanti and Chris Fedak, teleplay by Marc Guggenheim and Phil Klemmer, directed by Dermott Downs, DC Entertainment, and Warner Bros. Television, 2016.

Penny, Laurie. "Culture." *Bitch Doctrine: Essays for Dissenting Adults*. Bloomsbury Circus, 2017, pp. 95–161.

"Pilot, Part 1." *DC's Legends of Tomorrow*, written by Greg Berlanti, Marc Guggenheim, Andrew Kreisberg, and Phil Klemmer, directed by Glen Winter, DC Entertainment, and Warner Bros. Television, 2016.

"Present." *The Flash*, story by Aaron Helbing and Todd Helbing, teleplay by Lauren Certo, directed by Rachel Talalay, Berlanti Productions, DC Entertainment, and Warner Bros. Television, 2016.

"Return of the Mack." *DC's Legends of Tomorrow*, written by Grainne Godfree and Morgan Faust, directed by Alexandra La Roche, DC Entertainment, and Warner Bros. Television, 2017.

Rhodes, Richard. *Hedy's Folly: The Life and Breakthrough Inventions of Hedy Lamarr, the Most Beautiful Woman in the World*. Vintage, 2012.

"Shogun." *DC's Legends of Tomorrow*, written by Phil Klemmer and Grainne Godfree, directed by Kevin Tancharoen, DC Entertainment, and Warner Bros. Television, 2016.

Simone, Gail. *Women in Refrigerators*. http://www.lby3.com/wir.

"The Virgin Gary." *DC's Legends of Tomorrow*, written by Phil Kelmmer and Grainne Godfree, directed by Gregory Smith, DC Entertainment, and Warner Bros. Television, 2018.

Wanner, Kevin. "'And, erm, religious stuff': Islam, Liberalism, and the Limits of Tolerance in the Stories of Faiza Hussain." *Muslim Superheroes: Comics, Islam, and Representation, op. cit*, pp. 40–47.

"Welcome to the Jungle." *DC's Legends of Tomorrow*, written by Ray Utarnachitt and Tyron B. Carter, directed by Mairzee Almas, DC Entertainment, and Warner Bros. Television, 2017.

Yanora, Mercedes. "Marked by Foreign Policy: Muslim Superheroes and their Quest of Authenticity." *Muslim Superheroes: Comics, Islam, and Representation, op. cit*, pp. 110–133.

"Zari." *DC's Legends of Tomorrow*, written by James Eagan and Ray Utarnachitt, directed by Mairzee Almas, DC Entertainment, and Warner Bros. Television, 2017.

The Problematic White Woman in *Black Mirror*'s "Crocodile"

Spinster Eskie

After Brett Kavanaugh was accused of sexually assaulting the highly credible Dr. Christine Blasey Ford, Congress had the audacity to insinuate a comparison between Brett Kavanaugh and Tom Robinson from *To Kill a Mockingbird*. Tom Robinson is a black man falsely accused of rape. Brett Kavanaugh is a supreme court justice with a degree from Yale and the unwavering support from some of the most powerful men in the United States. Like many congressional moments, this was one that highlighted how horribly dense most people are about the concepts of privilege and power. Those who don't seem to realize their position exempts them from crying victimhood, seem to cry victimhood the loudest. This can only be categorized as an unapologetic, brazen mentality that white people's pain and problems are somehow worse or more important than the pain and problems of others. No episode of Netflix's brutal science-fiction series, *Black Mirror*, exemplifies this notion of the modern subconscious better than that of Season 4's "Crocodile."

It may be ironic that writers Charlie Brooker and John Hillcoat are two white men that quite frequently spell out the themes of racial tension in a number of episodes. In fact, *Vice Magazine* likens *Black Mirror* to torture porn, stating, "As progressive as the dystopic methods in each episode are, the age-old message remains ironically regressive; that Black pain, Black trauma, and Black bodies are meant to be on literal display for an audience's enjoyment" (Addawoo). While it may be true that the show focuses on the world's open wounds, it seems necessary that Brooker and Hillcoat speak directly to the well-off liberal whites that make up *Black Mirror*'s audience. The implications and undertones of "Crocodile," in particular, reveal an important truth about white privilege and white supremacy that often get lost in most white narratives.

127

It is the tale of two women. They are both successful, intelligent, beautiful, and with loving families. They are both dedicated to their careers. They both have warm and supportive husbands. They both have everything to lose, but one woman is white and the other is quite possibly of Middle Eastern descent. Whose life, then, matters more?

"Crocodile" is as much horror as it is science-fiction, and as socially relevant as it is viciously chilling. Of course, that is what we have come to expect from a show that began its dark and compelling vision with a politician fucking a pig ("The National Anthem"). *Black Mirror* has an ingenious way of stabbing its viewer right where it hurts. For entitled white folk, fear of giving up the power is where it hurts the most.

Most white women may assume a lesson about racism doesn't apply to them. "Oh, I'm not racist! I voted for Barack Obama twice!" As they insist this, they continue to not show up for "Black Lives Matter" protests and they indulge in all the benefits with which this world provides. Therefore, "Crocodile" is not about the typical interpretation of racism. Mia (Andrea Riseborough) is not a blatant racist, like members of the alt-right movement. She never says anything remotely cruel about Shazia's heritage. In the beginning of the episode she mentions "injustice and intolerance" in an acceptance speech she is practicing in the mirror. She probably has brown friends. She probably loves Middle Eastern cooking! However, Mia's racism is evident in her entire lack of regard for Shazia's humanity. Thus, it is not Mia's words that show an inherent idea of superiority. It is her actions.

This would not be the first time *Black Mirror* exposed the subtleties of casual racism. *Splinter News* noted that in the episode "Nosedive," "The majority of service roles like baristas, airline booking agents, car rental attendants, airport security—apparently associated with lower rankings—are played by people of color" (Aran). The technological trend that is critiqued in the episode is one that involves people rating each other based on their everyday social interactions. What better way for people of color to earn the approval of white people, than by granting a service?

It is unclear if Charlie Brooker and John Hillcoat's casting intentions for "Crocodile" included race as a factor. Nonetheless, racial tension is very much an issue that lies on the surface of society, and most competent writers and storytellers are not ignorant to this reality. Therefore, even if actress Kiran Sonia Sawar auditioned and was cast in the most colorblind of circumstances, her ethnicity and the ethnicity of her character mattered in a story about murder for the sake of maintaining the perfect life.

Mia is a renowned and celebrated architect, when she discovers that the life she has built is about to come crumbling down. In a domino effect spiral, Mia begins to kill anyone who could potentially squeal and cause her downfall. Her first victim is an old friend, Rob, who has withheld a secret the two of them had shared for fifteen years. During their partying days they had participated in the hit and run killing of a cyclist. They threw his body into the ocean and vowed to never speak of the deed again. At the time, Mia seemed like an innocent bystander, pressured into covering for the friend behind the wheel. However, years later, when she learns of his recovery from alcohol and desire for redemption, she's horrified at his plan. He wants to write an anonymous letter to the dead man's wife, who still awaits his return. "Look, when I quit alcohol, they told me to make amends with anyone I've ever hurt. Who have I hurt more than her?" he explains.

"You'll open up God knows what, you'll just rake it all up," she protests. "'Cause they can trace it back. They can trace it. They'll find the body, they'll find us." At this stage of the story, she makes a good point. Rob has put her every accomplishment at risk with his threat to admit all to the cyclist's widow. Jassie Justice of *Medium* explains:

> Listen, we want Mia to be a good person because she possesses and performs all the traits our racist, colonial, and neoliberal society tells us that a "good" person should. She has used her class mobility to secure wealth, she has an elite job where she is considered a visionary architect "not just of buildings, but of communities," while being a mother of a beautiful son. In fact her doting husband seems happy to take on the role of stay at home parent. She epitomizes the white feminist ideal. In fact I think its brilliant how adeptly these tropes are established early on as they feed into the audience's confusion as to how to understand Mia. We are made to look at our own justifications for Mia throughout this episode [Justice].

Mia promptly kills Rob and hides his body. Neither Rob, nor the cyclist, are people of color, and so Mia's murder spree does not begin with any racial motivations. It isn't until she meets Shazia that her superiority complex is really exposed.

Shazia works for an insurance company. The science-fiction twist is that her job is to collect memories from accident survivors and witnesses using a Recaller device that records images from the subject's mind. Since Mia witnesses an accident right after murdering Rob, Shazia convinces her to consent to her memories being viewed. Sure enough, Shazia catches glimpses of Mia's violent past, leading Mia to frantically attack her. After, Mia panics. "What am I gonna do with you? I mean, I can't let you go. You're gonna tell someone, aren't you? [She makes muffled sounds] I know, but even if you say you won't, your recollections are all recorded."

As Mia is not necessarily a murderer by nature, she does not kill Shazia immediately. Instead, she ties her up and questions her in order to find out if anyone else is aware she would be visiting that day. Mia learns that Shazia had informed her husband, Anan, that she would be arriving at Mia's residence. This is where Mia's narcissism becomes extremely evident. Though Shazia clearly has a full life to return to, Mia does not see it as valuable as her own. Indeed, Mia never outwardly says, "my life is more important than yours," but her subsequent actions suggest her truest and deepest beliefs. From there, Mia unravels and slaughters not only Shazia, but Shazia's family, including her baby, in order to destroy any possible path of witnesses that would lead the police to her. "Mia's knowledge of the wrongness of her crimes, nor her horror and physical sickness in the face of them do not stop her at any point. There are so many moments where she pauses, and is given by the story a chance to just come forward and face her crime. Or at least try and stop her murderous rampage. She does not. She cries, sobs, vomits; but doesn't stop" (Justice).

Mia's one motive is to hold on to her exquisite lifestyle, so her villainy does not lie within contempt or hatred. Her evil is her inability to feel compassion and empathy for anyone outside her own selfish sphere. "I can almost taste how much she thinks she deserves the accolades, money, success and security she has. I can hear how progressive she believes she is, she even 'devotes her life to social change' and believes she is building a better future. How many white rich liberals can you imagine justify their untold violences by repeating to themselves how they are part of a solution that centres them" (Justice).

"Her performing white motherhood throughout this episode as a justification for her evils is powerful, to walk into her son's play to see his shiny, white, monied face singing about Bugsy Malone while she herself is covered in the blood of a mixed race black and brown baby speaks volumes to me" (Justice). Justice catches up to Mia toward the end of the episode, and it is implied that she meets her fate when police swarm her son's school musical. At this point, Mia is visibly shaken and disturbed by her recent experiences, but not because she feels for Shazia and her family. As *Digital Spy* put it, "Now she cries—crocodile tears, which feel like they're from exhaustion rather than a mass killing spree. These are not crimes of passion but the chilly, dispassionate acts of a ruthless creature" (Fletcher). This is the inspiration for the episode's symbolic name. Even the bitter, mountainous setting of "Crocodile," which takes place in remote Iceland, adds to the themes of emotional vacancy. Mia is a killer whether she likes it or not, because she does not see others as equals, only obstructions that stand in her way.

So many white women in my personal life after seeing this episode seem utterly confused and disturbed—how could she do this? They find every answer except the obvious. Mia thinks she deserved to be innocent and continue her rich, white, powerful life unspoiled by consequences. I genuinely feel that she is emboldened further to murder an entire family of black and brown people not simply because Shazia discovered her wrong doings, but because she understood that this is a murder that she could get away with. Mia knows and believes deeply that in society she is worth more than Shazia and her family. Their collective humanity means far less than Mia avoiding prison and the potential loss of her own family. As Mia brutally murders Shazia she asks her to close her eyes. Even as Mia is bludgeoning a woman of colour to death, she requires that woman to ease the process [Justice].

When police officer Amber Guyger shot her neighbor, Botham Jean, she may not have planned to murder a person of color that day. Many specifics of the case are still publicly unknown. *The New York Times* reports that on September 6, 2018, the unarmed, twenty-six-year-old African American accountant was watching TV in his apartment, when Guyger, returning from her shift (and apparently on the wrong apartment floor), burst in and shot him. Afterward, she claimed she had mistaken his home for hers and believed he was a burglar invading it (Hassan). However, if the defense proves that her actions were not racially motivated, that does not make Guyger any less of a white supremacist, because she did not see Jean as a whole person, only a dark figure that posed a threat. Daryl K. Washington, a lawyer for the Jean family, pointed to what he called "serious training issues" in Dallas, and said departments everywhere needed to delve deeper into disproportionate use of force against African Americans (Hassan). An alarming number of similarly racially-tinged incidents have appeared throughout history, even as witnesses today make more of an effort to document and expose these crimes on social media. White supremacy is not just about discriminating against people of color: it is about the deep-seeded ideology that white people matter more. It is this sick and vile ideology that has poisoned humankind for centuries and influences some of the world's most powerful leaders.

Since 2016, racist incidents have strikingly risen in the USA, with many culprits insisting that the 45th president, Donald Trump, supports their actions. The National Association for the Advancement of Colored People (NAACP), the nation's premier civil rights organization, revealed that hate crime totals for the ten largest cities rose to the highest level in a decade. "The NAACP believes there is a direct relationship between the rise in hate crimes exemplified by the continual #LivingWhileBlack incidents and other reported crimes and President Donald J. Trump's xenophobic rhetoric and racist policies." According to the report, racially-motivated crimes comprise nearly 60 percent of overall crimes, and African Americans remain the most targeted group. Overall, "anti–Black, anti–Semitic, anti-gay and anti-Latino were the most common type of hate crimes," said the study authors. NAACP President and CEO Derrick Johnson adds, "From campaign to election, this president has spewed the language of division and hate, and it has manifested in not only racist policies but in racist acts against people of color and other groups" (NAACP).

While Season 4 of *Black Mirror* is often praised for being carried by strong, dynamic, female characters, the final episode of the season also touches upon racial inequalities. The episode entitled "Black Museum" follows the solitary young Nish (Letitia Wright) to an eerie and unsettling gallery that exploits the suffering of a black death row inmate. The white proprietor Rolo Haynes (Douglas Hodge) "the man to blame for this repulsive amusement park" explains the attractions in three interlocked flashback stories (Nkadi). "There's a sad, sick story behind most everything here," he tells Nish. The first two introduce "a borderline–BDSM neurological hat that allowed a doctor to overdose on sexual pleasure from his patient's pain, a neurological device that evicts a person's consciousness from their body to live rent-free in someone else's mind" (Addawoo).

As the third story relates, Clayton Leigh (Babs Olusanmokun) was innocent of the charges of murdering a white woman, but his pardon fell through (due, in part, to negligence on Haynes' end). He was executed but first convinced to sign over the rights to his post-death consciousness in exchange for money to help support his family. Now Clayton is a fully-conscious hologram with a ghostly appearance, doomed to be eternally executed (and feel real suffering) whenever visitors pull the lever on his virtual electric chair. Haynes smirks, "I knew just seeing the guy walking around captive, that was good, but that wasn't much of a draw. But pulling the lever yourself? Now, that's an attraction." He calls the hologram "a conscious sentient snapshot of Clayton … perpetually experiencing that beautiful pain. Stuck forever in that one perfect moment of agony. Always on. Always suffering." The image crouches in his cell, fragile and ghostlike in his flickering transparency. Of course, sadists and racists crowd the museum. Visitors can even leave with a key chain souvenir containing a preserved, and fully independent, copy of Clayton eternally in agony. Reviewing this episode, critic Ashley Nkadi criticizes how much America's history has depended on torture of black people as well as its commodification—beyond slavery and lynching to selling postcards of both for white people to mail their friends. She goes on:

> Today these "snapshots" take the form of enterprises like the rap industry, in which artists recount trauma, suicidal thoughts and drug addiction while listeners sing along, or museums where people line up to pay to get a glimpse at the bloody slab of concrete where Martin Luther King Jr. took his last breath, or hashtag T-shirt companies whose sales literally depend on continued fatal encounters between black individuals and police officers. As James Allen expressed, "In America, everything is for sale, even national shame" [Nkadi].

However, the heroine strikes back. In an end-of-episode twist, Nish reveals herself as Clayton's daughter. Her father was innocent, and protestors marched against the cruelty of the program. As Nish continues, "His wife started a campaign, got some momentum behind it. Guess you'd call it virtue-signaling bullshit, but I know it hurt your attendance. And even the protesters got bored after a while. As soon as it was clear the state wouldn't do a damn thing about clearing him, they just moved onto the next viral miscarriage of justice they can hang a hashtag off of. But they did their job, right? This place was on the shit list." Most of the attendance vanished, but the "supremacist sicko demographic" kept coming. Of course, this fully reflects reality. "In the cycle of the commodification of black pain, we become desensitized to black suffering in every form, even death" (Nkadi).

With her father tortured beyond sanity, her mother killed herself. Now, Nish has come to settle the score. When Haynes collapses from the poisoned water she's provided, Nish transfers his consciousness into Clayton's hologram. She pushes the electric chair simulation to its maximum, allowing Haynes to experience the full force of the torture and destroying her father's consciousness. She gets herself a souvenir keychain of Haynes in perpetual agony, starts a fire, and leaves happily as the museum burns down. Equally joyful is her mother's consciousness, preserved within her own mind as one of the previous stories set up. Her carrying of her mother is significant: *Vice Magazine* describes the character of Nish as one who "reflects the unspoken grief that black people—particularly black *women*—carry" (Addawoo). This is what *Black Mirror* does. It takes the worst of humankind and then displays the extent of its grotesque vulgarity through the use of technology, which keeps us as disconnected as ever. Similarly, "Crocodile" draws attention to the hostility of privilege and the false tears of white people who are clenching on to their power as tightly as possible, terrified that it will soon be taken away.

Then there are the educated white feminists that reject hatred and bigotry, but still greatly benefit from their whiteness. What does "Crocodile" make clear to this particular audience? An article floating around Facebook called "Why We Should Say 'Female Genital Cutting' and Not 'Mutilation'" by Louisa Leontiades caused an uproar among white feminists who were bothered by the suggestion of using a euphemism for an act of abuse. The headline appeared to trigger readers who made assumptions based on their Westernized understanding of the practice. However, the article does not promote female circumcision, but instead promotes allowing women of color to choose the language for their experience. Those are the moments white feminists need to reflect upon. If the goal is to counteract the lingering normalization of white supremacy, those that seek justice must re-evaluate their thinking and develop an awareness of how white supremacy has infiltrated the beliefs and actions of everyday existence.

Referring to the Season 4 finale of *Black Mirror*, the magazine *The Root* reminds readers that although it's easy to blame neo–Nazis for current societal problems, if "even the most benevolent, well-meaning white liberals, look in the mirror, they'll find that it is they who are holding the money to pay to get on the ride" (Nkadi). Storytelling is indeed a mirror held up to reflect society, and "Crocodile" is the reflection of the comfort white women take in their privilege. The vast majority of white people on this planet are prone to separating the concepts of white privilege and white supremacy, in order to distance themselves from kyriarchy. However, white privilege and white supremacy are clearly codependent entities and one does not exist without the other. To ignore this fact is to participate in the perpetuation of systematic oppression.

WORKS CITED

Addawoo, Lindsey. "*Black Mirror* Is Obsessed with Black Suffering." *Vice Magazine*. 8 Jan. 2018, https://www.vice.com/en_us/article/mbp9my/black-mirror-is-obsessed-with-black-suffering. Accessed 8 Dec. 2018.

Aran, Isha. "Black Mirror's 'Nosedive' Isn't Just About Social Media, It's About Race." *Splinter News,* 24 Oct. 2016, https://splinternews.com/black-mirror-s-nosedive-isn-t-just-about-social-media-1793863113. Accessed 8 Dec. 2018.

"Black Museum." *Black Mirror,* season 4, episode 6, 2015. *Netflix.*

"Crocodile," *Black Mirror,* season 4, episode 3, 2015. *Netflix.*

Fletcher, Rosie. "What Does the Title of Black Mirror's 'Crocodile' Mean?" *Digital Spy,* 1 Feb. 2018, https://www.digitalspy.com/tv/ustv/a846493/black-mirror-crocodile-episode-title-explained. Accessed 8 Dec. 2018.

Hassan, Adeel. "Former Dallas Officer Amber Guyger Charged with Murder for Shooting Man in His Apartment." *New York Times,* 30 Nov. 2018. https://www.nytimes.com/2018/11/30/us/amber-guyger-botham-jean-indicted.html.

Justice, Jassie. "Crocodile Tears: The Violence of White Womanhood in Netflix's *Black Mirror* Episode "Crocodile"—Part One." *Medium* 31 Dec 2017. https://medium.com/@theperfecttension/crocodile-tears-the-violence-of-white-womanhood-in-netflixs-black-mirror-episode-crocodile-3ccdf9d08ed7.

Leontiades, Louisa. "Why We Should Say 'Female Genital Cutting' and Not 'Mutilation.'" *The Body Is Not an Apology,* 4 Nov. 2018. https://thebodyisnotanapology.com/magazine/interview-on- female-cutting-louisa. Accessed 8, Dec. 2018.

"NAACP Sees Continued Rise in Hate Crimes, Legacy of Trump's Racism." *NAACP,* 29 June 2018. https://www.naacp.org/latest/naacp-sees-continued-rise-hate-crimes-legacy-trumps-racism.

"The National Anthem," *Black Mirror,* season 1, episode 1, 2015. *Netflix*, https://www.netflix.com/watch/70264857.

Nkadi, Ashley. "*Black Mirror*: 'Black Museum' Reckons with America's History of Commodifying Black Pain." *The Root,* 8 Jan. 2018. https://www.theroot.com/black-mirror-black-museum-reckons-with-america-s-histo-182181435. Accessed 2, Feb. 2019.

"Bloke Utopia"

Bill Potts, Queer Identity
and Cyborg Narratives in Doctor Who

Sarah Beth Gilbert

Introduction

One of the brilliant and lasting traits of science fiction, no matter its form or medium, is its ability to show both possibilities of better worlds and ways to better our own world. The vast reach that comprises science fiction has been widened through its adaptation of narratives onto film and television, termed sci-fi on these mediums. No matter the medium, Carl Freedman's theories on science fiction remain true as a realm of work "whose initial act … is to refuse the status quo in favor of a social alternative which is not ours but which, for better or worse, could, at least in principle, become ours" (188). The shift from science fiction literature to sci-fi film and television happened in the mid–20th century as televisions became more accessible to all. In adapting to film and television, sci-fi has brought fanciful storylines, characters, and worlds to the mass public. *Doctor Who* was originally aired in 1963 to be a children's history show using the narrative framing of time travel to allow BBC to present past histories in an engaging way to viewers.[1] Since then, the realm of sci-fi has expanded enormously to include independent and blockbuster films, prime time television and streaming TV shows, as well as YouTube created narratives and storylines. Despite the widening of source material across mediums for science fiction and sci-fi, representation of anyone not white, male, and heteronormative has been extremely low. Not until 1979 with Sigourney Weaver's role of Ellen Ripley in *Alien* did sci-fi really begin to feature strong female protagonists that didn't need to be saved by the male protagonist. Even now in sci-fi, it is hard to find a female protagonist who is not forced to deal with a romantic side plot while she simultaneously worries about saving the world. This is a narrative trope into which *Doctor Who* has also fallen.

After a mid-season break of 16 months, Season 10 of the British sci-fi television show *Doctor Who*[2] has aimed to stay culturally and politically relevant. It features Peter Capaldi as the 12th Doctor but introduces a new companion named Bill Potts who is played by the talented Pearl Mackie. Since its reboot in 2005, improved technology and storylines have kept up the significance of *Doctor Who*, while diverse representation has been absent. In her book titled *Dancing with the Doctor: Dimensions of Gender in the Doctor Who Universe*, Lorna Jowett succinctly attributes this to how "Doctor Who valorises 'universal' values and ideals—yet these values are ingrained with (possibly unconscious) white, middle-class, male privilege that goes generally unremarked because of its pervasiveness in UK television" (139–140). In the show's history, all of the Doctors have been white males and only one full-time companion, until Bill Potts, was a person of color. Similarly, only one companion previous to Bill in the history of the show has been part of the LGBTQIA+ community, and he, Captain Jack Harkness, tended to play comic relief. Working off of Lee Edelman's anti-normative theories of queer agency in *No Future*, Bill Pott's character in Season 10 of *Doctor Who* calls attention to the constraining nature of the roles to which queer women in sci-fi are subjected. The rigid structure of female roles in sci-fi are made more noticeable by establishing a true female characterization of Bill Potts that positions itself as anti-normative to the structural role of the companion.

Theoretical Approaches

Queer theorist Lee Edelman further analyzes the ways that anti-normative queer positions can navigate power, specifically examining the ways that conservative politics locates futurity in the Symbolic Child. Edelman explains how ideas of the future are often wrapped up in biological reproduction, thus aligning the future with the Child whose survival solidifies the existence of the human race. Queerness, he argues, works against this notion of futurity because it "dispossesses the social order of the ground on which it rests" (6). Queerness has, historically, been a position of being outside of the norm which has led to an embracing of an anti-normative stance. Edelman calls for queerness to rupture the notion of futurity in the Child by embracing the power of anti-normativity in order to locate a new future that is not defined by gender and reproductive status. Similarly, Alexander Doty analyzes the ways in which queerness is both represented and consumed by the public by focusing on its effects in Pop Culture in his book *Making Things*

Perfectly Queer. Doty theorizes that queer representation doesn't only have to occur in explicitly queer texts. Rather, there can be "queer moments" in cultural texts that are accessible and identifiable to straight identifying viewers. The presence of these queer moments work to destabilize heteronormative ideologies in ways that can "create a more consistent awareness within the general public of queer cultural and political spaces" (4). Finally, Heather Walton's article titled "The Gender of a Cyborg" takes Donna Haraway's ideas about cyborgs and applies them to cultural representations to analyze the ways that the cyborg either supports or subverts cultural norms such as gender identity, sexual identity, and other dominant cultural symbols. All three of these theorists' work applied to Season 10 of *Doctor Who*, specifically Bill Pott's character and narrative, reveals which ways queerness is represented, subverted, or reinforced through Bill's anti-normative characterization as a companion, how that creates queer moments for straight identifying viewers, and what notions of futurity the use of the cyborg as the Cybermen create.

Anti-Normative and Queer Moments

In the first episode of the season, titled "Pilot," Bill's clever characterization asserts her as anti-normative to the functional role of the companion. Historically during the classic run of *Doctor Who*, the companion played a supportive role to the Doctor and his adventures. Quite simply, the companion set up the exposition for whatever new planet, alien species, race, or law of gravity was foundational to understanding that narrative. Richard Wallace's article on the narrative function of the companion references an interview with Nicola Bryant (who played companion Peri in classic *Doctor Who*) in the documentary *More Than 30 Years on the TARDIS*, in which she comments that "'apart from being lovely to look at,' the role of the companion is to 'ask a lot of questions ... to make the Doctor look very clever ... to let the audience know what's going on ... and to reaffirm the patently obvious'" (104). This function of the companion rests on the groundwork of a lack of knowledge on the companion's part in order to refract the focus onto the main character, the Doctor. Much of the "new companion" narrative in the establishing episode in which he or she is introduced is still written to allow the Doctor to show off because "without the baseline of others' lesser knowledge and experience, the Doctor's abilities would seem much less impressive" (Jowett 15). Recently with the reboot, *Doctor Who*'s companions have been as vital to saving worlds and planets from destruction as the Doctor is. Nothing is more relevant than "The End of Time" two part finale of Series 4 in which eight previous companions join forces to help the Doctor save multiple worlds. The Doctor, increasingly, just cannot do it alone anymore. Nonetheless, even with the expanding depth of the role of the companion since the reboot, companions have still been written to marvel at the spaceship, the technology, or the Doctor's brilliance in a wide-eyed naïve way.

Nonetheless, Bill Potts rejects this norm and enters her first adventure fully capable of understanding the complexities of time travel. The spectacle of explaining its splendors isn't necessary because Bill is quick and intelligent. When Bill is told that the TARDIS is a spaceship, instead of gaping open-mouthed at the idea, she points out that it doesn't make sense that the TARDIS' signs would be in English if the Doctor is alien since English clearly wouldn't be his native language ("Pilot"). The majority of the explanatory moments the Doctor normally is allowed with a new companion are subverted by her intelligence. At the end of the episode, the Doctor tries to wipe Bill's memories of their encounter, only to be admonished by her; "I've seen movies. I know what a mind wipe looks like!" ("Pilot"). For the viewers, it is as if Bill has also seen episodes of *Doctor Who* the way she sees through his tricks. Here, Bill's characterization is privileged over her narrative function as she is allowed to call out the absurdity of assuming that a millennial in 2018 would not have seen enough sci-fi to understand the basics of mind wiping and space ships. Furthermore, her knowledge disrupts the narrative focus on the Doctor and "dispossesses the social order of the ground on which it rests" by shifting the focus of new companion narrative back to her, the new companion (Edelman 6). Immediately, Bill quickly establishes a character whose intelligence and cleverness about space travel takes an anti-normative stance in opposition to the typical young, naïve, female stereotype that has found itself played out in the role of past companions.

By reclaiming the new companion narrative, Bill also is given room to establish her identity outside of her relationship with the Doctor. Since the reboot, most companions have been straight, white, and female. Of five modern female companions, all of their narratives, except Donna's, have romantic elements (and even her first and basically last appearances feature her weddings). This has been an unfortunate consistency that has established companions who feel "unrequited love for [the Doctor], or certainly feel a strong attraction to him, despite other, ongoing relationships" (Jowett 18). Again, Bill shatters this trope in the first episode by being clearly interested in another girl named Heather. In a scene solely meant to develop Bill's character, she sits listening to her foster mom warn against being too trusting of men. Bill remarks, halfway under her breath, "Men aren't where I keep my eye actually" ("Pilot"). Within the first ten minutes, the narrative establishes that there will be no romantic love plot between the Doctor and Bill through establishing her identity as a queer character. It is notable that this is stated by Bill, who is given the voice to assert what type of Doctor/companion relationship she is looking for rather than allowing the Doctor say he isn't interested in her first. Nikki Sullivan seamlessly summarizes Doty's work on queer moments, like this one, for straight identifying people to see Bill "destabilise heteronormativity and the meanings and identities it engenders" by rejecting the trope that a leading woman must fall in love with the leading man; a trope that consistently constitutes the majority of female representation in film and television (191). This queer moment helps viewers actively question the heteronormative logic behind such representations and experience a queering of the Doctor/companion relationship as it takes a platonic, antinormative approach that gives the show the "shot in the arm" that "even institutions need" every now and then (Hughes).

Tackling the subject of sexuality has been a lightly treaded area since Russell T. Davies was the showrunner for the first four series. While the show has strayed away from making any large statements about understandings of sexuality, the Doctor/companion romantic narrative has ideologically established a heteronormative stance. Even with Captain Jack Harkness being a secondary companion for awhile, his sexuality was never explicitly stated, which seemed to leave the responsibility of interpretation on the viewer.[3] In a stand-alone episode titled "Eaters of Light," an episode that does not contribute to the season's narrative, Bill and the Doctor go to second-century Scotland in order to figure out what happened to the legendary Ninth Legion of the Roman army. Bill finds herself trapped in a cave with the Ninth Legion and talking to a Roman soldier named Lucius. After it is clear that Lucius is flirting with Bill, she explains to him that she only likes women, to which he replies:

> LUCIUS: I don't think it's narrow-minded. I think it's fine. You know what you like.
> BILL: And you like both?
> LUCIUS: I'm just ordinary. You know, I like men and women.
> BILL: Ha! Well, isn't this all very modern.
> LUCIUS: Hey, not everyone has to be modern. I think it's really sweet that you're so restricted ["Eaters of Light"].

Here a queer moment is established for straight identifying viewers not by Bill but by historical characters. By flipping the heteronormative view that heterosexuality is correct and any deviant sexuality is wrong, the dialogue overturns the established associations of the terms "modern" and "restricted" as Lucius finds Bill's attraction to just one gender restrictive no matter the gender. This is a moment where the show allows "straight-identified audience members to express a less-censored range of queer desire and pleasure than is possible in daily life" (Doty 4). When the Doctor is absent from scenes, Bill is the character with whom most viewers identify since she is the character they have known for the second longest. By identifying with Bill, straight identifying audience members relate to the identification of being attracted to *one* gender, regardless of the question of *which* gender. The dialogue then plays on the idea that this type of attraction is restrictive by limiting attraction to one of many genders. Further, the dialogue then establishes bisexuality as the normative sexuality in this context, which puts straight identifying viewers in the positions of identifying as the anti-normative sexuality. This queer moment helps straight viewers to question heteronormative standards that influence their identities by assessing those beliefs and characters on screen—an assessment which ends in the realization that both straight identifying viewers and Bill find common ground when it comes to their sexuality.

Agency and Queer Moments

The eighth episode of the tenth season, "The Lie of the Land," stands at the end of a three-episode narrative arc featuring aliens called the Monks who want to control the Earth in return for preventing the end of the world—a mishap in a laboratory. "The Lie of the Land" opens with the Monks transmitting mind control and rewriting history to convince humans that life has always been controlled this way. The first scene shows Bill clearly resisting the mind control, trying to hold on to her real memories, and searching for the Doctor. Once they are reunited they find the original transmitting location and break in, hoping to destroy the transmitter. The Doctor realizes that the only way to break the world's mind control is to project pure, uncorrupted memories into the transmitter, which would snap humans' brains back to their original memories. The norm of the show has always privileged the Doctor's 200 years of knowledge over companions' as we are quite frequently reminded just *how much* the Doctor has seen and experienced in his life which allows him to save the Earth and humanity so frequently. However, in this episode, the Doctor's memories aren't powerful enough and he fails: "Who ends up saving humanity? Bill Potts. Bill, who has watched the Doctor save the day enough times to know that if you see your chance, you can't hesitate" (Villanueva). Since Bill knows that the Doctor won't allow her to use her own memories, she ties him up while he is passed out and takes control. It is important to note that Bill's assertion of her ability and agency to save the day only can happen once the Doctor is restrained, by her, from stopping her.

Although the Doctor's conrol stems from his care and desire for her not to die, it consistently and ideologically pushes the idea that women need protection from men and should not choose to sacrifice themselves. Narratively, the Doctor doesn't ever willingly lets his companions have the same agency to decide to sacrifice themselves the way that he does time and time again. When characters do sacrifice themselves, as Rose Tyler does by being banished to an alternate universe, it happens as a narrative decision that is out of the companion's hands. In Series One, the tragedy revolving around Rose and the Doctor is that they did not choose to be separated. Similarly, the tragedy with married companions Amy and Rory being sent back in time during Series 7 is the same; they were forced to stop traveling with the Doctor. Thus, here, Bill is taking an anti-normative approach and undermining the female sacrifice trope since she isn't being *forced* by the narrative. Rather, she is making the decision herself and rejecting the companion role in which the Doctor wants her to stay.

Narratively, this goes against the institutional makeup of the show which puts the Doctor in impossible situations and has him work himself out of it. By privileging her agency over his, the show also creates another queer moment that disrupts and destabilizes heteronormative logic. Bill's memories are the memories that are pure enough to break all of the mind control over the entire planet. As Bill puts her hands on the transmitting device and her memories flash up behind her on the screens they show Bill as a child running in a field, the PRIDE flag, Bill and Heather, Bill's adventures with the Doctor, and her memories of her mother ("The Lie of the Land"). These uncorrupted memories are the ones that allow humans to break the mind control by glimpsing truth and freedom. Bill's anti-normative stance as companion not only then disrupts the show's heteronormative logic that the Doctor must always save the human race, but also locates the actual futurity of the human race in Bill's experiences as a queer woman. This allows a sci-fi show able "to conceive a future without the figure of the Child" when depicting the future of the human race (Edelman 11). It also makes sense that the future of the human race should not rest on the experiences and memories of an alien Time Lord. The fact that the show locates its savior in a "gay, black, and working class [woman] is another welcome step in Doctor Who's ability to reflect the entire spectrum of who enjoy the show," which moves the ideology of who can and cannot save the world away from the dominant heteronormative male narratives that have been perpetuated by sci-fi and *Doctor Who* (Wilkins).

Queer Futurity in Cybermen

In addition to looking at characterization and agency in episodes of television shows, it is also important to consider what the entire narrative of a character's story does. This is quite often hard to do with *Doctor Who* while the show airs since viewers are watching week by week. However, in hindsight, once a season or storyline is over, one can look at characters' narratives as a whole to determine what the show does and does not do. An example of this would be the way that *Doctor Who* established the ability for Time Lords to change genders as they regenerate. In Season 10, the Doctor's childhood friend and enemy, the Master, is brought back into the narrative regenerated as a woman, now called Missy (Michelle Gomez). Lorna Jowett notes that many fans had read into the Master and Doctor's original relationship homosocial if not homosexual possibility; "It was therefore a disappointment to many that only when the Master became a woman was this relationship depicted in physically intimate or sexual terms. In this sense, what can be seen as advancement in relation to depictions of gender within the series results in a regression in representations of sexuality" (91). Even though the inclusion of a LGBTQIA+ character may indicate a step in the right direction, the narrative afforded to that character may not. Although the possibility for Time Lords to change genders opens up the Doctor's characterization, the Master's change of gender led to the heteronorming of the Doctor and Master's relationship.

More than locating the power of queer politics in being anti-normative, Lee Edelman also analyzes the notion of the Symbolic Child as heteronormative society's depiction of the future. He explains "the Child has come to embody for us the telos of the social order and come to be seen as the one for whom that order is held in perpetual trust" and then calls for a rejection of the Child as the notion of futurity (11). A way to disrupt the tying of futurity to reproduction is seen in the genre of sci-fi through the progress of technology. If the hope for humans is to continue to survive then technology has the ability to rupture that goal from notions of reproduction through the cyborg. Heather Walton discusses in her article "The Gender of Cyborg" how the cyborg and its cultural representations have the ability to disrupt and lend analysis to the "dominant cultural symbols" and "practices and privileges" created through "the material practices of symbolization" (33). Due to the non-genderedness of the cyborg, it has the ability not only to disrupt "our binary and hierarchical understandings of masculinity and femininity" but all "essentialist constructions of human nature" (34). This analysis can lend itself to a study of how innovation and technological advancements are represented in cultural texts as well as creating the ability to locate futurity in a non-flesh alternative, the cyborg. Simply, in depicting the cyborg as a symbol of the future, one is not tied to the physicality of gender—which is inextricably at the basis of the majority of our systems of power. This power in disrupting heteronormative futurity is quite similar to the same power to disrupt that Edelman locates in queerness.

Doctor Who's second most notorious villain is the Cybermen. Arguably tied with the Daleks, the Cybermen have played key roles in multiple storylines throughout all seasons since the start of *Doctor Who* in the 1960s. The Cybermen are technologically "upgraded" humans whose origins are often explained by their desire to keep only what is necessary for survival. Centered around the question of futurity, the Cybermen's response to death is to upgrade everything about the human from flesh that fails to metal that lasts in order replace anything that encumbers humans' survival, including emotions and pain. Therefore, emotionless, the Cybermen are "the archetypal TV monster: evil, remorseless and emotionless cyborgs that are prepared to get what they want" (Geraghty 86). In the two-episode season finale narrative directed by Rachel Talalay and written by showrunner Steven Moffat, the Doctor, Missy, and Bill seek out a spaceship's distress call and transport on board. Once they're on the flight deck, an alien emerges, telling them that monsters are coming to take whatever human life was just detected on the ship. Bill, being the only human on the ship, is then suddenly, shockingly killed by the alien so that the Cybermen won't have a reason to come all the way up to the level they are on ("World Enough and Time").

The last episode opens with the Doctor attempting to escape from the Cyberman and finding a past reincarnation of the Master (John Simm). The Master tells him the story of why these Cybermen were created: the people on the lower levels of the ship were poorer and thus subjected to worse living conditions. The fuel from the ship compromised all of the atmosphere on their level, making it near impossible to live. In order to rectify this, doctors at the hospital started created "better" body parts to replace the flesh ones that could not last in the conditions they were in. This forced them to begin "upgrading" all of the humans to a new form that could withstand their economic and environmental conditions ("The Doctor Falls"). This origin story focuses on the ways that flesh has failed humans. Even when the humans are continuing to reproduce and have children, those children cannot withstand the conditions around them in the spaceship. Thus, in this narrative, "if there is a baby, there is a future, there is a redemption" no longer rings true due to the fact that the babies cannot live long enough to create a future or redemption for the human race (Edelman 13). The "pro-procreative ideology" Edelman locates in society is rendered useless in this society on the spaceship and gives way to a materiality that is necessary for survival. Since flesh cannot survive, humans need to turn their bodies into a different material. Nonetheless, in that process, the pain of the transformation still remains, which leads them to get rid of feeling and pain. In this origin story, there could be said to be a queerness in the way that the future is located in Cybermen as it subverts the "foundational faith in the reproduction of futurity" as reproduction through the flesh must give way to replication through the "upgrading" process and locates the future of the human race in metal and technology (Edelman 17).

Moreover, if notions of futurity in this narrative are not tied to gender's relation to sexual organs and reproduction, then the question to pose should be why gender the cyborg at all? The villainous race are, always in *Doctor*

Who, Cyber*men*, even when being men and male is no longer necessary to this society. The narrative explanation behind why the Cybermen are the way they are often revolves around the idea that humans wanted to take the *best* of everything. This justification then indicates that being male is the best and strongest gender to accept if the human race is to survive. Here we see the cyborg reproduced culturally to indicate the future in a way that ties futurity and survival to our present "dominant gender forms" (Walton 35). The reasoning for the gendered form of cyborgs pushes the ideology that the male is the more powerful, strong, and worthy gender since it is worthy of keeping in the "upgrades." Again we see what seems like a step forward by including cyborgs, which have the potential to disrupt current societies' hierarchical positionings, fall into privileging the dominant male/female gender dichotomy. Moreso, part of the Cybermen's villainous success is that they are able to be a ruthless, killing race who prioritizes surviving by embodying typical male stereotypes, like aggression and strength. Even though the notion of futurity in the Cybermen takes a step away from relying on reproduction, and thus heteronormative mating, it takes a step back by reinforcing the same damaging hierarchies that stem from the "most enduring cultural anxieties" around gender (Walton 36).

However effective the Cybermen are at playing the villain and being worked into the narrative as a worthy opponent for the Doctor and companions to vanquish, they are unnecessarily gendered male. The effect of this, while inherently reinforcing existing notions of male superiority, becomes even more significant when Bill Potts is "upgraded" into a Cyberman. After being shot at the start of "World Enough and Time," Bill is taken by what seems to be hospital personnel and wakes up with a metal heart on a lower level of the ship. The rest of the episode features Bill waiting for the Doctor to make it down to her level of the spaceship, where time moves slower. Due to the time difference, Bill is stuck waiting years for the Doctor to save her, an unfortunate trope seen in many of Moffat's companions, particularly Amy Pond and River Song. During that time, hospital personnel come back to finish the procedure for Bill and "upgrade" her to a Cyberman, before the Doctor finally makes it to her ("World Enough and Time").

Bill spends the next episode hiding out in a barn in a upper level farm on the spaceship because she scares the children there. When the Doctor finally comes to explain to her that she has been changed into a Cyberman, she doesn't accept it. The cinematography alludes to this by filming Bill in a Cyberman suit while the Doctor is talking to show what he sees, only to show human Bill during scenes when she is talking to show how she sees herself. What is communicated to the viewers, then, is that she still retains her memories and identity as Bill Potts even though physically she is a Cyberman. More disturbingly, Bill is re-gendered as male in a narrative choice that ultimately "straightens" her, since we can assume her identity remaining intact means that she is still Bill and thus still attracted to females. At the end of the episode during a fight between the adults on the farm and the Cybermen from the lower levels, Bill and the Doctor stay to fight, knowing that they will probably be killed. While it is notable that the Doctor allows her to stay and fight, the narrative only allows Bill full agency to make a final stand with the Doctor once she is regendered as a Cyber*man*. This clashes with the way her character has been anti-normative to the role of companion because it only allows her to be equal to the Doctor and help with the fighting once she is *physically* an equal match. Bill's ability to save the Doctor at the end of the episode reinforces the stereotype of the male savior. Bill is only capable of saving the Doctor as a companion once she is no longer physically female.

In addition to this, the Doctor and Bill are fighting in order to hold off the Cybermen from capturing the local children while they escape to a higher level. Their third companion, Nardole (male but also queered as an alien robot) takes the classic feminine companion role of fleeing along with them. Meanwhile, Bill and the Doctor's final fight aligns them fighting against the notion of futurity in cyborgs and positions them to fight *for* the notion of futurity in the Child. Ideologically, this establishes the belief that if the children survive, (cyber)Bill and the Doctor have died *for something*. Thus, both Bill and the narrative that have depicted queer anti-normative representations and storylines give way to the heteronormative re-gendering notions of futurity. Predominantly, the final fight of the season reinforces heteronormative notions of strength, life purpose, and futurity. Even though Bill's final moments in the show do not end with the battle and instead feature her being "saved" and turned back into a human by Heather, her love interest from the "Pilot" episode, the narrative points to how companions will not be able to do what the Doctor does or be considered equal until they lose part of themselves and mirror his heteronormative male centered traits. Thus, the only real power anyone can have in the show is found when they mimic and act like the white, heteronormative, male Doctor. From the gender statement to the pat rescue by a "love interest" with whom Bill only ever shared a few minutes' conversation, it's a disappointing endto such a vivacious, endearing character, even as the season appeared to take such bold strides.

Conclusions

Overall Bill Potts' character served to express and represent a characterization of a non-heteronormative identity through her role as companion to Peter Capaldi's Doctor. Through this strong and true characterization, the show presented both queer moments and notions of futurity that undermined the hetero-normative ideologies most often perpetuated by television. More, Bill's narrative points to the idea that non-heteronormative and fully rounded characters will only find tension between the agency they wish to express and the role of the companion as long as it is in relation to a white, male Doctor on *Doctor Who*. Since the Doctor/companion dynamic has, historically, represented a dichotomy that privileges white males as the Doctor, the show's inclusion of women, minorities, and LGBTQIA+ characters will always create a strain if they are only limited to the companion part of the dichotomy.

In a genre that works to stand against norms, sci-fi film and television can be one of the most accessible tools to be used to challenge and redefine notions of what and who is normative, important, and powerful. Season 11 of *Doctor Who* has already taken steps to do this by featuring the first female Doctor, played by Jodie Whittaker, and a cast of companions that include Yas, a female millennial Pakastani police officer, Ryan, a black millennial male, and Graham, Ryan's older, white stepfather. The dynamic of the Doctor/companion relationship has changed dramatically in this season as the Doctor assumes a female identity and takes a less authoritative approach to being the center of the solving of mysteries as well as featuring multiple companions who represent various backgrounds that better reflect the show's viewers. Further research could seek to analyze the ways that Jodie Whittaker's Doctor and companions' characterizations and narratives either work undermine or reinforce cultural power relations and dominant ideologies often found in sci-fi. Regardless of how it is approached, the application of queer theory and anti-normativeness to the sci-fi genre is capable of opening up discussion around the way the genre has worked as a white, male dominated institution in order to bring conversations forward and to the attention of those with the ability to choose what storylines and what characters are represented.

NOTES

1. For more information about the history of the show, see the "Doctor Who" article written by the official Tardis Wiki.

2. Known as Series 10 in the U.K

3. For more information about Jack Harkness' time on the show, reference the "Jack Harkness" article written by the official Tardis Wiki.

WORKS CITED

Alien. Directed by Ridley Scott, performances by Sigourney Weaver, Tom Skerritt, and John Hurt, Twentieth Century-Fox Productions, 1979.

"The Doctor Falls." *Doctor Who*, season 10, episode 12, BBC, 1 Jul. 2017. Amazon Prime, https://www.amazon.com/Doctor-Who-Season-10/dp/B06XPTWTGN.

"Doctor Who." *TARDIS FANDOM powered by Wikia*, http://tardis.wikia.com/wiki/Doctor_ Who.

Doty, Alexander. *Making Things Perfectly Queer: Interpreting Mass Culture*, University of Minnesota Press, 1993. ProQuest Ebook Central, https://ebookcentral.proquest.com/lib/villanova-ebooks/detail.action?docID=310246.

"The Eaters of Light." *Doctor Who*, season 10, episode 10, BBC, 17 Jun. 2017. Amazon Prime, https://www.amazon.com/Doctor-Who-Season-10/dp/B06XPTWTGN.

Edelman, Lee. *No Future: Queer Theory and the Death Drive*. Duke University Press, 2004.

"The End of Time: Part One." *Doctor Who*, BBC, 26 Dec. 2009. Amazon Prime, https://www.amazon.com/End-of-Time-Part-1/dp/B003LWI7EK/.

"The End of Time: Part Two." *Doctor Who*, BBC, 2 Jan. 2010. Amazon Prime, https://www.amazon.com/End-of-Time-Part-1/dp/B003LWI7EK/.

Freedman, Carl. "Science Fiction and Critical Theory." *Science Fiction Studies* vol. 14, no. 42, 1987, pp. 180.

Geraghty, Lincoln. "From Balaclavas to Jumpsuits: The Multiple Histories and Identities of Doctor Who's Cybermen." *Atlantis, Revista De La Asociacion Espanola De Estudios Anglo-Norteamericanos*, vol. 30, no. 1, 2008, pp. 85–101.

"Jack Harkness." *TARDIS FANDOM powered by Wikia*, http://tardis.wikia.com/wiki/Jack_Harkness.

Jowett, Lorna. *Dancing With the Doctor: Dimensions of Gender in the Doctor Who Universe*. I.B. Tauris, 2017.

"The Lie of the Land." *Doctor Who*, season 10, episode 8, BBC, 3 Jun. 2017. Amazon Prime, https://www.amazon.com/Doctor-Who-Season-10/dp/B06XPTWTGN.

More Than 30 Years in the TARDIS. Directed by Nicholas Courtney, BBC, 1994.

"Pilot." *Doctor Who*, season 10, episode 1, BBC, 15 Apr. 2017. Amazon Prime, https://www.amazon.com/Doctor-Who-Season-10/dp/B06XPTWTGN.

Sullivan, Nikki. *A Critical Introduction to Queer Theory*. New York University Press, 2003.

Villanueva, Michelle. "Doctor Who Season 10: Why It's the Perfect Palate Cleanser for the Current Political Climate." *SYFY Wire*, 5 Jun. 2017. https://www.syfy.com/syfywire/doctor-who-season-10-palate-cleanser-current-political-climate.

Wallace, Richard. "But Doctor?—A Feminist Perspective of Doctor Who." *Ruminations, Peregrinations, and Regenerations: A Critical Approach to Doctor Who*, edited by Christopher J. Hansen, Cambridge Scholars Publishing, 2010. ProQuest Ebook Central, https://ebookcentral.proquest.com/lib/villanova-ebooks/detail.action?docID=1114353.

Walton, Heather. "The Gender of the Cyborg." *Theology and Sexuality*, vol. 10, no. .2, 2004, pp. 33–44.

Wilkins, Alasdair. "Doctor Who returns at long last, and it's got us a brand new companion." *AV/TV Club*, 15 Apr. 2017. https://tv.avclub.com/doctor-who-returns-at-long-last-and-it-s-got-us-a-bran-1798191033.

"World Enough and Time." *Doctor Who*, season 10, episode 11, BBC, 24 Jun. 2017. Amazon Prime, https://www.amazon.com/Doctor-Who-Season-10/dp/B06XPTWTGN.

Girl-Centric Kids

Rebelling Heroines

Hera, Sabine and Ahsoka
in Star Wars: Rebels

STEPHENIE MCGUCKEN

> I want to believe we're doing good, making a difference, but
> sometimes it seems like the harder we fight, the harder
> things get out there. I feel like we can't take down the Empire
> on our own. That's why I need to know this isn't all for noth-
> ing. I need to know that I am not walking into another
> nightmare here.
>   What you need is faith. Faith that there is a long-term
> plan that's bigger than you or me, bigger than Lothal, bigger
> than the entire Outer Rim. Have faith in that and in us....
> We are making a difference, Sabine. And I promise: we won't
> always be fighting this battle alone.
>   —Sabine Wren & Hera Syndulla (*Rebels*,
>   Episode 105: "Out of Darkness")

> This is a new day, a new beginning.
>   —Ahsoka Tano (*Rebels*, Episode 115:
>   "Fire Across the Galaxy")

Fourth wave feminism has been marked by the continuation and elab-
oration of intersectional feminism, a growing deployment of Social Media,
and the questioning of how women can truly promote equality in society for
themselves and their allies, including trans populations and racial minorities.
In her related book, Prudence Chamberlain has noted how the wave, and
feminism more broadly, must look forward as it looks backwards, creating a
"deviant" approach to patriarchal society whose "progress is not only met by
resistance, but also by regression" (47, 49). The quotes above, taken from the
three rebelling heroines of the essay's title, echo parallel worries and hopes

within the *Star Wars* universe at the time of the animated series *Star Wars Rebels* (2014–2018). The series tells the story of teen Jedi-in-training Ezra Bridger after he joins the crew of the ship the *Ghost*, captained by Twi'lek revolutionary Hera Syndulla. The crew also includes Kanan Jarrus, Jedi knight; Garazeb "Zeb" Orrelios, a Lasat Honor Guard; Sabine Wren, a Mandalorian warrior-artist; and the astromech droid Chopper. Throughout the first season the crew make reference to a secret informant, codename Fulcrum, who provides valuable intelligence for the crew and their missions; in the second season Fulcrum is revealed to be Ahsoka Tano, Anakin Skywalker's former Padawan and costar from Lucasfilm's previous *Star Wars* animated series, *The Clone Wars* (2008–2014). The *Rebels* crew are framed as a sort of familial Robin Hood–esque band who work to thwart the Empire. Within the *Star Wars* cinematic universe, *Rebels* begins five years before *A New Hope*; references to familiar characters from the original and prequel trilogies, *The Clone Wars* (2008), and *Rogue One* (2016) were incorporated throughout its four-series run. While *Rebels* follows Ezra's arc as he learns the Force and aids the Rebellion, the show also features three powerful female characters: Hera, Sabine, and Ahsoka. It is their journeys across the show that create the possibility for a discussion around feminism and its current developments toward the fourth wave.

Feminism and the Fourth Wave: Defining the Unknown Future in a Galaxy Far, Far Away

The *Star Wars* cinematic universe has been seen as fertile grounds for discussion of female representation and feminism in science-fiction and fantasy. Countless academics and bloggers alike have dealt with the issues of *Star Wars* and feminism, with recent studies and articles by Valerie Estelle Frankel (2018), Jeffrey Brown (2018), Derek Johnson (2014), Diana Domniquez (2007), and Veronica Wilson (2007), considering aspects of (post)feminism and its intersection with merchandising and character development. Amy Ratcliffe's recent coffee-table encyclopedia *Women in the Galaxy* identifies some seventy-odd female characters from the films, television series, books, and comics.[1] Ratcliffe's book brings female characters to the center of conversation and reveals how these characters have impacted and inspired women, including artists and the actors who bring them to life.

In general, the women prior to those in *Rebels* can be identified with the different waves of feminism, even as they set the stage for the show. For instance, Leia is a product of the second wave in that she is representative of the female who pushes against a male-dominated world, demanding her voice and talents be recognized. She is also the archetype of the universe that combines the stereotypes of female representation into one character. From her role as Princess-diplomat and Princess-warrior in the original trilogy (1977, 1980, and 1983) to her role as Mother-General-Wise Woman in the sequel trilogy (2015, 2017, and 2019), Leia embodies a variety of roles that establish the pattern of *Star Wars* female characters challenging commonly-held assumptions about women in film and society. Importantly, nowhere is she solely an object; rather, she is an active agent.[2] The importance of Leia as a "foundational text" or figure cannot be overstated: each female character in the franchise is compared to her in some way. Moreover, as suggested by Dominquez, Leia is also the fulfillment of Padmé Amidala, her mother, whose story develops in parallel to Anakin Skywalker/Darth Vader in the prequel trilogy (130).

Since Leia is influenced—in creation and reception—by the early waves of feminism, it might be expected that Padmé is illustrative of a more developed feminism. Padmé can be connected to the third wave and postfeminism; the critiques of Padmé as a character can largely be interpreted as pushback against the empowered woman as queen and senator, which parallels what Dominquez identifies as an "unconscious reflection of the vocal and often virulent backlash against feminism" in the United States at the time of the prequel trilogy's release (1999, 2002, and 2005). Moreover, Dominquez has also connected Padmé to rising domestic abuse statistics, which further demonstrates the problematic nature of her characterization and her relationship with Anakin, while also acknowledging that domestic abuse is not simply a feminist issue of the past and can be found at all levels of society, including those who are otherwise privileged in society (Dominquez 124, 129). In the same volume, Wilson argued that Padmé "rediscovered some of her old spirit only to be nearly killed for it in the end," highlighting the ways in which female characters are often silenced or punished for the perceived transgressions against a patriarchal authority (141; see also Tasker 134–141).

That then brings us to fourth wave feminism. Within the cinematic universe, Rey is the most obvious candidate for an ideal fourth wave feminist idol. In the words of Megan Garber, "Rey is a woman who refuses to be defined as one" even as she embodies a moment that "replac[es] feminism-as-a-movement with feminism-as-a-way-of-life." Garber also quotes actress Daisy Ridley, who plays Rey: "She doesn't have to be one thing to embody a woman in a film. It just so happens she's a woman, but she transcends gender" ("*Star Wars*: The Feminism Awakens"). Rey, then, is heralded as a hero whose gender is unimportant to her characterization. If the fourth wave looks to establish femininity as multivalent and more than gender or traditionally gendered roles within society, then Rey's portrayal as a sort of genderless femininity, coupled with her acceptance of different voices (her best friend is, after all, a former stormtrooper) and her commitment to the Resistance's ideas is reflective of fourth wave feminist concerns of inclusivity and globalization. A character such as Rey has been a long time coming in the *Star Wars* cinematic universe, but her development has been foreshadowed within *Star Wars* lore by the women of *Rebels*.

Each of the women in the wider *Star Wars* universe is without a doubt a warrior who thus challenges female representation (see Tasker 14–34 for the ways female warriors do so in different cinematic traditions). Still, throughout the universe, their warrior ethic is tempered by more traditional female roles, including wife and mother. Padmé is critiqued for the way her feminism never manifests (Dominquez 121–128); Leia's struggle to balance motherhood and her role within the New Republic is documented in the larger *Star Wars* canon, including books such as Daniel José Older's *Last Shot*, and hinted at in her estrangement from her son and husband in *The Force Awakens* and *The Last Jedi*. The women of *Rebels* are no different: they might be first and foremost warriors, but they are always something else. More than tempering female ambition, it can be interpreted more feminist-friendly. Women, fourth wave feminists have argued, are something *more* than the roles they inhibit: they are whatever they want to be, and female identities can be multiplicitious. Women can be women, warriors, teachers and professors, executives, mothers, leaders, rebels, and artists, to name a few of the options that we see within the *Star Wars* universe. The women of *Rebels* build on these expectations and the contexts they operate within while reflecting fourth wave feminism's desires to question and problematize the definition of a woman, the roles she is assumed to embody, and the expectations put upon her. No one enforces a *feminine* set of guidelines, for either behavior or dress, on Hera, Ahsoka, or Sabine; no one comments that because they are women, they cannot do something, and anyone who suggests otherwise is soon corrected. Unlike Ahsoka in *The Clone Wars* with her iconic tube top, the women of *Rebels* are never objectified through their clothing. While Ahsoka's costume is similar to that in *The Clone Wars*, it does not show her midriff and is comparatively more reserved, even if it is the most revealing of the three characters' costumes. Hera is most frequently shown in a practical jumpsuit and Sabine wears Mandalorian armor that she has painted. The dress in each case emphasizes individuality, competence, and personality. Moreover, the paring of Hera and Sabine allows them to escape the "one woman in the galaxy" pattern that too often dominates Leia, Padmé, and Ahsoka's stories.

Still, while the women certainly meet fourth wave criteria, they also reflect traditional female roles and suggest an inherent tension in defining female, femininity, and feminism itself. This reflects divisions and important factors in identifying the fourth wave, which is marked by a multiplicity of definitions and contradictions—and a welcoming of them in order to better understand the next steps within the feminist project. Nicola Rivers, acknowledging that "feminism(s) have always been characterized by a degree of internal disagreement and critique," defines the fourth wave broadly as "associated with a surge in online activism and the utilization of new technology, or coupled with an evolving understanding of intersectional feminism" and notes that much of the fourth wave can be found in earlier waves (2, 5). Rivers later expands her definition of the fourth wave to include a "renewed commitment to offline activism" (134). Alison Dahl Crossley argues for a waveless conception of feminism after defining the fourth as similar to the third "but with more emphasis on transgender issues and the value of online feminism" (19, 20). Angela Smith traces its roots to "the use of Web 2.0 as women join up online to raise their voices to campaign for greater equality" (Nally and Smith 1). Ealasaid Munro noted that fourth wave culture "is indicative of the continuing influences of the third wave with its focus on micropolitics and challenging sexism and misogyny insofar as they appear in everyday rhetoric, advertising, film, television and literature, the media and so on."

These definitions of fourth wave feminism, then, can be crystallized for our purposes. The fourth wave is multiplicitious, defined by activism and an online presence, and concerned with the continuation and advancement of concerns of earlier waves and moments in feminism. It also looks to push feminism further, recognizing and addressing intersections of race and class with gender. Fourth wave exemplars promote these ideals in different ways while challenging long-held assumptions about feminism(s), femininity, and gender more broadly; Moreover, fictional fourth wave exemplars in popular culture represent negotiations within feminism rather than proscribed checklists. For instance, the women of *Rebels* seemingly challenge an attempt to define female exemplars as can be done with earlier waves and demand that our assumptions of and expectations for feminist-media be constantly evaluated. Furthermore, *Rebels*, like other *Star Wars* narratives, is basically a journey based on activism and the desire for evoking change—in this case overthrowing a tyrannical government rather than feminist cultural change. Still, a clear overlap appears, including promoting ideologies through media in new ways, amplifying voices traditionally overlooked aiming to promote equality among all groups, and environmental protections.[3]

A further aspect of fourth wave feminism is an enhanced understanding and promotion of ideas related to intersectionality. Intersectionality, at its most basic, is acknowledging the intersections of race, gender, sexuality, and socio-economic status as all forming justification for varying levels of discrimination. Recognizing and promoting minority voices, then, is integral to the fourth wave project. While this has been ascribed to the third wave (see Rivers, Crossley, and Munro) as well, it is the fourth wave that truly raises the awareness and social conscious of the importance of intersectionality. Through online activism, minority voices and the related calls for recognizing how the minority experience is different from the heteronormative white experience are being amplified. Various activist groups, such as Black Lives Matter and the Women's March, are partially products of grassroots intersectional desires to recognize minority voices and concerns on a national platform.

Rebels in its broader narrative mirrors this, seeking to free Lothal while exploring the presumed genocide of the Lasat people, through its survivor, Zeb. While the intersectional moments of *Rebels* are often more problematic than its feminist moments, they acknowledge that activism and struggles against an oppressive government are felt differently by different people—whether male, female, Jedi, Rebel, citizen, or Imperial agent. As Frankel noted for *Rebels,* and is certainly true for intersectional fourth wave feminism, "representation for women merges with representation of people of color" (118). In many ways, *Rebel*'s intersectional voices are often masculine: Zeb, Kallus, Ezra and Kanan play a key role in promoting these ideas in particular despite the actuality of their female counterparts' leadership. At the same time, we see in *The Last Jedi* that the male voice is capable of challenging the female only to realize the errors and be "converted" to the intersectional way of thought, as Admiral Amilyn Holdo teaches Poe Dameron, and Rose Tico teaches Finn. For many fans, these moments echo challenges that women in power and women of color face within society; in fact, this interpretation led to a backlash against the film for being too feminist and too intersectional (see Busch, Hillman, Weekes, and Zakarin).

As with #HeForShe, it is the masculine voice that legitimizes the female struggle: while women can and will acknowledge societal problems, it is not until their voices are collectively heard and authorized by a male counterpart that they are taken seriously. In both the case of *The Last Jedi* and *Rebels*, the masculine bends to support the feminine—or other minority—only after they have experienced a hardship that attunes them to the other perspective (see the Canto Bight narrative in *The Last Jedi*; in *Rebels*, this is evident in the larger story arc between Zeb and Agent Kallus, as well as in Kanan's characterization of Hera's duties, in particular in episode 111, discussed below). For men who do speak to largely feminist and related minority issues they are themselves victimized and feminized (for example, see the responses generated to Terry Crews's outspoken participation in #MeToo and commitment to raising awareness of male sexual harassment and rape on his Twitter—@terrycrews). While this is arguably a setback in fourth wave goals and a problem that deserves more consideration than what can be given here, it is also indicative that fourth wave, intersectional, and social media-backed voices are heard and are challenging the status-quo, testifying to the wave's agency, and ability to bring wider recognition to issues that it wishes to adopt. In terms of *Rebels,* and *Star Wars* more broadly, this reinforces the importance of the work that the storytellers are doing with the universe in order to make it more inclusive, and therefore more feminist-friendly.

Contemporary trends in feminism, witnessed by *Rebels,* then, are by no means perfect, but its imperfections not only further open the discussion on what feminism can achieve in its latest iteration, but also testify to its importance and ability to push boundaries, striving for the larger equality that fourth wave feminism and feminism generally espouses. These imperfections, contradictory definitions, and negotiations of the problematic are seen within individual *Rebels* characters. What follows is a more focused consideration of Hera, Sabine, and Ahsoka in light of the current state of fourth wave feminism and the *Star Wars* universe as it works to keep up with and develop socio-political and cultural trends.

Hera: Warrior Mother

Hera Syndulla is the captain of the *Ghost,* and a key Rebel general. At the outset of the show, Hera is clearly more knowledgeable than the rest of her crew about the Rebel Alliance and its secret workings to draw support in its battle to overthrow the Empire. In the course of the show, we learn that Hera's mother was killed in the Separatist invasion; her father, Cham, is an important freedom fighter on her home planet of Ryloth and wants his daughter to stay and fight within her own system. Hera, then, is a born fighter and Rebel Alliance leader. Further, she is a minority with a planet subjugated by the Empire and as such has a true stake in the conflict.

Throughout the show, the *Ghost* crew is constructed as a family, with Hera as its matriarch. In Episode 202 Hera tells Ezra and Sabine "Alright kids, do Mom and Dad proud," referring to herself and Kanan; in Episode 302 after Sabine returns from reuniting with her biological family, Kanan comments that "the family's together again"; in 411, Hera adds a memento of Kanan to her kalikori (sacred Twi'lek family tree). Thus, Hera, as the crew's leader, is framed as Mother to Kanan's Father. At last, in the show's epilogue in the series finale, she becomes a biological mother to Kanan's son Jacen. The importance of Hera's motherhood is noted by fans in their nickname for her: "Space Mom" (Ratcliffe 77). The question of Hera's feminism is whether her motherhoods undermine her warrior status or promote Hera as the quintessential warrior-mother in the *Star Wars* universe, building on the legacies of Padmé and Leia.

In speaking about Hera, her actress Vanessa Marshall describes her as a mother, but more than just that:

What I love about Hera is that she manages to be very nurturing and kind, and everything we would want in a mother figure, but she's also very fierce and strong, and her talents in the areas of fighting and flying are also very impressive. Not that those things are mutually exclusive, but I think that she has such an elegant combination of those things, that she makes a pretty powerful icon for young women to look up to. I think anyone can draw strength from her [qtd. in Ratcliffe 75].

While Marshall obviously admires Hera's mothering, her desire to acknowledge her skills as a flyer and to note that they are not mutually exclusive reflects a greater societal desire to examine both sides of Hera's characterization—that as pilot/general/warrior and mother—and see how they relate to or contradict one another. That Marshall identifies her as a "powerful icon for young women" based on both of these aspects before acknowledging that *anyone* could see her as a role model prioritizes Hera's appeal to a female audience over a male one, while acknowledging that a male or gender-neutral audience can also identify with her strength.

Such descriptions of Hera fit into Allison Palumbo's framework for understanding fighting females in romantic narratives. Palumbo describes how "fighting female narratives afford contradictory viewing pleasures that reveal both new expectations for and remaining anxieties about the 'strong, independent woman' ideal" and highlights how "certain fighting female romance narratives expand and represent actions of femininity. Being tough, autonomous, intelligent, aggressive, and rational is now more compatible with being vulnerable, emotional, and interdependent" (Palumbo 26, 235). Hera meets all of Palumbo's checklist, and because of her subsequent physical motherhood, creates expectations for female science fiction and popular culture exemplars; yet, in the moments where her place as captain is questioned, contemporary anxieties are also recognized.

Importantly for the conception of fourth wave feminism, the ways these anxieties are handled is equally important. Whenever Hera is challenged, her rightful place as captain is shortly reaffirmed through an active display of bravery, as well as a general eye roll to the person questioning her—even if it is her partner, Kanan. In episode 111 ("Idiot's Aray"), Kanan acknowledges that Hera's "job is harder than it looks" after having stepped in as captain to fulfill their current mission. In 201 ("The Siege of Lothal"), it is Kanan again who tries to overrule Hera's decisions, but eventually submits to her authority while acknowledging the importance of the Rebellion itself. Despite his reservations at times and missteps, Kanan is clearly an appropriate partner for Hera and supports her decisions. Palumbo acknowledges that "for any feminist-friendly romance fantasy to work, the men who love them must prove they can be compatible with such a fierce, powerful, and unafraid agent" (Palumbo 236). Not only is *Rebels* part of the development of fourth wave feminism on screen, then, it is also a witness to the development of fighting multifaceted female characters whose male partners accept both sides of their characterization. The fact that Kanan is not perfect in this acceptance can be taken as an allegory for the unfinished work of feminism—even allies make missteps and can learn from them. For fourth wave feminism, this is important for the online activism which consistently challenges voices who would belittle, override, or otherwise leave out aspects of the feminist project as it stands today, especially regarding intersectional concerns. Kanan serves as a foil to toxic masculinity and masculinity that is threatened by a strong, empowered femininity.

Hera, like the successful Leia, though unlike Padmé, is not punished for her participation in the rebellion through death or the threat of and actuality of rape or sexual harassment, as women are elsewhere in cinema. While she is tortured as part of her capture (episode 410, "Jedi Night"), it is the same treatment that Kanan receives during his capture (episode 114, "Rebel Resolve"); it is also akin to that Han Solo undergoes in *Empire Strikes Back* and Rey in *The Force Awakens*. In her work on cinema in the eighties and nineties and the muscular body, Yvonne Tasker noted that heroes often encounter the threat of physical violence, which, for female characters, "is easily mapped onto the sexualized violence of rape" (Tasker 151). The lack of sexualized physical violence reinforces the idea of the female warrior in *Star Wars* as ubiquitous. Thus, Hera's loss of Kanan is not figured as a punishment, but rather an accepted—and to some degree expected—part of the war. Kanan's sacrifice to save her and the other crew members ultimately allows for their success in this mission, and the wider Rebellion. While the fourth wave, then, seems to promote an outspoken, active heroine, it does not exclude the possibility of physical trials or loss, or indeed the adoption of feminine attributes and actions, but rather welcomes struggle that does not foreground her female body through torture or threats of rape.

Sabine: Warrior Artist

Sabine Wren joined the crew of the *Ghost* after leaving Mandalore; her family, Clan Wren of House Vizla supported the Empire at the start of the series while Sabine embraced the Rebel cause, in part because of her personal experience with the Empire. In descriptions of her both in the show and within wider *Star Wars* and *Rebels* press and literature, she is consistently noted as both ammunitions expert and artist. Her explosives are typically defined by colorful detonations that emit paint to mark the enemy and obscure their vision. Thus, her explosives expertise and artistry go hand-in-hand throughout the series in such a way that they cannot be separated. In one of the junior novelizations of the show, *Sabine's Art Attack*, readers are told that "she loves to paint. She is an artist. She is also a rebel. She fights for what is right" (Heddle and Weisman 2, 3). In both of these instances, it is Sabine's art and her ability to fight against the Empire that define her character. In describing Sabine for *Women of the Galaxy*, Amy Ratcliffe notes that "with freedom of expression at odds with the Empire's vision for the galaxy, Sabine uses her art to make a statement. She's the first character in the *Star Wars* galaxy to rebel through creative means by tagging Imperial outposts with the symbol of the phoenix" (189). Moreover, when there is the opportunity to separate it, the art is rendered in service of her crewmates (including when she decorates Ezra and Zeb's compartment and repeatedly paints Chopper to disguise him on missions) or the wider Rebellion (painting a stolen TIE-fighter, signaling her victory in the theft and the adoption of her phoenix/Rebel symbol). Her art, then, forms a key part of her identity as a warrior. In terms of fourth wave feminism, this serves to highlight how female identities can be manifold and contradictory. An explosives expert might be synonymous with a destructor, but an artist is synonymous with a creator; in Sabine, these two contradictions exist without comment.

While it is tempting to argue that her creativity links her with traditional feminine roles, in episode 401/2, "Heroes of Mandalore," her father comments that her artistic talent comes from him, and her talent for fighting and explosives comes from her mother. Ezra displays surprise at this, informing the audience that his universe holds traditional gender expectations. Further, as in '80s action movies, she is supplanting her father as the local hero, or heroic artist (see Tasker 25). Here, however, the *masculine* trait is her artistic talent, her productive means which proliferate and act as a fertile symbolism that grows alongside the Rebellion. This inversion comments on audience expectations, ultimately forcing them to question their own biases within the *Star Wars* universe and science-fiction genre more broadly.

In the third season, after discovering the Dark Saber, traditionally wielded by the leader of Mandalore, Sabine enlists Kanan and Ezra to help her train with it. During one of their sessions, Kanan forces Sabine to acknowledge why she left her birth family. In an impassioned speech, Sabine declares:

> I left to save everyone. My mother. My father. My brother. Everything I did was for family. For Mandalore. I built weapons. Terrible weapons. But the Empire used them on Mandalore. My friends. My family. People that I knew. They controlled us through fear. Mandalore in fear of weapons I helped create. I helped enslave my people. I wanted to stop it. I had to stop it. I spoke out. I spoke out to save them. To save everyone. But when I did, my family didn't stand with me. They chose the Empire. They left me. Gave me no choice. The Empire wanted to destroy worlds. They did. They destroyed mine [Episode 315, "Trials of the Darksaber"].

Sabine's hurt, her desire to forge a new family with the *Ghost*, and her hesitancy to carry out orders of uncertain impact are revealed as the result of her family's desertion. (In episode 401/2, it is her weapon that threatens to destroy the newly reunited family, highlighting Sabine's horror and guilt over what she has created.) For Sabine, the warrior ethic is not necessarily problematic in and of itself; after all, she uses her expertise for the Rebellion after accepting its importance and ability to do good. Unlike the patriarchal Empire, however, the Rebellion, comparatively feminized, uses her skillset and weaponry to protect her families. In this way, the Rebellion becomes an allegory of fourth wave feminism: it protects and amplifies feminine and minority voices and environmental concerns (as in episode 405, "The Occupation").

In discussing the differences between male and female superheroes created by men, Victoria Ingalls notes that the female superheroes she considered were more likely to be driven to action in order to save a family member, rather than, as male superheroes do, seek revenge and/or advance their own image (214). She concludes that female heroes are often inspired by their family and they "may actually be stronger when working with other family members, and the needs of the family often stimulate the courageous acts of the hero." Sabine, like Hera, is driven by her family, both biological and adopted. After her fleeing her family to protect them, her adopted family inspires her, giving her a mission that eventually allows for her return. Furthermore, Sabine, unlike Inglis's description of male superheroes, is clearly not concerned with her image, prioritizing instead a form of revenge against the Empire closer to activism, to overthrow the status-quo in favor of a more equitable society for both her families.

Sabine challenges expectations and thus fits within the fourth wave model of heroine who successfully juggles her roles while looking forward to enacting widespread change that challenges a patriarchal tyranny. Sabine, like the others considered here, is more than a type deployed to fulfill audience expectations of gendered roles.

Ahsoka: Warrior Wise Woman

Ahsoka Tano is the only female character of *Rebels* whom audiences witness growing from child to mentor across multiple series and media. Ahsoka, like Kanan, also bridges the past from the height of the Jedi Order under the Old Republic to the current Jedi Order, which is all but extinct after Order 66's mass execution of Jedi. Unlike Hera and Sabine whose concerns with family (and art) complement her battle against tyranny, Ahsoka's characterization is more akin to the tradition of the lone wise woman or widow in folklore and literature. To speak of Ahsoka is to queer gender identities in the style of fourth wave feminism, where roles and assumptions are queered to challenge dominant patriarchal constructions. Where not recognized and promoted as queer, such figures are easily claimed by the patriarchy to uphold traditional boundaries.

Ratcliffe describes Ahsoka's journey from Padawan to "a Jedi hero of the Clone Wars, to the Rebel agent Fulcrum, to a wise mentor" (19). As noted, Ahsoka was introduced in *The Clone Wars* as Anakin Skywalker's Padawan. The sharp-tongued talented Jedi-in-training's fanbase grew as her *Clone Wars* narrative became more serious, with her storyline apparently ending after she was framed for the bombing of a Jedi temple, and most of her teachers turned against her (episodes 518–520, *The Clone Wars*). Importantly, Ahsoka *chooses* to leave the Order after Anakin proves that Ahsoka's friend and fellow Padawan Barriss Offee is behind the attack; Ahsoka questions her own confidence in and knowledge of herself because of the Jedi Council's lack of faith in her. The novel *Ahsoka* describes some of her adventures between *The Clone Wars* and *Rebels*, in which she eventually joins the Rebellion in exchange for Senator Bail Organa (Leia's adoptive father) protecting Force-sensitive children in danger from the Empire. In *Rebels*, Ahsoka first appears as the spy Fulcrum; initially, only Hera knows Ahsoka's identity.

Through her role as Fulcrum and her interactions with Ezra and Kanan as a Jedi mentor, Ahsoka becomes a wise woman. Ratcliffe describes Ahsoka as "an enigmatic figure of mystical wisdom" after her reappearance in the finale of *Rebels* (episode 415/16, "Family Reunion and Farewell"), but her wisdom is evident throughout the run of *Rebels*. In discussing the archetype of the mentor, Jung notes that the "old man always appears when the hero is in a hopeless and desperate situation from which only profound reflection or a lucky idea … can extricate him" (Jung 113). Further, Lichtman has argued that the crone—unlike male equivalents—"connects back to the virgin stage as mentor or teach for other young women beginning their own hero cycle" (9). Ahsoka, to borrow Jung's description of the old man, "represents knowledge, reflection, insight, wisdom, cleverness, and intuition … [and demonstrates] goodwill and [a] readiness to help" (Jung 118). As Fulcrum, her knowledge and insight into where the crew are needed is key to the success of the *Ghost*'s missions and development of the Rebellion. Shifting to an active member of the crew, Ahsoka's cleverness and intuition, for which she was noted as a Padawan, ensure the success of the missions. Ahsoka's desire and readiness to help—despite her break with the Jedi Order and Old Republic—reflects her wise womanhood without undermining her past. Importantly, where female Jedi knights and instructors have been comparatively absent in the *Star Wars* canon to date, Ahsoka becomes an important one in a post–Jedi era.

In the second series, Ahsoka confronts her former master, battling Anakin/Vader in the season finale as his perfect nemesis—the former trainee who adored him as a big brother. Though the battle's end goes unseen, Vader appears to kill her, but a final shot that pans from Vader limping from the temple to Ahsoka's owl-like companion, Morai, flying toward a cavern where a figure, remarkably similar to Ahsoka, is shown fading into the shadows. This final moment undermines Ahsoka's apparent death, suggesting she somehow survived the battle. In Episode 413 ("A World Between Worlds"), Ezra accidentally finds a portal that allows him to pull her from the battle, thereby saving her life. These narrative moments bring together different aspects of the wise woman as Ahsoka inhabits her. Shortly after Ezra has saved Ahsoka, Ezra realizes that he could similarly save Kanan and finds a portal to that moment: "If I can change your fate, I can change his." Ahsoka stops him, saying, "Ezra, Kanan gave his life so you could live. If he's taken out of this moment, you will all die. You can't save your master, and I can't save mine. I'm asking you to let go." She has learned for her battle, and now passes on the wisdom to the next generation. Ezra accepts Kanan's death in this moment and proceeds to destroy the temple to protect it and its powers from the Empire. Here, Ahsoka is a bridge between time—not just between the old and new orders—with her timeline jumping as Ezra pulls her through; this betweenness is alluded to in Yoda's earlier appearance in 218 ("Shroud of Darkness") when the old master acknowledges Ahsoka symbolically as part of the Jedi Order in its current state. While Ezra's actions save Ahsoka, she goes off alone after strategizing Ezra's next step, only to once again rejoin the Ghost's community after the Empire has been defeated. Her escape from Vader after Ezra saves her implies new life and new adventures, though the audience is currently left without the knowledge of these; her subsequent return at the end of *Rebels* functions similarly as it is implied that she and Sabine will now bring back Ezra, which has the potential to complete his journey.

Unlike Hera and Sabine who speak to specific moments within fourth wave feminism, Ahsoka queers our understanding of feminist mainstream figures at this moment. With both her constructed families, Jedi and *Ghost* crew, she remains outside yet an accepted part. She also queers time with her appearances and disappearances in ways that question a linear interpretation. In this way, Ahsoka reflects Crossley's conceptions of, and becomes an analogy of, the waveless feminism in how she is both active and seemingly inactive (Crossley 20). Like apparent downturns in feminist mobilizations Crossley identifies as part of the waves, Ahsoka clearly works through these (or despite them), as her novel *Ahsoka* demonstrates, as well as the intelligence she provides throughout *Rebels*. Like the relationships established between feminists and others in these moments, Ahsoka's work lays the foundation for furthering larger goals, and bridges past, present, and future.

164 Section IV: Girl-Centric Kids

Conclusion

What then can we say about *Rebels* as evidence of fourth wave feminism in the *Star Wars* universe? While *Star Wars* fans are certainly familiar with the female warrior through Hera, Leia, Padmé, Rey, and Admiral Holdo, they are tempered through more stereotypical feminine representations of motherhood (Hera, Leia, Padmé), romantic subplots (Hera, Leia, Rey, Padmé), and feminine dress (Leia, Padmé, and Admiral Holdo). Individually the recognizable feminine traits call into question the progressiveness of the roles and the universe more broadly; collectively, however, they demonstrate that traditionally feminine traits do not undermine a character's position or respect within the universe, but can serve to enhance it.

To return to the quotes at the opening of this essay, Sabine and Hera demonstrate the worry that comes with any new moment or movement. Their conversation in "Out of Darkness" could easily represent a discussion on the worries about a successful feminist wave, including whether it is impacting its audiences and supporters in the ways it should. The Rebellion and the surrounding worries as voiced by Hera and Sabine, parallel Chamberlain's comments about feminist waves, nothing that they "exist in a tension of past pessimism and future optimism, with both creating strong affective ties amongst feminist subjects" (189). Past and present, allies and enemies, converge with individual memories, usually traumatic, to create a tension that defines the relationship between Hera and Sabine at this moment. Moreover, Hera and Sabine's ability to juggle roles and responsibilities to biological and constructed families and the Rebellion illustrates larger concerns of contemporary feminism, including whether it is possible to have it all. "I think it's going to be hard to find the family/career balance. I don't know what's looked down on more now, a woman who gives up her career to have a family, or if a woman gives up someone she loves for a career." As Crossley notes, the student has no answer, but can readily vocalize a perceived problem and challenge to feminism as it is understood by the student in that moment (41). Sabine and Hera, especially, offer a positive outlook on such contemporary concerns: there will be loss and difficult choices, but ultimately women can have it all.

Furthermore, Ahsoka, Sabine, and Hera fight for equal rights by protecting those who the Empire targets while embracing their own femininity in different ways. The different feminine voices exist largely in harmony, recognizing the strengths of each as they overcome individual challenges collectively. This teamwork further demonstrates their place among fourth wave feminism's popular culture exemplars.

The characterizations and stories of *Rebels* are an intersectional narrative against a patriarchal regime that seeks to consolidate its own power to the detriment of those it is meant to serve and protect. Throughout *Rebels*, differences are cast aside to achieve common goals. As fourth wave feminism works toward equality, it will encounter similar challenges and obstacles. The show may not be a road map for the fourth wave's success, but it does offer a hopeful vision of what success could look like, while acknowledging ongoing difficulties with achieving equality. Its greater focus on intersectionality, having it all, and activism positions it as a new moment within the history of feminism that requires new characterizations of male and female, as well as the popularization of queer figures. It is, in Ahsoka's words "a new day, a new beginning."

NOTES

1. All of the women identified in the book are considered canon—the Extended Universe's female characters are predictably absent. Work on the differences in portrayal of women prior to Disney's acquisition of Lucasfilm and *Star Wars* and the portrayal in the Disney canon needs to be undertaken to better understand the development of female representation, as well as how Disney has "Princess-ified" female characters, such as Leia and Rey.

2. While some have argued that the slave costume objectifies Leia, her ability to act within it to aid in the plan to rescue Han demonstrates that she is still an active agent, regardless of the objectivity the costume introduces. The balance here between objectified female and active agent is something that is seen throughout the cinematic universe until Rey.

3. For instance, Sabine's art can be paralleled in the history of feminist artistic practise. The "guerrilla" dispatches of the Rebellion share a similarity to not only early feminist zines and other publications, but also to the platforming that occurs at events such as the Women's March and is repeated in videos on social media; both serve to make the goals of the movement readily available to wider audiences through easily-digested and emotive soundbites.

WORKS CITED

Brown, Jeffrey. "#wheresRey: Feminism, Protest, and Merchandising Sexism in Star Wars: The Force Awakens." *Feminist Media Studies*, vol. 18, no. 3, 2018, pp. 335–48.

Busch, Caitlin. "The Best Responses to the Crazy Men-Only Cut of *The Last Jedi*." *SyFy Wire*, 16 Jan. 2018, https://www.syfy.com/syfywire/the-best-responses-to-the-crazy-men-only-cut-of-the-last-jedi.

Chamberlain, Prudence. *The Feminist Fourth Wave: Affective Temporality*. Palgrave Macmillan, 2017.

Cochran, Kira. "The Fourth Wave of Feminism: Meet the Rebel Women." *The Guardian*, 10 Dec. 2013, https://www.theguardian.com/world/2013/dec/10/fourth-wave-feminism-rebel-women.

Crossley, Alison Dahl. *Finding Feminism: Millennial Activists and the Unfinished Gender Revolution*. New York University Press, 2017.

Dominquez, Diana. "Feminism and the Force: Empowerment and Disillusionment in a Galaxy Far, Far Away." *Culture, Identities and Technology in the Star Wars Films: Essays on the Two Trilogies*, edited by Carl Silvio and Tony M. Vinci, McFarland, 2007, pp. 109–33.

Filoni, Dave, Simon Kinberg and Carrie Beck, creators. *Star Wars Rebels*. Lucasfilm Animation, 2014–2018.

Frankel, Valerie Estelle. *Star Wars Meets the Eras of Feminism: Weighing All the Galaxy's Women Great and Small*. Lexington, 2018.

Garber, Megan. "Star Wars: The Feminism Awakens." *The Atlantic*, 19 Dec. 2015, https://www.theatlantic.com/entertainment/archive/2015/12/star-wars-the-feminism-awakens/420843.

Heddle, Jennifer, and Greg Weisman. *Sabine's Art Attack*. LucasFilm Press, 2015.

Hillman, Melissa. "Why So Many Men Hate *The Last Jedi* But Can't Agree on Why." *Bitter Gertrude*, 4 Jan. 2018, https://bittergertrude.com/2018/01/04/why-so-many-men-hate-the-last-jedi-but-cant-agree-on-why.

Ingalls, Victoria. "Sex Differences in the Creation of Fictional Heroes with Particular Emphasis on Female Heroes and Superheroes in Popular Culture: Insights from Evolutionary Psychology." *Review of General Psychology*, vol. 16, no. 2, 2012, pp. 208–21.

Johnson, Derek. "'May the Force Be with Katie': Pink Media Franchising and the Postfeminist Politics of Her Universe." *Feminist Media Studies*, vol. 14, no. 6, 2014, pp. 895–911.

Lichtman, Susan. *The Female Hero in Women's Literature and Poetry.* The Edwin Mellen Press, 1996.

Lucas, George, creator, and Dave Filoni, developer. *Star Wars: The Clone Wars.* Lucasfilm Animation, 2008–2014.

Munro, Ealasaid. "Feminism: A Fourth Wave." *The Political Studies Association: Insight Plus*, 5 Sept. 2013, https://www.psa.ac.uk/insight-plus/feminism-fourth-wave.

Nally, Claire, and Angela Smith. *Twenty-First Century Feminism: Forming and Performing Femininity.* Palgrave Macmillan, 2015.

Palumbo, Allison. *Strong, Independent, and In Love: Fighting Female Fantasies in Popular Culture.* University of Kentucky, 2016, http://dx.doi.org/10.13023/ETD.2016.152.

Ratcliffe, Amy. *Women of the Galaxy.* Chronicle Books, 2018.

Rivers, Nicola. *Postfeminism(s) and the Arrival of the Fourth Wave.* Palgrave Macmillan, 2017.

Schaeffer, Elizabeth, and Kevin Hopps. *Hera's Phantom Flight.* LucasFilm Press, 2015.

Smith, Ann. "A Force for Good: Why *The Last Jedi* Is the Most Triumphantly Feminist Star Wars Movie Yet." *The Guardian*, 18 Dec. 2017, https://www.theguardian.com/film/2017/dec/18/star-wars-the-last-jedi-women-bechdel-test.

Tasker, Yvonne. *Spectacular Bodies: Gender, Genre, and the Action Cinema.* Routledge, 1993.

Tasker, Yvonne, and Diane Negra. "Introduction: Feminist Politics and Postfeminist Culture." *Interrogating Postfeminism: Gender and the Politics of Popular Culture*, Duke UP, 2007, pp. 1–25.

Weekes, Princess. "The Treatment of POC & Women in *The Last Jedi*." *The Mary Sue*, 22 Dec. 2017, https://bittergertrude.com/2018/01/04/why-so-many-men-hate-the-last-jedi-but-cant-agree-on-why/.

Wilson, Veronica A. "Seduced by the Dark Side of the Force: Gender, Sexuality, and Moral Agency in George Lucas's Star Wars Universe." *Culture, Identities and Technology in the Star Wars Films: Essays on the Two Trilogies*, edited by Carl Silvio and Tony M. Vinci, McFarland, 2007, pp. 134–52.

Zakarin, Jordan. "How the Alt-Right and Nostalgic Trolls Hijacked Geek Pop Culture." *SyFy Wire*, 17 Jan. 2018, https://www.syfy.com/syfywire/how-the-alt-right-and-nostalgic-trolls-hijacked-geek-pop-culture?fbclid=IwAR0ngj1zw28vNWgWLFW-wbgTZN-L-vEXZu-IoOOhfscHwV1fIlFifPjdFgM.

DC, *Marvel* and *Star Wars* for Girls

The Transmedia Online Adventures

VALERIE ESTELLE FRANKEL

For decades, parents have known that little boys wanted to be action heroes while little girls wanted to be princesses. Cartoons, films, toy aisles: all pushed this philosophy down to the navy and pink décor. However, the last decade has shaken up the stereotypes with new branding—superheroes just for girls. This is a delightful message, countering the gamergate trolls who insist that girls don't belong in their *Star Wars* and *Ghostbusters* (where they nevertheless are showing up anyway). Several cartoon lines set out to welcome girls into the worlds of superheroes and *Star Wars* ... with cooperative, mostly nonviolent adventures aimed specifically at the newest generation. Unlike in the eighties' *She-Ra: Princess of Power*, no one is hypersexualized, and unlike Barbie, they're not obsessed with fashion and glamor. In fact, the cartoon heroines are capable, clever, ordinary girls who emphasize how much they can share in their franchises even while offering a protective space for the youth. All three series offer gateways to the larger franchises of comics and films for younger fans, even while creating uplifting short stories just for them.

Transmedia Power: DC Super Hero Girls

The transmedia franchise *DC Super Hero Girls* launched in 2015. While DC has always been most famous for Batman and Superman (with Wonder Woman in an arguable third place), this line creates a superhero high school starring only the heroines, intended for an enthusiastic female audience. "It was a full day meeting with reps from Mattel, DC and others involved in the launch of this new universe. I heard of their market research including that they found no gender difference in superhero worship. Girls like 'em as much as boys do. Surprise! Surprise! Not," reports critic Veronica Arreola, on being invited to help with market research. With no Superman, Batman, Green Arrow, or other central superheroes (though with a few boys, like Cyclops and Beast Boy from the *Teen Titans*) the girls are free to excel without competition. The brand appeals to small children six to twelve, but perhaps closer to the younger end, as the episodes are just two to three minutes. The uplifting theme song "Get your Cape On!" instantly captivates.

The franchise quickly spread into novels, picture books, sticker books, comics, clothing, two sizes of action figures, Lego character playsets, and other toys. There are dedicated Twitter, Facebook, and Instagram accounts too. The cellphone app boasts, "Play mini-games with your favorite Super Heroes, unlock action-packed photo filters, and explore Super Hero High." Creator Diane Nelson gives a perfectly polished soundbite, saying:

> My leadership team has a strong and active goal: to create diversity by making sure that we have a diverse staff and content that is diverse. In the last few years, girl empowerment has come to the fore, and the consumer products department saw this opportunity. We have strong female characters in the DC universe, and decided that creating a program around female teenage super heroes could give young girls role models they've never had before [Eng].

As Nelson adds, "The characters wear practical uniforms instead of swimsuits and high heels. We have 12-inch action dolls and 6-inch action figures. There's a great Wonder Woman shield, capes that appeal to younger girls, and novels that appeal to older girls" (Eng). Arreola adds that the action figures were quite appropriate:

> The action figures stand on their own. Christine Kim, the lead designer, said she made sure that the dolls could stand on their own. After a false start on the dolls, she told her team to use photos of athletes and dancers as models. This is why these dolls have muscle tone. Sure the legs are longer than this short lady would want, but I was told it's about the fact the dolls have a lot of joints so they can be posed in many different positions.

In episode one, Wonder Woman, the new kid, tours the school and meets the teachers including Principal Amanda Waller. However, she's assigned the incredibly irritating Harley Quinn as her roommate. This Harley is an irritating prankster but not a wicked person. Jennifer Kluska, the franchise director, adds: "Harley loves very hard and she loves her friend Barbara and she makes bad choices for love … but there's good in her" (Knight et al.).

> We saw a clip from the cartoon where Harley Quinn is so excited to have Wonder Woman as a roomie that Wonder Woman is annoyed to death. We've all been there

right? We pull back and the annoying friend walks away. I've also been that annoying friend and it feels terrible. Wonder Woman realizes that Harley is just excited and goes over to hang out with her. It was a sweet moment. And while not all depictions of superheroes shows the villain getting killed, they rarely turn the villain into a superhero. Maybe, just maybe this cartoon will give boys an image that not all "bad guys" are bad, but are people who do bad things. I know, it's a lot to expect from a cartoon and a plastic doll [Arreola].

Each mini episode features a new challenge, from P.E. to exams, all presented sympathetically. Super Hero High School has clubs like Playing with Poisons, Cooking with Swords, and Knitting and Hitting. The classes include Flyers' Ed, Weaponomics, Heroes through History, and costume design. P.E. involves tossing trucks, running a fifty-mile obstacle course, and swimming with hungry sea serpents (Yee, *Wonder Woman* 115). The girls have food fights, pie-eating contests, and plenty of pranks even as they gush about smoothies and their favorite bands. Dating and flirting are at a minimum. Still, in *Finals Crisis,* Wonder Woman rescues cute smoothie barista Steve Trevor, who babbles, "I'm always falling for you. I mean, you're always catching me." While she takes on the villain, he stands there and cheers. Clearly, traditional gender roles have been tipped out the window.

Lauren Faust, the show's executive producer, worked on *My Little Pony* and *The Powerpuff Girls.* For too many shows, she remarked at a Comic-Con panel: "It's not about entertaining or inspiring little girls—it's about telling them how to behave." She prefers to tell a good story. As she explains, "If it's good anybody will watch it. No pun intended, we're not pulling any punches" (Knight et al.). Stories often end without much resolution, though the central figures model positive qualities such as resourcefulness and determination, with friendship the central theme. Occasionally the girls (especially the villainesses like Harley Quinn) try to undermine their classmates' hard work and act generally spiteful. Still, there's a major emphasis on making friends and seeking help from one's peers. Several episodes focus on the "Hero of the Month"—for each, their friends are asked to give quotes in an example of solidarity and friendship. There's a strong emphasis on turning villains into friends. As one Arreola suggests, "Boys are much more likely to want the bad guy to die or be locked up, while girls want the superhero to talk some sense in the villain and convert them into a hero."

The episodes' presence on the internet reaches out to the new market there—since the episodes are available on YouTube, they have a very egalitarian reach. On Twitter, fans of all ages use the hashtag #dcsuperherogirls or #DCSHG to post fan art and memes. With this, they claim and repurpose the series for themselves—a huge innovation that's marked all levels of internet fandom. Meanwhile, #DCSHGBookClub encourages interaction and discussion with the novels. Because of their expansion on the original stories, the longer works especially explore multiculturalism, like Bumblebee's inter-actions with her loving family or Katana's Japanese background as her sword is left to her by her superheroic grandmother. The author, Lisa Yee, explains:

> We know who they are, but don't know why they are. When writing Katana's story I wanted to explore how her ancestors and culture led her to be the superhero she is today. Like so many of us, Katana as a teen was unaware of her family history. I decided that her grandmother's secret would be that she was the world's first female samurai superhero. To research, I visited the Samurai museum in Tokyo and even took ninja lessons to learn how to fight and use swords. I also wove haiku riddles into the novel and ancient legends to enrich the story and to reflect on Katana's character and her journey.

With this, Yee invited young readers into Japanese culture, expanding their awareness of the larger world.

Season 2 features the next fish out of water, Supergirl, coming to the school. She's incredibly powered but clumsy and lacks training. At least she's used to American culture, while Wonder Woman the perfect Amazon has a harder time fitting in. Supergirl's problem is the legacy of Superman, the school's "most famous student." "Superman's famous. Supergirl has the same powers but no one's heard of her and if you were a teenage girl, how would you feel?" asks Faust (Knight et al.). The stories offer sympathy and support for girls dealing with excelling in men's shadows, though they encourage independence more than outright rebellion.

Season 3 features Batgirl, who makes herself a hero without powers. Though she's not a student or Batman's protégé, Barbara Gordon is a gifted inventor with her BAT gadgets—Barbara Assisted Tech. In fact, she loves bats because they "use the talents they have," turning their blindness into a strength with echolocation, an excellent lesson for young fans (Yee, *Supergirl* 150). Their Weaponomics teacher, meanwhile, emphasizes that "there was a time in the history of super heroes when one needed to have special pow-ers—but that's not so anymore" (Yee, *Batgirl* 108). As he teaches the girls that their most powerful weapon is "your brain and your ability to access it to its fullest" (Yee, *Batgirl* 109), the story emphasizes the Batgirl model of heroism without powers. A few novels later, Bumblebee succeeds Batgirl as another tech genius, building her own shrinking and flying suit—with strength and sonic blasters. At the climax of her novel, she realizes she needn't rely on the technology. "All this time when I thought I didn't have any power, I was wrong. It was always there, whether or not my battery pack was working," she decides (Yee, *Bumblebee* 185). She adds that the real power is in her head.

The first three novels parallel these three seasons, while the next three star Bumblebee, Katana, and Harley Quinn—four white heroines and two of color, while the white heroines lead most episodes and stand centrally in the pictures on products, much like the Disney Princess line. It's not perfect representation, but there's some. Season 4 begins with Jessica Cruz chosen as Earth's new Green Lantern. The characters fall into high school archetypes: Green Lantern is the activist. Catwoman is the shoplifter. Zatanna is the showoff. Giganta is the bully. "Harley is that girl—every school has one—and she's going to juvie" (Knight et al.). Bumblebee is the rookie. "As a teenager, she's the nobody" so she creates her special scent to get noticed (Knight et al.).

The 2017 DVD film *Intergalactic Games* challenges the young heroines on a more personal level, as Starfire's snobby sister Blackfire and Big Barda's former sisterhood show up to compete with them. Their arrival hints at a more global (or rather universal and multiversal) community, sympathizing with the exchange students' foreign perspectives. As the story continues, Lena Luthor, the neglected IT girl, attacks the entire competition in a super-powered suit complete with kryptonite. Empathetically, Wonder Woman talks her down though she fails to make the other woman turn good. Further, Wonder Woman and Supergirl each rescue Steve Trevor, flipping the gender roles.

Just like the MCU, Harry Potter, or any of these ever-widening brands, these giant franchises make enormous amounts of money as they spread to videogames, clothes, snacks and new products. An article from *License! Global* noted that while *Thor* (2011) made an impressive $1.5 billion in ticket sales, the profits from related merchandise were far higher: "On the licensing side of the business, the Marvel franchises represent $6 billion in retail sales of licensed merchandise worldwide in 2011" (qtd. in Brown 22). As *DC Super Hero Girls* adds birthday party themes and Legos to the mix, they're likewise snowballing. Aaron Taylor argues: "These contemporary blockbusters exemplify the new industrial logic of transmedia franchises—serially produced films with a shared diegetic universe that can extend within and beyond the cinematic medium into correlated media texts" (qtd. in Brown 22).

Lego DC Super Hero Girls: Brain Drain (animated and direct-to-video) showed a new avenue for adaptation and marketing as the two franchises combine. This one stars Wonder Woman, Supergirl and Batgirl (yet again). Bumblebee and Katana attack, and the three central white heroines are problematically pitted against the two heroines of color. They wake the next morning discovering they've lost an entire day, while Bumblebee and Katana appear to be working for Lena Luthor and Eclipso. The three girls investigate and discover an evil plot of mind control and magic. In a twist, Eclipso drains Wonder Woman's and Supergirl's powers, but the pair realize that Batgirl's inventing brain and hacking abilities still remain. "The only way we're most likely to succeed is by working together," Batgirl pronounces loyally. They do so and finally save the day.

Intersectionality in the superhero world not only considers issues of race and socioeconomic status but labeling. *Lego DC Super Hero Girls: Super-Villain High* follows on and addresses the underlying conflict of the heroes and villains being mixed up together as the villains are encouraged to find a new school. Lena Luthor frames the villainesses Harley Quinn, Frost, Catwoman, Poison Ivy and Cheetah to encourage them to quit. Even as the central heroines quest to clear their friends (and Bumblebee and Katana engage in a friendly competition rather distant from the main plot), the villainesses get together to stew over their discomfort. "At Uber High, they're all about letting you be you," Lena Luthor promises, disguised as the girls' new peer Divide. However, Lena uses her new school to get the students to commit crimes. Though Uber High offers a constant dance party, most of the girls miss their old school. Batgirl finally gives Catwoman a speech about how the villains challenge her and her friends to do better. "You girls make us better heroes. We don't just respect you—we need you." Eventually, the villain girls choose their friends and turn on Lena. In a massive team, they face down Lena and her giant robot armor to save the day with cool vehicles of their own (since it's a Lego story after all). "Who needs superpowers when you have these," Frost quips. Coach Wildcat wraps up the show with the admission that "while competition is important, it's not as important as working together." This is typical of the stories—emphasizing turning bullies and mild villainesses into friends with compassion and grace. As such, these modestly dressed friendly heroines provide strong models of cooperation.

At last, *DC Super Hero Girls* went on to Cartoon Network to reboot with more of an anime style, reaching out to a new audience. In the first episode, a reporter notes, "Metropolis is still in need of super-help." Wonder Woman promptly shows up to save the day. Barbara (Batgirl), meanwhile, is off to Metropolis High, over her frantic protests at starting at a new school, where she must presumably leave superheroism and her old friends like Harley Quinn behind. However, Kara (Supergirl) is sent there too to help with her "impulse control." Bumblebee, Zatanna, and Green Lantern show up, and a superhero lineup is all ready to go. After the obligatory superhero battle (in this case a food fight), the heroines find commonality. As they take Wonder Woman shopping and show her how to be a typical teen (phones, ice cream, burritos, movies, and amusement parks), they celebrate the high school experience while enjoying their differences. The new format includes both full episodes and tiny shorts to appeal to different audiences. Meanwhile, all the episode titles are styled as social media hashtags preparing in advance for the episodes to be discussed online with fan art and media. It's a new era, and the show is taking full advantage.

Star Wars' *Girl Line*—Forces of Destiny

This Marvel model, adapted from its comic book origins, of branding an entire universe as a related franchise, has proven incredibly profitable and Disney has stated their desire to replicate it with the Star Wars universe that it purchased from George Lucas in 2012 for $4 billion. Taking note of Disney's success with the Marvel Cinematic Universe, the other Big Six media corporations are striving to expand their properties into entire universes. J.K. Rowling and Time-Warner are expanding the Harry Potter universe through prequels and spin-offs, NBC Universal is updating and extending its classic horror properties into a Monster Universe, and Viacom's Paramount has plans to develop a larger and more cohesive Transformers Universe. Most importantly. Time-Warner has moved to mimic Marvel's success integrating their multiple DC Comics properties into a unified DC Extended Universe [Brown 22–23].

Following the Disney buy-out and release of *Star Wars: The Force Awakens*, the new era reached out to girls. In fact, echoing the *DC Super Hero Girls* model, *Star Wars Forces of Destiny* short cartoons are centered around *Star Wars'* various heroines: Jyn, Rey, Leia, and Padmé, but also the heroines of the children's shows *Clone Wars* and *Rebels*. "We're telling stories from all eras," senior editor Denton J. Tipton added. "There's original trilogy, there's prequels, there's sequels, *Clone Wars, Rebels*. We're doing it all" ("NYCC").

Also in the tradition of *DC Super Hero Girls,* the show was comprised of two- or three- minute shorts released online, accompanied by two sizes of posable action figures, plastic weapons, and several age levels of books and comics. Hasbro even gave every doll an action move: squeezing the legs makes Leia ready her blaster or Rey swing her lightsaber. Ashley Eckstein (the voice of *Clone Wars* teen Jedi Ahsoka Tano) explained, "I loved the Disney princess movies growing up, but that's not who I wanted to be. I wanted to be the Jedi. I wanted to play with the boys and use the lightsaber. There are a lot of girls who would prefer to carry around a lightsaber than wear a tiara." At last, there are products marketed for them.

Two releases of cartoon runs, each eight mini episodes, premiered on Disney's YouTube channel on July 3, 2017. Maz Kanata, Rey's mentor in *Force Awakens* and the first wise crone of the *Star Wars* universe, introduces all the episodes with a quick and simple "The choices we make, the actions we take, moments both big and small, shape us into forces of destiny." Most of the original actresses reprise their roles, from the *Clone Wars* and *Rebels* stars to Felicity Jones and Daisy Ridley from the films. Rostislav Kurka writes in "*Forces of Destiny* Review: What Is Its Value?": "Episodes are exactly the right length that parents can let their little daughters (or sons) watch it as part of their *Star Wars* education. The appeal at young audience as the target group is obvious, starting with the style, through the fairly straightforward plots,

74

174   Section IV: Girl-Centric Kids

the 'right' mixture of characters being 'cool' and some cute elements" (Kurka). Marissa Martinelli of *Slate* notes how it ties into the larger universe as "a midyear snack designed to keep *Star Wars* fans sated between the franchise's feature-film releases."

The art is softer and more approachable than that of the mainstream shows, tying it closer to its Disney creators. In fact, the art has "a less stylized, more cartoon-y look than that of the Genndy Tartakovsky *Clone Wars* series," as Martinelli decides. "But what makes *Forces of Destiny* truly unusual for Disney-era *Star Wars* is the way it leans into that childishness." The shows are light, fun, mostly nonviolent adventures with clear lessons for young viewers. "I could actually see *Forces of Destiny* being a vanguard to some actual Disney Star Wars Princess movie," Kurka concludes.

The plots stress cooperation, cleverness, and kindness. Most are set in tiny in-between moments, giving Rey and BB-8 an adventure on Jakku or Leia more time with the Ewoks. "Of course, in three minutes, you don't have enough time to explore deep, intellectually rich themes of the SW universe. The connection to the lore is enough, however—we see shapeshifter assassins on Coruscant, we see the bounty hunter droid IG-88 (who appears in *The Empire Strikes Back* and has even much richer record of extra-canon appearances), we see Wampas or denizens of Jakku" (Kurka). On Hoth, Leia and R2-D2 go hunting Chewie, who's vanished (in a cut subplot from *Empire*). As it happens, a wampa has adopted him, and Leia must hypnotize it with her lantern so they can get away. With this, she models teamwork, courage and ingenuity. Martinelli explains:

> These vignettes don't offer any major revelations for fans, unless you've spent the past three decades lying awake at night wondering where Leia managed to find a human-sized dress in the middle of the forest in *Return of the Jedi* [The answer: Ewoks are apparently very speedy tailors.] Because the shorts mostly act as prequels to or "deleted scenes" from the movies and television series, you won't find clues about Rey's identity or the fate of Ahsoka Tano here—nor, sadly, any long, choreographed lightsaber battles. Instead, the self-contained stories tell side adventures that we didn't get to see in the movies, while delivering some basic life lessons along the way: Help those in need. Be kind to others. Fight for what you believe is right.

On another inserted backstory adventure, Padmé and Ahsoka (Anakin's trainee and partner through the show *Clone Wars*) hold a diplomatic event but must protect each other with chairs and vases when a bounty hunter attacks. In another episode, Sabine from *Rebels* persuades her former best friend Ketsu to leave the criminal organization Black Sun and join the Rebellion. This is prompted by their team-ups in which they save a koala-like Chadra-Fan child from Imperials and steal crates of food for the Rebels. Caring for the oppressed and starving thus is featured. The stories don't stress difference, but they do teach viewers to protect those in danger, even at serious risk to oneself. Queen Amidala spends one episode aiding an apparent sea monster who actually is in distress because its child is lost. Likewise, "Bounty of Trouble" shows young Leia playing both sides and pretending to cooperate with Stormtroopers while sneaking intelligence to the Rebel Alliance. After their partnership, Sabine tells Leia, "You keep fighting on the inside. I'll keep fighting on the outside," modeling their different paths to power. Of course, these small plots emphasize that girls can have their own adventures in the *Star Wars* universe. The episodes are tiny and juvenile, but that's their intent: "Adults are not the target demographic for *Forces of Destiny*, which sets it apart from previous, more sophisticated animated *Star Wars* series. The *Forces of Destiny* shorts stick to simple messages, uncomplicated humor, and easily solvable problems" (Martinelli).

Emma Carlson Berne's *Forces of Destiny* books are about a hundred pages with three stories each. As with *DC Super Hero Girls*, the stories adapt the episodes, only longer. The stories are framed by Maz, once again, who invites the reader to sit and join her for tea. In the first volume, she emphasizes the lesson of each tale, and their collective point that "being a hero means ... stepping forward. No matter the outcome" (119). "Thank you for listening to my stories, my friend" she concludes sweetly and tranquilly (119). Here, some of the language choices in the six heroines' stories is especially nice: Leia's helping with the early rebellion is framed as a metaphor for childhood: Maz the narrator explains, "If you are something very small fighting against something very big, finding a good place to hide is important." This is clever and also encourages young fans to relate to Leia's abstract rebellion. "I wonder if you have ever felt like Sabine?" in the next story is less subtle. Each story has a blatantly spelled-out moral, as Maz explains, "Heroes like Padmé often try to carry the weight of the galaxy on their shoulders. But a galaxy is much easier to carry when you have a friend to help you do the lifting" (Schaefer).

Of course, if readers weren't frustrated by reading the same stories, they might have been more so when the 2017 holiday gift book of the *Forces of Destiny: Tales of Hope & Courage Replica Journal* was released. By Elizabeth Schaefer with art by Adam Devaney, it's quite pretty, with the characters' written comments and drawings included in the journal. However, once again, it retells the same stories from the cartoons and books, in the lazy side of transmedia.

Volume two, released in October and November 2017, offers another tiny eight cartoon episodes. More missing scenes from the films appear as Rey and Han fly together before reaching Maz's planet. These fun bits of trivia often don't give the characters much time to stand out. "Objectively, did we need such scenes? No. But they are not entirely without value, either. Think of them as of a DVD bonus" (Kurka 2017). Leia and Hera team up in one, delighting fans as the live and cartoon series were bridged at last. Kurka explains, "The chief value of these scenes [is] that they establish or expand existing relationships. Rey and BB-8, Leia and Ahsoka, even Leia and Sabine (these two have practically zero interaction just on their own apart from this). We, as the audience, can get better sense of what do these characters mean to each other." Likewise, when Jyn sees a fleeing Sabine and helps her escape Imperials in "Accidental Allies" (113), Sabine compares how they've each chosen to rebel against Imperials, noting sympathetically, "I used to work alone too. But these days I can't just think about myself." Jyn is persuaded by her friendly lack of judgment.

"Traps and Tribulations" (214) shows the giant beast for which the Ewoks were setting the meat snare in *Return of the Jedi*, while also teaming up Leia with Hera on Endor. This redefines canon, merging the shows, but fans got a bigger surprise with another team-up: In her own story, little Ahsoka reveals that she knows Padmé and Anakin are a couple when she catches the pair embracing in "Unexpected Company" (202). Back home, Anakin tells Ahsoka he's glad she came. Padmé privately tells her, "You and Anakin make a good team."

"Thanks.... I could say the same of you." Padmé quietly thanks her, sharing the secret between the two of them. Still, while the women are always presented as strong, clever, and capable, they don't always get perfect respect. In "An Imperial Feast" (114), Leia discovers Han and Chewie on Endor snickering and preparing to watch the Ewoks eat the Stormtroopers.

> As Leia upbraids them and they smirk, the audience has more sympathy for the men than their chiding mother figure. Meanwhile, Hera (charmingly established in this scene as still alive and part of the Rebels after the Battle of Endor) only agrees to send over rations if Han admits the Ghost outshines the Falcon. Thus, she joins in on the silly macho posturing, while Leia bosses everyone around as the adult. Everyone's gender roles are thus problematic here [Frankel].

Another issue is the lack of intersectionality, or even minority issues in *Star Wars*. True, the universe appears post-racial among humans of color, but most humans are privileged colonizers while Wookies are enslaved and Hera's people the Twi'lek have been conquered by the Empire. Still, neither Chewie nor Hera brings up these issues on a personal level (though they do in the original *Rebels* show, films, and novels). Ahsoka the Togruta is even more problematic as in six seasons of *Clone Wars* she almost never performs rituals of her people or meets with them, instead recreating herself as a perfectly assimilated Jedi. Meanwhile, those who are less fortunate appear in *Forces of Destiny* as background alien children or lost animals, whom the heroes generously help while the show keeps them cute and very impersonal. This is a flawed model as it's kindly charity but not friendship or respect between equals.

The exploited minority who is in fact angry enough to fight for her rights with every line is L3-37, the rebellious droid of the 2018 film *Solo.* Memorably, she responds to Lando's "You need anything?" with "Equal rights." Sassy and assertive, she wants to be treated decently, not dismembered or enslaved as space junk. "And, sadly, that resonates in 2018, when too many people—and one person alone would be too many—are feeling emboldened to treat others as lesser-than, whether it's because of their gender, race, ethnicity or immigrant status," notes Julie Hinds in her admiring newspaper review. Hinds concludes, "L3 is a freedom fighter, just like any ordinary person who's speaking out these days against actions and beliefs that just aren't right. In short, her feminist credentials are impeccable, as are her humanitarian ones. So when's her spin-off movie?" Not in *Forces of Destiny,* though this might have provided an ideal vehicle. She is not included, leaving the heroines sweet and helpful but failing to demand an end to exploitation.

Season 2 (released March 19, 2018, and May 4, 2018) brought more new adventures with the *Last Jedi* stars' voice talents: Mark Hamill (Luke), Daisy Ridley (Rey), John Boyega (Finn), Lupita Nyong'o (Maz), and Kelly Marie Tran (Rose). The *Clone Wars* and *Rebels* stars also returned: Tiya Sircar (Sabine), Ashley Eckstein (Ahsoka), Vanessa Marshall (Hera), Catherine Taber (Padmé) and Matt Lanter (Anakin), among others. It tied in heavily to *Last Jedi,* following Rose and Finn's trip to Canto Bright and giving them a space jellyfish encounter. The adored "Porg Problems" (208) has Rey playing with the porgs on Luke Skywalker's island when one steals her lightsaber. She freezes the bird in place in midair to reclaim it, while the porgs are delighted with the chance to become airborne. Chewie has his own encounter with the porgs as they tear up his ship for nesting materials, and he too must learn to compromise.

Many scenes tie the generations of *Star Wars* together. Chewie introduces Leia to Maz before *Return of the Jedi* in "Bounty Hunted" (206), to get help freeing Han from the Carbonite. Maz suggests Leia keep the bounty hunter outfit she's acquired and even approves the match. "I like this one, Chewie. Tell Han she's a keeper," she smiles, while mentoring Leia a generation before Rey. Yoda and Luke add a bit more to their training scene from *Empire Strikes Back,* while Ahsoka trains the characters of *Star Wars: Rebels,* tying her series to theirs. The show was capped off with a Solo tie-in, as Qi'ra's three-year gap is covered in "Triplecross," in which she outwits an assassin droid and the *Clone Wars* pirate Hondo Ohnaka. Certainly, these little moments promote and support the films, but they also invite young girls to enjoy them, emphasizing how much they're welcome in the franchise.

January 2018 added five comic books from IDW to the lineup, finally with three original adventures; these were titled *Princess Leia, Rey, Hera, Ahsoka & Padmé,* and *Rose & Paige.* Girly, rather pastel art once again reaches out to female readers. "The good thing about these *Star Wars* books is that they're all-ages, but they're not just for kids," comic book writer Elsa Charretier said ("NYCC"). Rey's and Ahsoka & Padmé's stories are adapted from the BB-8 adventure and dinner party, true, but the others offer longer, deeper insights into the characters. In a story penciled by Eva Widermann, Leia and Han not only team up on Hoth but ride with Hera, showing off a loyal partnership between characters and franchises. Hera teaches Leia that she must work with the Tauntaun instead of having a battle of wills with it—hilarious since the Tauntaun works as a metaphor for Han. In Hera's comic, she's traveling without her usual five-person team and even her ship. Still, she's formidable. Writer Devin Grayson explains:

> I'm glad we went with Hera the Leader, because it feels very timely to me. What better question right now than how do you inspire people to action when they're already feeling overwhelmed with the daily struggle of existence: their families and their communities and their jobs? How do you recognize when it's necessary to fight back and what are some ways you can do that without putting everything you love at even greater risk? Hera's someone who can answer those kinds of questions. She understands that to motivate people, you have to see both what they're capable of in that particular moment of time, and also what they have the potential to achieve down the line. I wanted to try to show what that might look like [Baver, "Raising a Rebellion"].

The "Rose & Paige" comic gave the sisters time together, something they'd received in an expanded universe novel and journal but not in the film. "This will be coming out right after [the film], so it will kind of get more into their backstories, so you can learn more about those characters," senior editor Denton J. Tipton says ("NYCC"). Writer Delilah S. Dawson comments, "To me, they're the heart of what the Resistance means: ordinary people willing to make sacrifices in the hopes that other people and planets won't have to suffer" (Baver, "They're the Heart"). The pair explore D'Qur (the world the Resistance evacuates from at the start of *Last Jedi*), while Paige sticks up for her shyer sister, insisting that the younger woman present her idea. General Leia receives it supportively and encourages Rose to use her engineering genius and build them wheeled vehicles. The older man Lazslo objects, but Leia overrides him, insisting, "Every idea has merit." Even as Rose tries to conquer her shyness, Leia and Paige continue to support her. Dawson adds: "In both of my Rose and Paige stories, I wanted to give Rose moments where she had an idea, doubted herself, was emboldened by Paige, failed a little, kept going, and ultimately succeeded. That, to me, gave her context for her increased confidence and strength in *The Last Jedi*" (Baver, "They're the Heart").

On the planet, Rose bravely tracks down her lost sister with the aid of silly-looking long-necked birds. Paige insists, "You're a genius, Rose. If anyone can get me out, it's you." Rose build a pulley and the girls ride the birds to safety, discovering many planetary resources on their way home. Meanwhile the sisters get to joke and goof around together. Nicoletta Baldari, the comic's artist, also worked on *Frozen* and explains, "…so knowing quite well the connection between Anna and Elsa has helped me a lot!" (Baver, "They're the Heart"). Baldari adds, "I thought, Rose and Paige have fun together, so they had to be funny, but at the same time they are Resistance girls, so they also had to have some pathos on display! So I focused on their actions" (Baver, "They're the Heart"). Dawson concludes, "Their love for one another and their drive to do what's right are definitely a chord they share" (Baver, "They're the Heart"). Their team-up is the perfect girl-power adventure: funny, charming, loving, and enduringly brave.

The Teen Adventure: Marvel Rising

"When Marvel first announced *Marvel Rising*, its new foray into animation, it looked to deliver something largely missing from the big-screen MCU: a focus on the comic publisher's younger crop of heroes, especially the women and people of color mostly relegated to sidekick status when it comes to the live-action films" (McLevy). Marvel's new diverse line had introduced many beloved characters, especially women, people of color, and queered characters, but these were slow to arrive on the big screen.

Miles Morales, the Afro-Latino Spider-Man invented in 2011, got a film in 2018 as *Spiderman: Into the Spider-verse* (alongside the comics' Spider-Gwen). 2017 featured the new female Wolverine, inheriting the role in *Logan*. Captain Marvel from 2012 arrived as the MCU's first central superheroine in 2019. However, this left many of the rest of the new lineup still unfeatured. Top fan favorites included Kamala Kahn, a Pakistani American teen, who took on the Ms. Marvel mantle in 2014. There was also The Unbeatable Squirrel Girl, invented as a joke in 1991 but given her own very assertive series in 2015. The subsequent relaunch, titled the *All-New, All-Different Marvel* (2015–2019) allowed the Squirrel Girl creators to brag they were getting two issue #1's in a year.

Among the new comics were *Spider-Gwen*, Thor's sister *Angela Queen of Hel, Captain Marvel, The Unbelievable Gwenpool, Patsy Walker A.K.A Hellcat* (herself a character on Netflix's *Marvel's Jessica Jones*), *Uncanny Inhumans, All-New Hawkeye* (Kate Bishop), *Mockingbird* (now a proud biologist-warrior saving male heroes bound captive in their underwear), *Spider-Woman* (reinvented as a single mother) and *All-New Wolverine* (Laura Kinney). *A-Force* produced a second volume, now an all-superheroine team on earth instead of Battleworld. *The Ultimates* relaunched with Black Panther, Blue Marvel,

Spectrum, America Chavez, and Captain Marvel. Likewise, Iron Man formed a new team of Avengers in the *All-New All-Different Avengers* series consisting of himself, the Vision, Nova (Sam Alexander), Ms. Marvel, Spider-Man (Miles Morales), Captain America (Sam Wilson), and Thor (Jane Foster). Along with several *X-Men* lines, *The Champions* launched as well, starring Ms. Marvel, Nova, Spider-Man (Miles Morales), Hulk (Amadeus Cho), Viv Vision and a teen version of Cyclops. The Champions are very modern teens, not only texting each other, but spending their collections running on the public approval of their internet fans. They mobilize their web presence through tweets and online videos to gain popularity … though they discover to their disgust that their logo has been copyrighted by someone else. The heroes are most excited to discover Viv generates wifi. As such, they're fun models in which young readers see themselves reflected. In the third volume, *Champion for a Day,* they team up with Rayshaun Lucas as Patriot, Falcon's protégé. Likewise, Nova recommends his girlfriend from another dimension, Spider-Gwen.

These new heroes—Ms. Marvel, Squirrel Girl, Spider-Gwen, America Chavez, Patriot, and Inferno (Dante Pertuz) from *Uncanny Inhumans*—debuted in a cartoon show aimed at children. Daisy Johnson (S.H.I.E.L.D. agent and Inhuman known as Quake) joined the team, played by Chloe Bennet, who also plays her on *Agents of S.H.I.E.L.D.* (2013—present). This ties the series into the larger MCU. There are no white men in the lineup and only two characters out of seven are white women (and both are part-animal mutants for a new type of minority). The franchise, *Marvel Rising,* was launched with a series of comic books, beginning in April 2018. Six four-minute shorts, titled *Marvel Rising: Initiation,* were released before the first television film, *Marvel Rising: Secret Warriors,* premiered on September 30, 2018, simultaneously on Disney Channel and Disney XD. On August 23, 2018, the film's theme song, "Born Ready," was released on Disney Records' YouTube channel.

The comic by Devin Grayson, Ryan North (of *The Unbeatable Squirrel Girl*) and G. Willow Wilson (of *Ms. Marvel*) flashes back to Squirrel Girl and Ms. Marvel's first meeting. A.I.M. goons attack, and Doreen Green breaks off teaching computer science to rush off and change. Kamala, her student, does likewise. As Squirrel Girl soars in and Ms. Marvel wields a giant boot, both are powerful while also cartoonish and nonsexualized (as these two heroines generally are).

Each politely calls herself a "huge fan" of the other, modeling teamwork and friendship. Kamala's comics in particular have helped teens see themselves, struggling with school and growing up in an increasingly divided America. "Kamala Khan, a 16-year-old child of Pakistani immigrants lives in Jersey City…. Kamala is a hero in the Peter Parker tradition: dweeby, self-doubting, unpopular. Like so many of today's teen geeks, she spends her nights resenting her parents and writing fan fiction for online forums" (Riesman). Her creator, G. Willow Wilson, explains that making her a fanfiction writer is particularly apt:

> Being a Muslim in America, I've noticed that there's a ton of crossover between the Muslim community and geekdom. Part of that is outsider culture: When you're growing up as a minority and you feel somewhat alienated from the mainstream, you're going to seek out other people who feel that way. That's what geek culture is traditionally about. And also, I wanted her to be fleshed out and have a real personality, rather than being a model minority. Plus, if you lived in a world where there were actual superheroes? Especially in a place like Jersey City, where you'd literally probably see Daredevil in the streets or Thor flying overhead or whatever. It made sense to me, in that situation, that Kamala would grow up looking up to these actual real-world superheroes and becoming a fan-fic writer [Riesman].

Squirrel Girl is born with bushy tail and proud of it, even as she summons a squirrel army on command. She too is a geek, constantly tweeting and expressing her love for the Avengers, whom she finally joins. With their shared interests, Ms. Marvel and Squirrel Girl make a particularly close partnership. Milana Vayntrub, the voice of Squirrel Girl, described the importance of that friendship, saying, "I am who I am because of the women in my life, hands down, and any time that we spend competing and comparing is not only time wasted, it's a step back, so I hope they sense that sisterhood and grow from it." (Steiner).

Ms. Marvel even launches Squirrel Girl in an X-Men "fastball special" so Squirrel Girl can let in her squirrel team to save the hostages. "I always had a feeling you'd get me," Squirrel Girl smiles. More teamwork and friendship are modeled for young readers. Later, they expand on this move with their own variation—Ms. Marvel twirling Squirrel Girl by her tail and hurling her like bolas. The two exchange puns, emphasizing that girls can be funny too. Contrasting them is Ember "Emulator" Quade, a loner bullied teen from a broken home, as the hacker villainess. The college boys bully her about her success, but she continues showing them up.

As the computer game monsters they're battling multiply, Inferno joins the team-up. Kamala, however, must warn Inferno, "You can't just fireblast your way to victory all the time," even as she uses computer-game know-how to win. Inferno, meanwhile, criticizes her insistence on reaching out to Emulator, adding, "When does that ever work?" Still, Kamala keeps empathizing with her, worrying, "I know what she's feeling right now. Creeped out. Angry. Confused. Afraid of her own power." America bursts onto the scene, notably taller and more muscled than they are, and calls both "children." This emphasizes her role as adult. Still, they learn to work together. Hurled into a computer game, they use their knowledge of the system to break out and save

Ember too for good measure. It's a sweet children's comic extolling the powers of camaraderie.

Along with clothes, school supplies, mugs, calendars, and phone cases, *Marvel Rising* is reaching out on multiple platforms. Linked with the Marvel.com site, artists offer drawing lessons, and actors answer internet questions. Further, Marvel created a live event in which students ages 11 to 13 would work with mentors to develop a three to five-page script featuring *Marvel Rising* characters and post them on Marvel's YouTube channel. Participatory web culture is running strong here. Likewise, Hasbro unveiled three varieties of action figures and the Ghost-Spider Web Slinger targeting kids ages 6 and up. The show, however, is central.

Marvel Rising: Initiation begins with Gwen "Ghost-Spider" Stacy (Dove Cameron, who also voiced Spider-Gwen in *Ultimate Spider-Man*), now on the run from her police-chief father, Capt. George Stacy and everyone else. (In her universe, she got the spider powers instead of Peter Parker). During the day, she's a normal high school kid who plays drums in a garage band with her friends Mary Jane Watson, Betty Brant, and Glory Grant. However, she's wanted as an outlaw wanted for supposedly killing an innocent teen— Gwen's high-school BFF Kevin. Stacy promptly calls in S.H.I.E.L.D. agents Quake and Patriot (Kamil McFadden) to bring in the murder suspect. "These are animated shorts aimed squarely at a tween demographic, with the attendant simplicity in form and execution (and length—each of the six initial installments clocks in around four minutes long). But the narrative doesn't shy away from the grounded life-or-death stakes kids and adults alike would expect from the source material," notes Alex McLevy in her *AV Club* review.

Over the six four-minute shorts, Ghost-Spider butts heads with the agents and then tussles with Ms. Marvel (*Avengers Assemble*'s Kathreen Khavari) and Squirrel Girl as the latter try a joyous team-up with Tippy-Toe the squirrel sidekick. Squirrel Girl even brings cupcakes as she drives up on a goofy motorbike with a sidecar for her pet. Ghost Spider smoothly defeats Patriot with a snarky "Captain America should've trained you better." However, Tippy-Toe (an ordinary but well-trained squirrel) cuts her webs and sends her tumbling. Squirrel Girl and Ms. Marvel take time for a cupcake break while the pair fight. It's a fun, silly scene. "Cameron makes for a brashly likable Gwen, all adolescent bravado and brushed-aside insecurities, while Khavari delivers on Kamala Khan's pragmatic wit. The best newcomer is Vayntrub, who takes Squirrel Girl's bubbly stream-of-consciousness logorrhea and makes it come alive" (McLevy).

There's also the heroines' status as competent, likeable superheroines. Kathreen Khavari says of playing Kamala, "It's a huge honor to be able to do this, because I think it's been a long time coming, I think it shouldn't have taken this long, and I didn't have that growing up, so it's wonderful to see that, to be a part of influencing a whole generation to see superheroes as not just boys and men ... there are female superheroes ... that to me is a responsibility, but it's the best responsibility I could ever have" (Steiner). Sana Amanat, the VP of content and character development at Marvel and executive producer of the film, explains of the project, "I started out as a comic book editor, and I've seen such an evolution of women coming into comics, girls coming into comics with such fantastic female heroes, and we (Marvel) have always had such fantastic female heroes, and these are the ones that people just wanted more content for, and we got lucky enough, Marvel let us take these characters into the next phase. People have been waiting for this for quite some time" (Steiner). G. Willow Wilson, meanwhile, notices how the demographic of comic book readers has changed.

> I think it's only really within the last couple of years that the conversation [about diversity] has gone truly mainstream and become something that everybody agrees we all need to tackle together. I think that's because fandom has reached a critical mass of people who are minorities but who make up a higher and higher percentage of fandom. Nowadays, when you go to a convention, it's pretty much a 50–50 split between male and female attendees. You have more and more LGBT people who want better and more accurate representation, more and more people of color who are interested in comics [Riesman].

Clearly, a show like *Marvel Rising* is reaching out to all of them. "Coupled with Squirrel Girl's penchant for self-narration and some nice hero-vs.-hero moments of splash-page-worthy animation, the series shows real potential for an inventive and big-hearted mini-universe of Marvel superheroes," McLevy adds.

Gwen wins the fight, but Squirrel Girl kicks it up a notch (with self-referential silliness) as she decides to fight "anime style." When the heroines hear Gwen's story, however, they want to help her. Likewise, when the S.H.I.E.L.D. agents catch her, Gwen's insistence that her friend was killed by an Inhuman with soul-sucking knives sparks recognition in Daisy. "I think something bigger is going on here," she says, concluding the episode arc.

Initiation sets the stage for the feature-length *Marvel Rising: Secret Warriors* film that follows. The movie, which premiered on Disney Channel, picks up where *Initiation* left off. Kamala kicks off the film as a devoted fangirl of Captain Marvel, with a room full of memorabilia. When she sees her hero cross the sky, she excitedly takes a video. "Carol's presence is tied into Kamala's nerdy love of comics, which includes being a fan of Ms. Marvel comics. Her status as a fangirl is an acknowledgement of the growing importance of the fangirl, who in addition to representing a large consumer base of comics, is also present at Comic-Con and other fan-based gatherings for comic books and the movies they inspire" (Arjana 52). As Hope Nicholson adds enthusiastically in her own book on superheroines, "Ms. Marvel is a fangirl turned superheroine. She showcases the power of fans who want to see themselves represented on the page. If Kamala Kahn signifies the future of the superhero genre in particular, then I think we can all look forward enthusiastically to the future" (Nicholson 229).

After the release of the *Captain Marvel* film, this is an even more delightful tie-in to the Marvel universe, as young Captain Marvel fans can instantly empathize. When the pair catch a glimpse of Captain Marvel soaring overhead, Kamala sighs wistfully: "I want to be her. So. Bad."

Doreen retorts: "We're totally her!"

Kamala decides, "We're weird."

Even the plot focuses on diversity: "The storyline aims at a brewing conflict between humans and an extremist group of Inhumans, the latter believing that a war between the two groups is inevitable. Khan ends up stuck in the middle, as an Inhuman herself who doesn't believe the conflict is needed," notes Mike Sorrentino in his review "*Marvel Rising: Secret Warriors* Tackles Diversity without Breaking a Sweat." This is a story of Kree invaders, as Ms. Marvel and Squirrel Girl literally stumble upon Dante (Tyler Posey), a teenage Inhuman with flame powers, battling another young Inhuman named Victor (Booboo Stewart). As such, it too sets up the feminist *Captain Marvel* film, while also tying into *Agents of S.H.I.E.L.D.* and *Guardians of the Galaxy.*

> The story of a young superhero struggling to understand and master their powers is not a new one (we've had nearly a dozen Spider-Man films covering this terrain) but seeing two girls (one a woman of color) navigating the experience is refreshingly original. The film is packed with powerful female characters, but the story is centered on the friendship between Kamala and Doreen. Kamala's hesitancy and reserve make her a great foil for the upbeat and wildly optimistic Doreen [Steiner].

The basically all-girl team shows that a world of superheroes that needn't rely on the men, just as *DC Super Hero Girls* does. It also welcomes a great deal of multicultural representation, like the recent Marvel comics. Kamala gets the others hooked on her favorite treats even as she struggles to balance life with her strict immigrant parents. "Kamala Kahn is a teenager. Her age plays a central role in the series, whether she is looking up to adults (other Marvel superheroes) or rebelling against them (her parents, her imam at the mosque)" (Arjana 51). Like Spider-Man, Kitty Pryde, and the Runaways did in their eras, she embodies the teenage struggle to fit in and balance changing responsibilities. "Kamala has superpowers, but she also has super heart, and her adventures are always tempered by her sense of morality and justice. She's an iconic superhero is the old school way; balancing her duties as a daughter and teenage student are equally important to her as saving the world" (Nicholson 229).

However, her story also features her friends being bullied because of their religion. She tries to please both family and peers, while her heritage complicates this balance. When one of the show's two main plot arcs appears—Inhumans being persecuted out of prejudice and fear—she and the other Inhuman Daisy must defend all those in trouble, in a plot that certainly resonates in 2018's anti-immigrant rhetoric.

> The film doesn't shy away from mature themes, using discrimination against Inhumans as a metaphor for prejudice. While chasing down pyrokinetic teen Dante (Tyler Posey), the heroes debate the threat of Inhumans, which drives a wedge between the Inhuman Kamala and Doreen. All the heroes in *Secret Warriors* are struggling with feelings of otherness and alienation, but create a found family in each other once they team up under the guidance of Captain Marvel (Kim Raver) [Steiner].

In this, the cartoon beats out its competition in metaphors for battling prejudice. Kamala's repeated pleas to stop pre-judging Inhumans and embrace them as friends and neighbors no different from other Americans is especially poignant from the Muslim American teen in the Trump era—her comics take this angle as well.

They begin investigating a global problem of disappearing kids, and soon encounter Quake and Patriot. Meanwhile, America Chavez (Cierra Ramírez) gets a brilliantly powerful entrance as she blasts into the show, riding her motorbike to Dove Cameron's theme song "Born Ready" that proclaims "One, two, time to be a fighter" in sassy fashion. She parks at the garage where she works, trades quips with her boss about the low pay, and gazes wistfully at two moms and a little girl … like her own lost family. "Her origin story, which sees Chavez's two mothers sacrificing themselves to protect their daughter, remains completely intact and sympathetic. Chavez herself demonstrates herself as a formidable ally, having super strength and the ability to fly. It's a nice start for LGBT representation on the animated side of the Marvel universe for now," Sorrentino notes. In this too, it has the other two cartoons beat.

When Victor (calling himself Exile) reveals his real agenda and kidnaps Kamala to serve Hala the Accuser of the Kree, America, an adult, haughtily calls Kamala "the junior Avengers" and refuses to team up. Before the film is over, S.H.I.E.L.D. arrests Daisy for breaking the rules to try helping the young Inhuman. Squirrel Girl, filled with guilt and desperation, finally entreats America's and Patriot's help. They arrange Daisy's jailbreak, and soon they have a real team. America proves the most powerful, blasting through walls and smashing S.H.I.E.L.D. agents across the room with her dimension-shattering punches as Gabi Sklar's song "Stay True" plays. To their delight, Captain Marvel (the strongest Marvel heroine) finally joins them.

Kamala, meanwhile, teams up with Dante and, as the theme song inspiringly plays once more, frees all the other Inhuman prisoners. This liberation of oppressed teen minorities like herself strikes a real blow against racism and tyranny. All the teens joyously unite to stage their revolution. "True warriors might know how to destroy, but they use their powers to protect," Kamala defiantly tells Hala. At the end, Kamala encourages Victor to accept that Hala has just used him. "I don't think it's us you really want to fight," she protests.

He puffs himself up into a giant monster and attacks her. "You've never felt threatened by my power, have you? Time for that to change," he blusters. However, the other heroes arrive and defeat him as a team, knocking him down to his human size. Divisiveness is the enemy, not other teenagers, and Kamala ends the threat by visually revealing how small he really is. They end the film with America offering them her garage as a home base for their ongoing hero team-up, reporting to Captain Marvel. Daisy, leader of the *Agents of S.H.I.E.L.D.* show, will be leading the *Marvel Rising* team as well. Squirrel Girl unofficially names them the Secret Warriors, and Kamala ends the show with an inspiring monologue:

> But it helps remind me of what I'm here for, what we're all here for—to find the truth. Now just about the world, but about who we are. And believe in it when nobody else does. I think that's what this whole thing's been about—going beyond where you think you can go. Reaching for what's true when it seems impossible to find. Rising to each challenge no matter the odds, because that's what heroes do. They rise.

Marvel Rising: Chasing Ghosts, written by Mairghread Scott, offers a 22-minute resolution to Ghost-Spider's story, as she stops Exile and a new villain named Sheath (voiced by Amanda C. Miller) who was responsible for Kevin's death. As she receives public acknowledgment of her innocence and a welcome to the team, she too is embraced by the larger sisterhood.

The next story, *Heart of Iron*, welcomes fan favorite Riri Williams, Iron-heart, a prodigy who has built her own Iron Man suit (adding a young black woman and STEM prodigy to the team). Riri, a prodigy at fifteen, has constructed her own suit and even A.I. (a beloved friend she calls Amy). Hala steals the suit and with it, releases a stream of anti-plasma that will doom the earth. Daisy leads brilliantly while Ghost Spider and Squirrel Girl reveal new powers. Meanwhile, Riri fights beside the Secret Warriors without her suit, emphasizing her toughness and courage. They need her science to save the day, as she calls the anti-plasma stream "a high energy matter state that can assimilate solid objects." Her A.I. can shut it down, but only if Riri builds a physical interface. She frantically reprograms her A.I. even as it points a massive blaster at her friends. However, saving the world requires sacrificing something she truly loves to save her new team. Meanwhile, Captain Marvel has been lured away so she fails to come save them all—the team do it all on their own. At last, Ironheart ends the story remodeling her suit in hot pink and black with a heart to give it her own style, like her place on the team.

Additional releases are coming, including the exciting *Operation: Shuri*. One assumes this one will stretch toward more global interests, emphasizing concerns besides American interests. With its pointedly multicultural emphasis from the start, *Marvel Rising* has the other franchises beat on the fourth wave front (as do its recent comics, compared with fewer diverse central characters from the other two lines). At the same time, all three shows emphasize that the real budget is going into the movies, which for all three franchises are largely white-able-bodied-cis-hetero-male-centric (with some characters like Iron Man and Batman fabulously wealthy enough to fund their entire teams). Marvel has had 20 starring white men or mostly so (and admittedly a few disability metaphors through the lineup), with one-and-a-half headlining women and one groundbreaking *Black Panther.* DCEU is at six mostly male films to one *Wonder Woman,* with *Birds of Prey* and *Wonder Woman 1984* set for 2020. *Star Wars* is arguably doing best in recent times, with Rey heading three films and Jyn one, in contrast with the more conventional *Solo.* Bringing in Rose, Maz Kanata, Captain Phasma, General Leia, and Admiral Holdo helps disperse the "one woman in the galaxy" trope that plagued Leia and even Wonder Woman, helping bring egalitarianism to the screen. Still, the franchises all have a way to go to even out the genders. Girl-centric cartoons are a start, but the spin-offs still need to go mainstream.

WORKS CITED

Arjana, Sophia Rose, with Kim Fox. *Veiled Superheroes: Islam, Feminism, and Popular Culture.* Lexington, 2018.

Arreola, Veronica. "Thoughts on DC Super Hero Girls." *Viva la Feminista,* 8 Apr 2015. http://www.vivalafeminista.com/2015/10/thoughts-on-dc-super-hero-girls.html.

Baver, Kristin. "Raising a Rebellion in IDW'S *Star Wars Forces of Destiny:* Hera." Starwars.com, 17 Jan 2018. https://www.starwars.com/news/raising-a-rebellion-in-idws-star-wars-forces-of-destiny-hera.

_____. "'They're the Heart of What the Resistance Means': Inside IDW's *Star Wars Forces of Destiny: Rose & Paige.*" *StarWars.com,* 31 Jan 2018. http://www.starwars.com/news/inside-idw-star-wars-forces-of-destiny-rose-paige.

Beck, Carrie, and Dave Filoni, producers. *Star Wars: Forces of Destiny.* Lucasfilm, 2017–present.

Berne, Emma Carlson. *Star Wars: Forces of Destiny. Daring Adventures: Volume 1.* Disney Lucasfilm, 2017.

Brown, Jeffrey A. *The Modern Superhero in Film and Television.* Taylor & Francis, 2017.

Charretier, Elsa, and Pierrick Colinet. "Star Wars Adventures: Forces of Destiny—Princess Leia." IDW, 2018.

Dawson, Delilah, and Nicoletta Baldari. "Star Wars Adventures: Forces of Destiny—Rose & Paige." IDW, 2018.

DC Super Hero Girls: Hero of the Year. Warner Bros., 2016. DVD.

DC Super Hero Girls: Intergalactic Games. Warner Bros., 2017. DVD.

Eckstein, Ashley. "One Part Pixie-Dust + One Part Midi-Chlorians = Ashley Eckstein." *Disney Unplugged,* 4 May 2011. http://www.disunplugged.com/2011/05/04/one-part-pixie-dust-one-part-midi-chlorians-ashley-eckstein.

Eng, Dinah. "Meet the DC Exec Turning Girl Superheroes into a 'Billion-Dollar Brand'" *Fortune,* 23 May 2016. http://fortune.com/2016/05/23/dc-super-hero-girls-diane-nelson.

Faust, Lauren, creator. *DC Super Hero Girls,* DC Comics, 2015–present. *YouTube,* https://www.youtube.com/channel/UCRdVJ9XqHCb6BqApCIO_TYg.

Frankel, Valerie Estelle. *Star Wars Meets the Eras of Feminism: Weighing All the Galaxy's Women Great and Small*. Lexington, 2018.

Grayson, Devin, Ryan North, G. Willow Wilson, et al. *Marvel Rising*. Marvel, 2018.

Hinds, Julie. "The Breakout Star in *Solo* Is L3–37, a Female Droid for Our Turbulent Time's Up Era." *Detroit Free Press,* May 20, 2018.

Knight, Rosie, Jennifer Kluska, Lauren Faust, Grey Griffin, Nicole Sullivan, and Marie Javins. "DC *Super Hero Girls* Special Video Presentation and Q&A." San Diego Comic-Con, 2018.

Kurka, Rostislav. "Forces of Destiny Review: What Is Its Value?" *Scifi Fantasy Network,* July 13, 2017. http://www.scififantasynetwork.com/forces-destiny-review-value.

Lane, Cort, producer. *Marvel Rising*. Disney, 2018–present.

Lego DC Super Hero Girls: Brain Drain. Dir. Todd Grimes. Warner Bros., 2017.

Lego DC Super Hero Girls: Super-Villain High. Dir. Elsa Garagarza. Warner Bros., 2018.

Martinelli, Marissa. "Disney's Charming Series of Animated Shorts Wants to Win Over a New Generation of *Star Wars* Fans." *Slate,* July 13, 2017. http://www.slate.com/blogs/browbeat/2017/07/13/star_wars_forces_of_destiny_reviewed.html.

McLevy, Alex. "The Animated Marvel Rising: Initiation May Be for Kids, but Its Heroes Contain Grown-up Potential." *The AV Club,* 8 Aug 2018. https://tv.avclub.com/the-animated-marvel-rising-initiation-may-be-for-kids-1828134732.

Nicholson, Hope. *The Spectacular Sisterhood of Superwomen*. Quirk Books, 2017.

"NYCC 2017: *Star Wars Forces of Destiny Comic Coming from IDW*." StarWars.com, 9 Oct 2017. https://www.starwars.com/news/nycc-2017-star-wars-forces-of-destiny-comic-coming-from-idw.

Riesman, Abraham. "Meet G. Willow Wilson, the Muslim Woman Revolutionizing Superhero Comics." *Vulture,* 20 Mar 2014. https://www.vulture.com/2014/03/g-willow-wilson-ms-marvel-kamala-khan-interview.html.

Schaefer, Elizabeth. *Forces of Destiny: Tales of Hope & Courage Replica Journal*. Illustrated by Adam Devaney. Disney Lucasfilm, 2017.

Sorrentino, Mike. "*Marvel Rising: Secret Warriors* Tackles Diversity without Breaking a Sweat." *CNet,* 30 Sept 2018 https://www.cnet.com/news/marvel-rising-secret-warriors-review-heroes-of-all-kinds-take-spotlight.

Steiner, Chelsea. "Review: Marvel Rising: Secret Warriors Is Empowering, Entertaining, and Radically Inclusive." *The Mary Sue,* 28 Sept 2018 https://www.themarysue.com/marvel-rising-secret-warriors-review.

Yee. Lisa. *Batgirl at Super Hero High* (*DC Super Hero Girls*). Random House, 2017.

_____. *Bumblebee at Super Hero High* (*DC Super Hero Girls*). Random House, 2018.

_____. Interview. By Valerie Estelle Frankel. 15 May 2019. Facebook Interview.

_____. *Supergirl at Super Hero High* (*DC Super Hero Girls*). Random House, 2016.

_____. *Wonder Woman at Super Hero High* (*DC Super Hero Girls*). Random House, 2016.

Rose Arisen

How the Children's Animated Show Steven Universe *Invented the "Reverse Fridge"*

Josephine L. McGuire

"We are the Crystal Gems We'll always save the day." Three colorful women stand in varying poses suggestive of strength, fun, and elegance before a rambunctious child jumps in front, laughing. *"If you think we can't we'll always find a way! That's why the people of this world believe in..."* Scenes flash of an ancient battlefield now covered in strawberries, an idyllic town. *"Garnet, Amethyst, and Pearl ... and Steven!"* In the final moment, the unlikely family of three magical aliens and their adopted child settle in to watch the sunset go down over their beloved home. This is the opening sequence in the children's animated television series *Steven Universe*'s theme song, but don't be fooled: the gorgeous animation and joyful song belies some quite thoughtful and surprisingly dark content.

Cartoon Network's first show solely created by a woman, *Steven Universe* (2013–2019) is an animated television series chronicling the adventures of Steven Universe, a half-alien half-human hybrid child who struggles to live up to the mission of Rose Quartz, his deceased mother, of protecting the Earth. Steven is raised by three maternal figures, the rebel Crystal Gems named Garnet, Amethyst and Pearl. All three are voiced by women of color and are suggestive of women of color in their outsider status and literal colorful skin. The show is famed for pioneering fourth wave feminist storytelling in children's entertainment, as well as for featuring a non-binary character, multiple prominent and explicit lesbian relationships as well as a variety of ethnicities within both the major and minor characters. One of the main differences between contemporary feminist storytelling and traditional narratives is the concept of the "fridge." The term "fridging" is derived from Gail

Simone, former fan blogger turned comics legend, and her 1999 website "Women in Refrigerators" (a list of female characters in superhero comics gruesomely violated, tortured, and murdered in order to propel male character's stories). As *Vox* notes, the trope is named after Alexandria De Witt, Green Lantern's girlfriend, whose corpse is butchered and hidden in the refrigerator for the hero to find. The trope was developed further by the online fandom community and is understood best from that perspective, due to the influence of online fandom on the emerging fourth wave feminist cultural conversation. The fan-culture archive Fanlore defines an act of fridging to be a plot device that rapes, tortures or kills a female character to advance the dramatic arc of a male character. "The male character then takes over the story and uses her tragedy as motivation, usually for broody manpain, violent revenge, or simply to become the best hero he can be." The trope aggregate site TV Tropes adds, "In some cases, the doomed character may be killed by natural forces or by a character who doesn't have the intent to cause someone else angst—in this case, the intent comes solely from the writer, who wants to rouse strong emotions in another character." Some examples of this trope include Barbara Gordon (the original Batgirl, who was crippled and photographed naked by the Joker in order to drive her father insane), Mina's extended rape in *League of Extraordinary Gentlemen,* and Jill Masterson from the James Bond film *Goldfinger* (who died screaming as she slowly suffocated by being encased in gold paint). The trope is prevalent in the literary canon as well, with such classics as *Hamlet* (Ophelia's drowning provokes a enraged duel at the story's end) and *The Picture of Dorian Gray.* Rebecca Sugar's show *Steven Universe* takes all of the components of the fridge as found in traditional narratives and reverses those elements to create a new and compelling take on female heroism. Rose Quartz's metamorphosis through childbirth deconstructs and redefines the "Women in Refrigerators" narrative trope. The Fridge encapsulates the androcentric vision, loss of female agency, and the patriarchal assumed world that the Reverse Fridge deconstructs, redefines and transforms.

Rose Quartz's death deconstructs the male gaze and as well as the glorification of hegemonic masculinity. The male gaze is the male perspective embodied by the use of the camera, filtered through the use of the fourth wall. Critic Robin James explains that one's pleasure in film of losing oneself in story or seeing oneself as the protagonist comes through camera angles … and often a particularly straight, male one focusing on "women's bodies as sexualized objects, women as problems to conquer[,] not people to interact with." The male gaze assumes a male camaraderie between the camera and the audience, a mutual sharing of cultural position. This means that most narrative perspectives, though perhaps nominally from a woman's point of view, still are ultimately masculine-oriented. In the fridge trope, even the suffering of a woman ultimately is still presented from the masculine viewpoint, narratively speaking. Secondly, hegemonic masculinity is best understood as "the normative ideology that to be a man is to be dominant in society and that the subordination of women is required to maintain such power.... While there are individual differences in male gender role socialization, this specific masculinity works to position men in a space of power, thus, it is often the ideal form of masculinity that men are socialized to achieve" (Smith). Men must be heroes, and women, victims to be rescued (or not). The male gaze concerns the way media is presented and its perspective, where hemogenic masculinity concerns the content and meaning of a story. When these two concepts overlap, they create a system of thought one might call the "Androcentric Vision."

The fridge is a logical byproduct of the androcentric vision's interpretation of male/female relationships. There are three reasons for this: first, it is a result of the commodification of women that the male gaze creates, second, it is a fetishization of misogynistic violence, and third, it is a glorification of hemogenic masculinity via a depiction of emotional endurance despite extreme suffering (this concept is called "man pain" by the wider online fandom community). Manpain is ubiquitous in hero stories everywhere and is often the first thing that comes to mind when one thinks of the modern broody hero. As Eva Óladóttir explains at length in her excellent essay "The Privilege of Pain: 'Manpain' and the Suffering Hero in the Supernatural Series":

> Manpain is a storytelling device that draws attention to the pain and suffering of a hero who is, almost without exception, a straight, white male. The narrative privileges the experiences of this character to the point where he becomes the only character with intrinsic value, and all experiences within the narrative come to belong to him. Manpain as a trope was originally identified and named by the fan community. The term seems to have been created in response to recent pop-culture narratives primarily in TV and gaming, but variations on the trope can be found in narratives stretching back throughout literary history. It also has a strong relation to other, older concepts, such as that of the Byronic hero and of the white man's burden, as it is heavily informed by patriarchal structures of privilege and deals with pain, sacrifice, and responsibility.

The traits of the classic man-pained hero include hierarchy of emphasis, a paternalistic sense of responsibility, and excessive suffering and/or reaction to suffering. In Oladottir's definition of manpain, some types of suffering are more valued, treated as more pressing or more justifying of bad behavior than others. An example of this trope in action would be the costumed vigilante Batman, whose personal tragedy is often treated as justification for violent behavior that another superhero character, say, the Flash or Martian Manhunter, would not be allowed to get away with either within the narrative or by the larger fan community. This creates a "hierarchy of emphasis" due to how narratives often rank some forms of suffering as deserving more emphasis than others.

Rose Quartz's story deconstructs the fridge by inverting the key components of the male gaze and hemogenic masculinity. One of the fundamentals of the fridge is that the fridged woman has no importance in and of herself and usually is only present in the story through the hero's emotions. This is a direct result of the male gaze's tendency of having the entire narrative's perspective seen through only male-coded eyes. However, in *Steven Universe,* the entire plot is based around Rose Quartz's legacy and posthumous character growth, inverting the commodification of the female perspective traditionally enacted by the male gaze. Remarkably, this inversion is maintained without negating the male hero and protagonist Steven's perspective and identity. In fact, the show even comments on this negation of perspective by having Steven struggle to define himself beyond Rose Quartz or Pink Diamond's legacy and identity, even as most of the Gems he encounters are convinced that he is merely a shapeshifted Rose or Pink. Unfortunately, this focus on Rose Quartz, both within the narrative and without, means that Steven is forced to pay for his mother's mistakes. *Steven Universe* both inverts and critiques hemogenic masculinity by ascribing the traits of the male hero onto the fridged woman and by depicting the deleterious effects this masculinity has on everyone in Rose Quartz's life. In *Steven Universe,* Pink Diamond and her alternate disguise/persona Rose Quartz are both leaders of their respective communities: Pink Diamond as one of the tyrant queens of Homeworld and Rose Quartz as leader of the rebel Crystal Gems. Her position in a masculine-style hierarchy emphasizes how even females in such a structure can enact male behavioral patterns. The show does not privilege her pain above the other characters but presents the character as operating from this place of unwitting privilege, viewing her suffering and desires as more important than those of others.

This privilege causes her a lack of empathy, despite her efforts to be something of an "all-loving hero." When Pink Diamond fakes her death so that she can live permanently as Rose Quartz, she uses her magic to place a bind of silence on her servant Pearl, permanently concealing Pink Diamond's plans. This has grave consequences for Pearl later when Steven (who was under the impression that Pink Diamond and Rose Quartz were separate individuals and that Rose Quartz had murdered Pink Diamond) asks Pearl for the truth. Her privileged position also leads to Rose Quartz's paternalistic sense of responsibility. All of her guilt and suffering causes her to keep secrets from her fellow teammates in order to protect them, instead of giving them the knowledge they needed to make choices for themselves—which she follows up with lies and manipulation in order to maintain those secrets. Her suffering is also extreme: not only is her whole army either killed or driven insane by her own abusive and cloistering sisters, all but three of her friends die and she is exiled to live on Earth forever.

Steven is confronted with the same temptation to succumb to the man-pain narrative as Rose Quartz, but ultimately overcomes it in a way she never does. In the episode "Full Disclosure," Steven returns home after having defeated a Gem named Jasper, who had held his friends and family captive in order to bring them in for punishment on Homeworld. His human friend, Connie, repeatedly calls him on his cell phone in a desperate effort to learn if he is safe. At first, he ignores her calls because he is overwhelmed and feels guilty over the destruction the battle with Jasper caused to his hometown, Beach City. As he contemplates how to respond to Connie's calls, Ronaldo (one of the citizens of Beach City) tells him that brooding is "just what people like us do. Suffer quietly, shouldering the knowledge no one else can bear … ordinary people fear the cold, leaded anchor of the truth…. This is no easy path we've chosen here…. It's our duty to let those simple people live out their simple lives, without ever knowing the burden of being friends with us" (04:07–04:39). Steven is then convinced that cutting off Connie in order to protect her from his life is the responsible action to take. However, when Connie confronts him, Steven quickly admits he doesn't want to cut her off, but that he is afraid that she will be hurt because of him and that it would be his fault. She tells him to stop "protecting" her and let her in, afterwards reassuring him that she wants to be there for him regardless of what happens. This episode directly rebukes the notion of manpain as heroic and instead emphasizes the importance of communication, vulnerability, and relationships. By having Ronaldo, one of the most foolish and self-involved characters on the show, be the spokesperson for this understanding of heroism, *Steven Universe* implies that so-called heroic stoicism is based on ego rather than true concern for others. It also points out that withholding emotionally from oneself leads to withholding from others—thereby destroying supportive relationships. The show consistently depicts trauma, bereavement, and guilt as best handled through forgiveness, community, and hope. Healing of trauma is the largest overarching theme of the series, with the episodes "Mindful Education," "Back to the Kindergarten," "Alone Together," and "Back to the Barn" being particularly prominent examples of this.

Not only does Rose Quartz deconstruct the fridge, but she also redefines it as a life-affirming sacrifice ultimately resulting in later empowerment and catharsis. In the episode "Lion 3: Straight to Video," Steven's magical pet lion, deftly named "Lion," attempts to cause Steven to fall into a portal located in his mane after overhearing Steven's private wish to know what his mother was truly like. Lion succeeds, and Steven is transported into another dimension filled with a sea of pink grass-like fur with a small mound where Rose

Quartz's belongings rest. He wades over to the mound and finds a mysterious VHS tape with his name on it. He then dives out of the portal and rushes to a nearby donut shop where his friend, Sadie, works. She lets him in despite the early hour, and they watch the tape together. It shows his father on the beach playing his guitar, while his mother's voice is heard for the first time in the series. "Isn't it remarkable, Steven? This world is full of so many possibilities. Each living thing has an entirely unique experience. The sights they see, the sounds they hear. The lives they live are so complicated and so simple. I can't wait for you to join them" ("Lion 3: Straight to Video," 09:44–10:07). Rose Quartz's death is not a murder. It is not a hideous, helpless, degraded slaughter solely meant to propel a hero on his journey and prove his emotional strength in the process. It still holds all the elements of the fridge: an idealized woman does lose her form and even her identity as herself to the hero's self and subsequent journey through her own death. Despite this, the construction and presentation are ultimately different. The fact that Rose willingly gives herself up for the betterment and opportunity of another rather than having been butchered means that her death is not deprived of agency. Her life is not stolen, it's gifted. Another crucial implication of "willing sacrifice" is that ultimately, Rose Quartz's death is not an antagonistic force to be overcome with emotional stoicism and repression but a choice that initiates Steven into a world of joy and pain and most importantly change—a choice to give the experience of life itself. The fridge in which Kyle Gardener's girlfriend was famously cut up and stuffed into has been redefined here as a womb.

This redefinition occurs through two key concepts: legacy and metamorphosis. In a typical fridge narrative, the woman has no true importance to the story, except for in the hero's emotions. Thus, the woman derives her value as a character only from her connection to the hero. This ultimately originates from the androcentric vision, but it is also a matter of pragmatics. The fridged character is dead, after all. Still, in *Steven Universe*, Rose Quartz has a legacy that continues to affect and interact with the narrative even after death; much like how in real life, the aftermath of a death isn't limited to one person's perspective. Though *Steven Universe* is the main protagonist, it is his mother, Rose Quartz, whose posthumous self-actualization propels the momentum of the show as the slow revelation of her true identity and character maintains the twists and turns of the plot. This redefines the fridge as a site of empowerment and agency. In Rose Quartz's tape for Steven in "Lion 3: Straight to Video," she continues, saying "We can't both exist. I'm going to become half of you. And I need you to know that every moment you love being yourself, that's me, loving you and loving being you" (10:13–10:23). This statement has a variety of functions, both from a character and narrative standpoint. It is literal; Rose does metamorphose into Steven on a biological and presumably psychological level. It is thematic; the ways one's identity can function as an extension of one's family is a recurring motif throughout the series. Most relevantly, however, it is metaphoric; Rose is carried in Steven's heart even after death. Fridging is primarily about trauma and ultimately the glorification of male failure to process and recover from that trauma. Rose's metamorphosis allows him to heal and move on from loss in a way that traditional fridging and manpain does not allow. Essentially, it permits her to keep on living through him on a metaphoric level through the power of legacy.

The fridge insists that the death of the woman be a tragedy. It is not merely her death that motivates the hero; it is the ugliness of it, the unfairness of it. Batman would hardly be Batman if his elderly aunt had keeled over due to liver failure. No, the fridge demands the blood of Bruce Wayne's parents be spilled before his very eyes as a young child. It requires his adopted son be beaten to death by the Joker with a crowbar after having been tortured physically and mentally for days on end. It commands that Jenny Calendar in *Buffy the Vampire Slayer* must not only have her neck snapped, but that Giles must find her broken corpse on her bed surrounded with rose petals on the night of their first official rendezvous. The very fact that this trope is so prevalent in American media implies a certain cultural belief that the world is inherently a dangerous place that unfairly victimizes people in general, but women in particular because of their vulnerable social status. In short, the fridge implies a belief in a world of misogyny. This is why works that are considered "gritty" or "realistic," such as *Kick-Ass* or *Sin City*, also often rely heavily on the fridge. Indeed, what is "fridging" or "manpain" other than a male-oriented perspective on female suffering? Whatever else the fridge might be, isn't it a symptom of a haunting fear that a loved woman in one's life might fall victim to the horrors many women in real life undergo?

However, Rose Quartz dies because the world is beautiful, not because it is ugly. In the traditional fridge narrative, life and death are opposing forces. The death of the loved one is unfair and needs to be somehow overcome by the protagonist if only in a metaphorical sense, such as taking revenge on the killer and thus restoring justice. Still, in the aesthetic put forth in "Lion 3: Straight to Video" (a standard aesthetic for the entire show) death becomes the reason life is worth living, its fragility as its preciousness. Rose understands human life and death in contrast to her own Gem immortality and timeless nature. Without the changes of time driving the process of physical maturation (Gems are born fully formed) and with Gem societal roles is tightly defined as they are, Rose Quartz sees the human paradox of life as simultaneously simple and complex as valuable in and of itself. In Rose Quartz's aesthetic, life is defined by death like the white space of a coloring book is defined by a black line. Traditional fridging posits life and death as opposing forces, but this aesthetic imagines life and death as complementary, with each defining the other—yin and yang. It is this idea of the necessity of change that compels Rose Quartz to metamorphose into Steven, who can change and so live the life she could never have.

Rose Quartz has played the role of the traditional manpained hero and suffered the consequences, so she turns instead to the fridge to find redemption through the metamorphosis of rebirth. In order to do so, she must undergo the New Heroine's Journey. *The New Heroines: Female Embodiment and Technology in 21st-Century Popular Culture* has a useful model on this alternative conception of heroism. The book sets up the potential that the heroine embodies as the center and origin of a community (or a network, as the author terms it) with the heroine herself serving as an interface between her own potential and her community. This system of potential, network, and interface undergoes change as the narrative continues, and if the heroine and her friends are successful, they will all mutually adapt despite the obstacles. In this understanding of heroism, The New Heroines explains, "What separates the New Heroine from the 'normal range' is not necessarily what she achieves or her commitment to the greater good. Instead it's her potential, the representation of a futurity tied to the present tense by the promise she holds" (35). For the New Heroine, it is what she might be—rather than who she is—that is the defining trait of her heroism. Pink Diamond instinctively understands this, taking on the identity of a Quartz soldier and all-loving Messiah figure in order to combat the injustices she was forced to perpetrate in her original identity as a Diamond tyrant. Even so, the highly idealized Rose Quartz cannot be truly realized, due to her past. It makes perfect sense, how and why she so adores the Earth: she yearns for its freedom and potential. In the episode, "We Need to Talk," her boyfriend and later father of Steven, Greg Universe, attempts Gem fusion with her through a dance with her. When Rose figures out his plan, she laughs at him, and in his hurt and exasperation this crucial line escapes Greg's mouth: "Can you just talk to me for one second, like a real person!?" The silence is visceral. He stands there, shoulders hunched defensively, his hands in fists—waiting for Rose to answer. A few painful seconds pass. Rose Quartz speaks. "I'm … not a real person. … Is this not how it works?" (00:8:17–00:8:37). When Rose tells Greg that she is "not a real person," this response reveals volumes about how Rose conceives of herself—for all her famed love of humanity, she can never truly be human. Later on in the conversation, Greg asks her if she misses her home planet, and she mildly replies, "No. Never." If she dissociates from her own species without a pang of regret, but consistently treats humanity—whom she has committed treason for—as some sort of adorable pet, where does she truly belong? If she has no solid identity as either Gem or human, is she even real? Rose is unable to interface between her network and potential because she has no ultimate identity in and of herself to serve as an interface. However, when she metamorphoses into Steven and attains the ability to grow, change, and determine her own destiny through literally being half of Steven due to her alien biology, Rose Quartz gains the self-actualization she could not as herself. Because Steven is half–Gem and half-human, he reconciles the two sides of her identity, while leaving behind the flaws inherent to Pink or Rose's way of thinking. In far too many stories to count, women are killed merely to further a man's plot. By contrast, in this case, instead of Rose dying so that Steven may live, Steven lives so Rose may die—realizing her legacy and mission in a way that even the good-intentioned but ultimately flawed Rose Quartz could not.

This redefined fridge is symbolic of the utopian aesthetic of the show; it questions and resolves the broken world of misogyny the traditional fridge narrative from which conceptually springs. Both the tropes of the fridge and manpain are experiences of a society defined by misogyny; it's simply that one is from the female-oriented role and the other from the male. The ubiquitous nature of narrative manpain exposes a male cultural fear that something terrible will happen to their female loved ones, and that as men, they will fail to protect the women in their care. After all, the logic goes, if a hero is not even man enough to protect his own loved ones, how can he be a hero at all? In the patriarchal world of the fridge, it's taken for granted that the men are naturally the strong agents, either for good or for ill, and the women are naturally defined as the frail subjects—either as cherished persons in relationship or as victims. From the fridge perspective, however, this conception of the inherent inequality of agent and subject, power and powerless, is the very thing that steals the life of the woman. Because if it was otherwise—if a woman had the same power as a man—she would not be dead. It's the patriarchy that kills her.

As previously discussed, Rose Quartz flips the paradigm as the agent who sacrifices herself in order to give up her own privilege. Still, either way, the fridge laps up yet another woman's blood due to a system of inequality and power imbalances. The Fridge and Manpain assume the patriarchy and its ensuing misogynistic violence is the natural state of the world. They don't do so with glee, despite often sexually fetishizing the victim, but with (admittedly self-centered) grief. Nonetheless, *Steven Universe* uses the Reverse Fridge as a utopian device in order to question the truth of and show a way forward from this cultural naturalization of patriarchy.

The Reverse Fridge mentality, as expressed through Rose's tape for Steven and her sacrifice to create him, is the moral aesthetic for the entire show. The fundamental presumption of *Steven Universe* is that life, despite and because all of its imperfections and mundanities, is inherently beautiful. Evil is only a refusal to accept and process the flaws and suffering of life and can always be redeemed in the end through the power of community and self-acceptance. This is a moral utopia, a conceptual space for imagining a world without sin. This beatific vision is innately queer in its idea of both evil and redemption. The Reverse Fridge mentality permeates the show through a repeated cycle of suffering and redemption. Among other things, subjects such as trauma, abuse, war, depression, anxiety, body horror, mental illness, and alienation have all been depicted on screen. What then of Steven Universe's utopian vision, its assertion that life is inherently beautiful? All of the characters grapple with this issue, but in observing the antagonists of the show one will soon notice a pattern: the characters' acts always arise from a lack of acceptance for imperfection. Whether it is Kevin and his compensation for his own insecurity or Jasper and her obsession with victory leading to a dependency on abusive relationships or the Diamonds' cruelty due to unchecked grief, these characters' refusal to accept and confront their flaws culminates in misery for everyone. Accepting, processing, celebrating and/or confronting limitation allows the character to come to terms with the imperfection and find enlightenment concerning the value of life, as Peridot does in "Back to the Barn" or as Lapis Lazuli does in "Same Old World." A refusal to acknowledge and celebrate imperfection will cause disaster and anguish, but this can be remedied if approached with the power of love and community. White Diamond is the most explicit example of this theme. White Diamond, in her own words, is "perfect." She is the source of the other Diamonds and the most powerful, as White contains all the colors in the spectrum. She has established an enormous empire dedicated to draining other worlds of their resources to create more Gems, and rigidly enforces an oppressively categorical society—every Gem has their place and purpose (including Pearls, who are required to be slaves) inherent to their type, with the Diamonds on top, of course. White Diamond is able to overpower other Gems' souls and project her "perfection" onto them, literally subsuming their identities and making them into mere mouthpieces of her personality. Nonetheless, there is still hope even for this monstrous tyrant. In the episode "Change Your Mind," after Steven confronts White Diamond in her spaceship, she rips his Gem out of his body in an effort to force Pink Diamond to resurface. When Pink Diamond instead appears in Steven's form, she throws something of a fit and accuses Steven of acting like a child. Steven's mature and reasonable retort causes her to blush pink in embarrassment. In the society White Diamond has constructed, being off-color, less than perfect in one's category, means being valued less and perhaps completely shunned and executed; blushing pink means that she, White Diamond, the "perfect" of perfects, is also an Off-Color. She and the other Diamonds are horrified by this revelation, but Steven quietly informs her that "if you just let everyone be whoever they are, maybe you could let yourself be whoever you are, too." Finally, she is brought to Earth to repair the broken minds of the forgotten Gems on Earth that she and the other Diamonds had corrupted and is brought into community with the rest of her kind at last. In "The Radical Arc of Queer Redemption in *Steven Universe*," Pitre explains, "As creator Rebecca Sugar has said, no character on the show is purely evil or unworthy of redemption.... One of the central themes of the series is the difficult journey of change, particularly when caught up in the fluid web of identity and self-discovery, and I find there to be something radically political in a cartoon forcing its audience to rethink conventions of violence, hostility, and evil in a way that ultimately articulates a space for queer utopia." Queer utopia is in this way demonstrated to be the escape of category and normativity and its subsequent isolation into a world of complete self-determinism and community.

José Esteban Muñoz's "Cruising Utopia: The Then and There of Queer Futurity" presents an understanding of queer utopia that illuminates some underlying principles of *Steven Universe*'s Reverse Fridge mentality. The three most relevant concepts include the quotidian, potentiality, and the collective. What makes a utopia queer is this sense of formlessness and category-defying, thrumming potential. Life on Earth, in the reverse fridge mentality of *Steven Universe*, is inherently a queer utopia, with the perfect being defined by in part by imperfection. This reading of the reverse fridge is clarified and enhanced by Muñoz's idea of the "quotidian." Muñoz states, "The utopian is an impulse that we see in everyday life. This impulse is to be glimpsed as something that is extra to the everyday transaction of heteronormative capitalism. This quotidian example of the utopian can be glimpsed in the utopian bonds, affiliations, designs, and gestures of the present" (22). The quotidian, then, is essentially the moments of everyday life and relationship that bring us transcendence, a vision of something more beautiful than could ever be in our present reality. The fridge assumes an ugly, patriarchal, violent world; but the reverse fridge, while acknowledging and grappling with violence, pain, and imperfection, assumes a better, brighter world that is both located in the present and in the future through potential. Gem society is essentially a factory empire; other forms of life on other planets are killed and their essence (or potential) are drained and converted into Gems, who are then sorted into permanent social roles. A Ruby or a Quartz must be a soldier. A Sapphire is an oracle. A Pearl, a slave. One is allowed to fuse only with Gems of one's own type and to do otherwise is to become an abomination. Fusion with a gem of a different type is too full of potential—no one knows what each will look like or who each will be, or even what type of Gem each will become. Muñoz defines queerness itself as the idea of futurity. "Queerness is a structuring and educated mode of desiring that allows us to see and feel beyond the quagmire of the present.... Some will say that all we have is the pleasures of this moment, but we must never settle for that minimal transport; we must dream and enact new and better pleasures, other ways of being in the world, and ultimately new worlds." In a rather poignant move, he adds, "Queerness is that thing that lets us feel that this world is not enough, that indeed something is missing" (1). The main conflict of *Steven Universe* is systematic suppression of individuality, or queerness, as expressed by the visual metaphor of White Diamond's ability to psychically puppeteer other Gems. Therefore, what is the Reverse Fridge's solution? It is relationship, or in Muñoz's thinking, the collective. In reference to the manifesto of the gay rights activist group "Third World Gay Revolution," he writes, "This 'we' speaks to a 'we' that is not yet conscious, the futurist society that is being invoked and addressed at the same moment. The 'we' is not content to describe who the collective is but more nearly describes what the collective and the larger social order could be, what it should be. This is to say that the field of utopian possibility is one in which multiple forms of belonging and difference adhere to a belonging in collectivity" (20). Collectivity is a unity of difference and a community. Steven learned that the manpain narrative cuts him off from his relationships that are the true source of his power, but he can now advocate for true community for the entirety of Gem society.

The fridge itself is not ultimately what is genuinely harmful. It is the ubiquitousness, the consistency, and the exclusivity of perspective that is truly problematic. This last one generates the Androcentric Vision, which in turn means that the experiences and suffering of women are placed below those of men, while the audience is expected to continue identifying and empathizing with the male-oriented role over the female-oriented role. In this way, male and female experiences are artificially divided and hierarchized. Instead of a depiction of how suffering is ultimately an affective experience that ripples across relationships, the hero must be alone; his greatest virtue being that he has no relationships to be responsible for (lest he potentially endanger them, of course). *Steven Universe* reintegrates male and female experience by literally simultaneously integrating Rose and Steven as a single entity. In the episode "Change Your Mind," Rose's past has finally caught up to her and her son, and her cruelest elder sister rips Pink Diamond's gem from Steven's body. She reforms; but instead of returning as Rose Quartz or Pink Diamond, she is now in Steven's form. When White Diamond demands she change to Pink, this new figure shouts in Steven's voice that "She's gone." They perform a fusion dance, and Steven is made whole. Yes, she is Steven, but she is also herself, and she is also the "part of [Steven] that loves him and loves being [him]." Rose and Steven are one. Steven's perspective cannot be separated and privileged above from Rose's own because they are part of each other, even though they are so different. The parallel to male and female experiences is obvious and beautiful. Thus, without that pesky male centricity polluting the narrative air-space, the whole construction of the fridge begins tottering dangerously. Rose Quartz's metamorphosis deconstructs, redefines, and replaces the fridge with the more humane Reverse Fridge.

Rose Quartz—War Hero, Gem Traitor, Diamond Brat, The All-Loving Messiah with a deficiency of empathy due to her own privilege—found herself redeemed and whole at last, despite the war and death and grief and lies, despite everything she could not face. The Fridge too is critiqued and deconstructed, yet is also redeemed, transformed, and forgiven: a site of misogynistic violence and eternal male trauma bent into a process for empowerment and hope for all, regardless of gender. The show *Steven Universe* opens a space for utopian thinking for ourselves as well, developing an imaginative space for us and our suffering world's grief finally being made right. This mythic reconfiguration paves the way for more thoughtful depictions of relational heroism in the future, both in real life and in the cultural narratives we construct for ourselves.

Works Cited

James, Robin. "Mulvey's 'Visual Pleasure & Narrative Cinema' Without All the Psychoanalytic Theory." *It's Her Factory*, www.its-her-factory.com/2016/10/mulveys-visual-pleasure-narrative-cinema-without-all-the-psychoanalytic-theory.

Muñoz, José Esteban. *Cruising Utopia: The Then and There of Queer Futurity*. New York University Press, 2019.

Óladóttir, Eva Dagbjört. "The Privilege of Pain: 'Manpain' and the Suffering Hero in the Supernatural Series." Diss. U of Iceland, 2014. Print.

Pitre, Jake. "The Radical Arc of Queer Redemption in *Steven Universe*." SCMS Annual Conference—Society for Cinema and Media Studies. Seattle. Mar. 2018. Reading.

Romano, Aja, and Alex Abad-Santos. "'Fridging,' One of Storytelling's Most Noxious Tropes, Explained." Vox.com, 24 May 2018, www.vox.com/2018/5/24/17384064/deadpool-vanessa-fridging-women-refrigerators-comics-trope.

Smith, Rachel M., et al. "Deconstructing Hegemonic Masculinity: The Roles of Antifemininity, Subordination to Women, and Sexual Dominance in Men's Perpetration of Sexual Aggression." *Psychology of Men & Masculinity*, vol. 16, no. 2, 2015, pp. 160–169.

"Stuffed into the Fridge." *TV Tropes*, tvtropes.org/pmwiki/pmwiki.php/Main/StuffedIntoThe-Fridge.

"Women in Refrigerators." *Fanlore*, 29 Aug. 2018, fanlore.org/wiki/Women_in_Refrigerators.

Wright, Katheryn Denise. *The New Heroines: Female Embodiment and Technology in 21st-Century Popular Culture*. ABC-CLIO, 2016.

About the Contributors

Audrey Jane **Black** is a doctoral student at the University of Massachusetts Amherst. She holds an MA in media studies from the University of Oregon and a graduate certificate in women, gender and sexuality studies from UMass. Her research focuses on the cultural politics of representation in film and television, emphasizing female-identifying and LGBTQIA+ populations.

Spinster **Eskie** has an M.Ed. in creative arts education and a background in women's studies. Her focus as a writer is to expose the female experience through unsettling tales that highlight the dilemmas of misogyny and oppression. Her work has been featured in various online magazines such as *Deadman's Tome, Bad Moon Rising*, and *69 Flavors of Paranoia*. She runs an online blog called Feminism in Horror.

Steven B. **Frankel** works as a high-tech project manager where he has been recognized for promoting women and people of color. He enjoys cosplaying as an airship officer or steampunk mad hatter with a collection of miniature steam engines and paneling and leading workshops decorating ray guns, parasols, and fans.

Valerie Estelle **Frankel** is the author of more than 60 books on pop culture. Many of her McFarland books focus on women's roles in fiction, from her heroine's journey guides *From Girl to Goddess* and *Buffy and the Heroine's Journey* to books like *Superheroines and the Epic Journey* and *Women in Doctor Who*. She teaches at Mission College and San Jose City College and speaks often at conferences. You can explore her research at www.vefrankel.com.

Resa **Haile** is the coeditor of *Villains, Victims, and Violets: Agency and Feminism in the Original Sherlock Holmes Canon*. She has been published in *The Baker Street Journal* and *NonBinary Review,* as well as Sherlockian anthologies. She cofounded two Sherlockian societies, the Original Tree Worshippers of Rock County and the Studious Scarlets Society (a group for women Sherlockian writers).

Sarah Beth **Gilbert** is pursuing an MA in English literature at Villanova University. She writes ELA curriculum at Great Oaks Charter School in New Jersey, where she previously spent two AmeriCorps service years tutoring and supporting the ELA department. Her interests lie at the intersection of science fiction and fantasy, pop culture, and gender and sexuality studies.

Stephenie **McGucken**, FSA Scot, obtained her Ph.D. from the University of Edinburgh in 2018. Her thesis focused on the representation of women and womanhood in late Anglo-Saxon manuscripts. She is the Project Chair for the Edinburgh Medieval Pigment Project and her research interests include how the portrayal of art objects and heritage sites in TV and film productions create new mythologies of the past.

Josephine L. **McGuire** is a screenwriter, poet, graphic novel scripter, and literary critic. She is working on her BA in English and a minor in film. She has a taste for superhero comics and obscurities/bizarrities of all types and mediums and hopes to make a change in the way our culture defines kindness, wisdom, and gender relations.

Katherine **McLoone** is a lecturer in the Comparative World Literature Program at California State University, Long Beach. She received her Ph.D. from UCLA in comparative literature with a focus on medieval romances. Her research areas are medieval engagements with—and portrayals of—reading practices, and television's engagement with literary techniques from close-reading to intertextuality.

Sumiko **Saulson** is a cartoonist, science-fiction, fantasy and horror writer, editor of *Black Magic Women* and *100 Black Women in Horror Fiction*, author of *Solitude, Warmth, The Moon Cried Blood, Happiness and Other Diseases, Somnalia, Insatiable, Ashes and Coffee*, and *Things That Go Bump in My Head*. She wrote and illustrated the comics *Mauskaveli* and *Dooky* and the graphic novels *Dreamworlds* and *Agrippa*. She writes for the SEARCH Magazine.

K. Jamie **Woodlief** teaches first year writing and literature at West Chester University of Pennsylvania. Her research focuses on pop culture pedagogy in the writing classroom including representations of gender in pop culture and exploring identity through social media. She has presented this research several times at the PCA/ACA national conference as well as regional conferences on the East Coast.

Index

abelism 9
abortion 11
abuse 11, 20, 21, 59, 65, 75, 77, 79, 82–88, 115, 133, 153, 193, 198
action figures 168, 173, 182
activism 11, 28, 116, 155, 156, 159, 161, 165
Adventure Time 13
The Adventures of Superman 3, 8
African 9, 33, 40, 102, 103, 105, 110, 114, 115, 123
African-American 3, 4, 6, 9, 10, 12, 23, 40, 42, 49, 86–88, 93–107, 112–114, 127, 130–133, 141, 146, 186
Afro-Caribbean 102
Afro-Latino/a 101, 102, 179
ageism 9, 23
agency 5, 10, 13, 20, 22–28, 51, 53, 58, 59, 80, 104, 120, 136, 140, 141, 145, 146, 157, 190, 194
Agents of S.H.I.E.L.D. 9, 180, 184, 186
aggression 144, 158
Agyeman, Freema 107
Ahsoka Tano 8, 13, 151, 152, 154, 157, 161–165, 173–178
Alien 49, 135
aliens 4, 6, 8, 13, 53, 104, 137, 138, 141, 143, 145, 176, 189, 197
ALS 84
Altered Carbon 40, 107
Always a Witch 107
Amanat, Sana 183
Amanda Waller 108, 168
Amazon 39, 44, 63, 170
ambition 67, 100, 154
America Chavez 180, 181, 185
American 5, 7, 10, 39, 40, 55, 79, 80, 81, 83, 94, 97, 98, 101–103, 106, 107, 110, 114, 116, 122, 170, 179, 185, 187, 195
American Gods 106, 107
American Horror Story 97, 98, 101, 106
Amilyn Holdo 156, 164, 187
Amy Pond 144
Angel 9, 102, 106

anger 12, 66, 84, 85, 99, 121
Angry Black Woman 106
animation 183, 189
anime 7, 172, 183
Ant-Man and the Wasp 103, 107
anthology shows 2, 3, 12
apocalypse 93, 95, 98
armor 13, 154, 172
Arrow 12, 52, 112, 113, 123
artist 33, 34, 64, 76, 85, 152, 159, 160, 179
Ashe, Tala 122, 123
Asian 10, 12, 40, 94, 95, 123
Aslaug 63, 64, 67–72
Atwood, Margaret 19–24
autogenesis 35
autonomy 72
Avengers 4, 180–182, 185

Baartman, Sarah 105, 106
babies 26, 53, 59, 130, 143
Babylon 5 8, 9, 32
backlash 13, 153, 156; *see also* toxic males; trolls
Badaki, Yetide 106, 107
Bassett, Angela 96, 98, 101, 104, 106
Batgirl 52, 170, 171, 172, 190
Batman 5, 52, 167, 168, 170, 187, 191, 195
Battlestar Galactica 5, 8, 49, 50
BBC 30, 39, 105, 135
beauty 52, 59, 60, 68, 101, 104, 116–118, 129, 132, 195–200
Being Human 103, 107
Berry, Halle 101, 102, 103, 107
bilingual 3
Bill Potts 12, 107, 135–140, 144, 145
The Bionic Woman 5, 49
Biopunk 30, 31
Birds of Prey 8, 51, 52, 187
bisexual 7, 10, 12, 34, 97, 100, 113–116, 123, 140
Black Lightning 9, 96, 107
Black Lives Matter 128, 156
Black Mirror 12, 14, 107, 127–133

Black Panther 14, 72, 96, 101, 103, 179, 187
Blaxploitation 5, 86
blogs 11, 152, 190
bodily autonomy 42
Bollywood 33
box office 96
Boyega, John 104, 177
Brazil 41, 42, 102
Britain 4, 33, 34, 37, 39, 44, 62, 66, 67, 72, 101, 103, 106, 113, 136, 146
Buffy the Vampire Slayer 6, 7, 9, 10, 52–59, 195
Bumblebee 107, 170–172
Burqa Avenger 120
Butler, Judith 35

Canada 34–36, 39, 121
cancer 67
Capaldi, Peter 136, 145
Captain America 78, 87, 180, 182
Captain Marvel 13, 14, 77, 179, 180, 183–186
cartoon 5, 7, 14, 112, 114, 167–169, 172–175, 180, 185, 187, 189, 199
casting 4, 12, 32, 40, 50, 99, 101, 102, 104, 110, 128
Cat Grant 53, 54
Catwoman 5, 171, 172
chains 99, 100
Charlie's Angels 5
Charlottesville 116, 118
Charmed 8, 52, 107
cheerleading 56
children's shows 3, 6, 13, 107, 135, 173, 189
Christian 32, 33, 42, 65, 67, 72, 122
civil rights 27, 131
classism 9, 43, 85, 111, 155
Cleopatra 2525 102
cleverness 68, 138, 162, 174
clothing 6, 19, 21, 52, 68, 75, 77, 79, 154, 164, 168, 172, 182; *see also* costume; dress; hair; leather jacket
colonialism 95, 99, 100, 105, 115, 176
Colter, Mike 79, 87
comic books 3, 8, 13, 40, 49, 51, 52, 53, 55, 59, 76, 78, 79, 86, 88, 94, 95, 101, 112, 113, 115, 120, 122, 124, 136, 152, 167–169, 173, 177–185, 187, 190
community 10, 11, 13, 34, 37, 60, 93, 111, 115, 116, 120, 122, 136, 163, 171, 181, 190–193, 196, 198–200
consent 8, 67, 72, 73, 78–82, 87, 129
cosplay 96
costume 8, 53, 75, 87, 104, 113, 116, 121, 154, 165, 169
counterculture 3
Crenshaw, Kimberlé 85, 111
The CW 49, 51–53, 96, 112
Cybermen 137, 142–145
cyberpunk 30, 35, 36
cyborg 12, 137, 142–144

Daenerys 98–100
Daredevil 181
Dark Angel 8, 52
Dark Phoenix 51, 101
daughter 23, 35, 40, 64, 66, 68, 72, 76, 84, 96, 98, 101, 107, 122, 132, 173, 184, 185
Davis, Viola 107, 108
Dawson, Rosario 102, 108
DC Super Hero Girls 14, 107, 167, 171–175, 184
Dead Lesbian Syndrome 97
death 2, 3, 20, 27, 34, 51, 57, 65, 67, 68, 70, 72, 80, 83, 84, 87–89, 95, 98–100, 128–133, 143, 159, 163, 168, 182, 186, 190, 192–197, 201
death row 132
decolonization 27
demographics 38
demon 79, 123, 162, 185
depression 27, 198
destiny 50, 57, 105, 123, 173, 197
digital 9, 111; *see also* internet
director 4, 33, 35, 84
disabled 1, 6, 59, 84, 98, 114, 187
Disney 3, 6, 7, 8, 10, 165, 170, 173, 174, 180, 183; *see also* cartoons; fairytales
diversity 1, 5, 7, 10, 12, 13, 14, 24, 28, 34, 37–40, 44, 49, 55, 104, 111–115, 123, 124, 136, 168, 179, 183, 184, 187
divorce 63, 69, 71
Doctor Who 4–9, 12, 49, 107, 135–142, 146, *see also* Amy Pond; Capaldi, Peter; Cybermen; Jack Harkness; Mackie, Pearl; Martha Jones; Missy; Moffat, Steven; River Song; Rose Tyler
Dreamgirl 55
dress 4, 6, 26, 28, 75, 174
drug 83–85, 132
dystopia 11, 19, 20, 24, 25, 96

Eckstein, Ashley 173, 177
Edelman, Lee 136, 138, 141–143
Einstein, Albert 118, 119
Elementary 49, 50
emasculating 79
Emmanuel, Nathalie 98, 99, 107, 108
Emmy 38, 42
emotional 37, 52, 59, 78, 84, 86, 87, 130, 158, 191, 194
empathy 79, 82, 111, 130, 192, 201
Empire 104
empowerment 2, 6, 8, 10, 14, 26, 36, 168, 193, 194, 201
equality 4, 5, 13, 35, 52, 65–69, 71, 73, 145, 151, 155, 157, 164, 165, 177
eugenics 36
executives 4, 35, 36, 52, 112, 169

Facebook 11, 94, 133, 168
fairytale 7, 68, 88
false consciousness 78

fan art 169, 172, 182
fan character 123, 181, 183
fan criticism 1, 11, 12, 190–192
fan fiction 181
fans 4, 6, 7, 11–13, 37, 38, 44, 50, 57, 59, 122, 142, 156, 157, 164, 167, 169, 170, 174–176, 180, 184, 190
Fantastic Beasts 107
fantasy 4–6, 9, 13, 14, 55, 77, 96, 97, 101, 102, 114, 158
father 35, 57, 59, 63, 66, 69, 72, 73, 82, 101, 105, 132, 133, 157, 160, 162, 182, 190, 194, 196
Faust, Lauren 169, 170
female genital mutilation 21, 24, 133
The Feminine Mystique 3
femininity 4, 7, 50–52, 56, 69, 75, 142, 145, 153–161, 164
feminism *see* empowerment; equality; first wave; fourth wave definition; second wave; third wave
financing 32, 39
Firefly 102
first wave feminism 1
The Flash 12, 52, 107, 112, 122, 123, 191
Flash Gordon 2
flashback 23, 27, 40, 75, 78, 132
Flockhart, Callista 54
fourth wave definition 9, 11, 85, 111, 151, 156; *see also* activism; fan protests; global feminism; intersectional; social media
freedom 20, 21, 27, 37, 84, 88, 100, 120, 141, 157, 160, 177, 196
fridging 13, 97, 99, 189–201
Friends 7, 38
friendship 5, 6, 35, 40, 54, 59, 68, 70, 77, 97, 160, 169, 172, 176, 180–186, 193, 196

Game of Thrones 13, 14, 37, 98–100, 107
gay 7, 10, 33, 35, 41, 43, 200; marriage, 7; metaphor, 6
gaze: female 77; male 77, 79, 105, 113, 114, 116, 190, 191, 192
geek culture 181
gender flipping 7, 14, 49, 51, 60, 86
genre *see* cartoons; children's shows; comic books; fantasy; horror; parody; romance; science fiction; sitcoms; Western
Germany 33, 40, 118
Ghostbusters 12, 14, 49, 50, 95, 108, 167
girl power 6, 8, 54, 56
girlfriend 2, 77, 79, 84, 103, 123, 180, 190, 194
GLAAD 10, 32, 38, 44, 97
global feminism 1, 9, 11, 12, 37, 39, 40, 111, 114, 116, 120, 123, 171, 185, 186; *see also* African; American; Brazil; Britain; Canada; German; Iceland; India; Japanese; Korea; Latin America; Mexican; multiculturalism; nonwestern models; Norse; Pakistan; Sweden
goddess 6, 43, 106, 201

gods 9, 43, 65, 66, 103, 106, 122
Gotham 108
Gothic 30
granddaughter 49, 105, 115
Guardians of the Galaxy 102, 184
gun 2, 42, 55–58
Gurira, Dania 95, 96, 101, 109
Guyger, Amber 131

hair 6, 9, 63
The Handmaid's Tale 11, 14, 19–29
Haraway, Donna 137
Harley Quinn 168–170, 172
hate crimes 131
Hawkgirl 112, 113
#HeForShe 156
Helen of Troy 110, 116, 118, 119
Hemsworth, Chris 50
Hera Syndulla 151–164, 175–178
hero's journey 62
Herter, Cosima 30, 36
heteronorming 115–116, 135, 137, 139–145
hierarchy 9, 20, 21, 31, 144, 191, 192
Hirst, Michael 63, 64, 72
Hollywood 23, 33, 38, 49, 97, 110, 116, 118, 119
homewrecker 69
homophobia 10, 97, 131
homosexuality *see* LGBTQIA+; queer
homosocial 142
horror 30, 77, 87, 88, 96, 97, 101, 102, 104, 106, 128, 130, 161, 173, 198
housekeeper 2
housewife 1, 34
How to Get Away with Murder 9, 10
Hulu 11, 19–24, 28, 44, 96
The Hunger Games 108
husband 1, 3, 20, 21, 23, 27, 51, 62–71, 95, 128, 129, 154
hybrid 105, 189

I Dream of Jeannie 4
I Love Lucy 1
Iceland 33, 63, 64, 130
imposter syndrome 56
incels 12; *see also* backlash; hate crimes; misogyny; prejudice; sexism; trolls
independence 11, 35, 39, 59, 73, 97, 98, 107, 132, 135, 158, 170
India 9, 33, 37
Inhumans 184, 185
innocents 76, 77, 80, 83–85, 129–132, 182
Instagram 168
internet 1, 9, 11, 12, 13, 54, 106, 169, 180, 182; *see also* digital; Facebook; fan art; fan fiction; Instagram; social media; Twitter; YouTube
interracial couples 95
intersectionality 1, 9, 12, 23, 31, 54, 77, 85, 106, 110, 111, 119, 121, 123, 124, 151, 155, 156, 159, 164, 165, 172, 176

intersex 34, 39
Iron Man 51, 107, 180, 186, 187
Ironheart 107, 108, 186

Jack Harkness 8, 136, 139, 146
Japanese 4, 7, 170
jealousy 70
Jessica Cruz (Green Lantern) 171
Jessica Jones *see Marvel's Jessica Jones*
Jewish 9, 121, 122
John-Kamen, Hannah 101, 103, 107, 108
Jordan, Michael B. 100
Judith of Flanders 66–67
Jyn Erso 173, 176, 187

kairos 26
Katana 170–172
Kavanaugh, Brett 127
Killjoys 108
king 2, 62, 65, 66, 68, 71, 73
kiss 7, 13, 41, 53
kitchen 51
Kitty Pryde 184
Korea 9, 33
Kravitz, Zoë 103, 107, 108, 109

L 3–37, 177
labels 34, 54
Lagertha 62–73
Lamarr, Hedy 110, 117, 118
Lapis Lazuli 198
Latin America 40
Latino/a 54, 94, 102, 113, 131
Laveau, Marie 98
law 10, 26, 33, 64, 68, 84, 98, 137
Law & Order SVU 35
leather jacket 56
legacy 56, 170, 192, 194, 195, 197
Legends of Tomorrow 12, 53, 105, 108, 110–124
Leia Organa 152–154, 157, 159, 162, 164, 165, 173–178, 187
Lena Luthor 171, 172
lesbian 7, 10, 12, 24, 33, 34, 43, 54, 57, 60, 96, 97, 107, 141, 189
LGBTQIA+ 5, 8, 10, 13, 21, 24, 31–33, 42–44, 60, 97, 111, 136, 142, 146, 183, 185
liberalism 10, 121, 122, 127
lies 10, 11, 26, 85, 128, 172, 192, 201
lipstick 6, 21
literacy 26
Logan 179
Lost 9, 42, 108
Lost in Space 49
love triangle 9, 113
loyal 62, 68, 85, 104, 178
Luke Cage 77, 79, 86, 87, 88, 108

Ma 106, 108
macho 83, 115, 119, 121, 122, 176
Mackie, Pearl 107, 136

Mad Max: Fury Road 108
Mammy 94, 96, 106
manipulation 80, 192
Manpain 190, 191, 193, 195, 197, 200
mansplaining 83
marginalization 9, 50, 85, 113
marketing 37; *see also* box office; Emmy; financing; Hollywood; merchandising; Oscar; producer; production; screenwriter; transmedia
marriage 7, 63, 66, 68, 69, 72, 73, 80
Martha Jones 12, 107
Marvel Rising 14, 107, 108, 179–187
Marvel's Iron Fist 12
Marvel's Jessica Jones 12, 13, 36, 75–89, 179
Marvel's The Defenders 12, 76, 88, 102, 108
Mary Jane Watson 182
The Mary Tyler Moore Show 3, 4
masculinity 23, 56, 77, 80, 83, 115, 117, 142, 156, 159, 160, 190–192
mask 87
Maslany, Tatiana 34, 35, 39, 42, 43
matriarchs 3
The Matrix 43, 44
Maud 3, 10
Maz Kanata 104, 173, 175, 177, 187
medieval 13, 64, 122
memories 27, 164; collective 116; in science fiction 129, 133, 138, 140, 141
merchandising 54, 106, 132, 133, 152, 168, 171, 173, 175, 182, 191, 192
#MeToo 10, 11, 28, 156
Mexican 9, 33, 34, 41, 101, 103
middle-class 12, 129, 136
Midnight, Texas 108
Miles Morales 179, 180
military 82, 83, 100
Millennials 138, 146
minotaur 98
misandry 117
Misfits 103, 108
misogyny 11, 12, 23, 35, 51, 52, 58, 67, 73, 118, 155, 191, 195, 197
Miss Sherlock 14, 49
Missandei 98–100, 107
Missy 142, 143
Misty Knight 108
mixed race 7, 23, 100–105, 113
modesty 26
Moffat, Steven 143, 144
morality 19, 22, 73, 81, 82, 84, 175, 184, 197, 198
morally ambiguous 58, 76
mother 2, 3, 9, 13, 35, 40, 84, 85, 94, 97, 98, 101, 104, 107, 120, 122, 129, 130, 133, 141, 153, 154, 157, 158, 160, 176, 179, 185, 189, 192–194
motorcycle 56
Ms. Marvel (Kamala Kahn) 120, 179–186
multiculturalism 7, 8, 170
Mulvey, Laura 114

Murphy Brown 10
music 6, 88, 113, 114, 168, 180, 185, 189
Muslim 12, 110, 114, 115, 120–123, 128, 181, 184, 185
My Little Pony 13, 169

naked 8, 13, 68, 190
Nakia 96, 101
Nazis 118, 119, 133
Netflix 11–13, 30, 32, 36–40, 42, 44, 75, 88, 102, 127, 179
New Orleans 105
Nicholson, Hope 77, 79, 81, 88, 183, 184
Night Nurse 108
1940s 1, 114–116
1950s 1–3, 51
1960s 100, 142
1970s 3–5, 7, 9, 21, 52, 96, 120
1980s 5–7, 9, 23, 159, 167
1990s 8, 54, 56, 101, 159
The 99 120
nonwestern models 14, 72, 111, 120, 133
Norse 14, 63, 65, 66, 73
Nyong'o, Lupita 96, 101, 103, 104, 106, 177

Obama, Barak 128
objectification 98, 107, 116, 117
Óladóttir, Eva 191
Once Upon a Time 10
The 100 97
oppression 6, 9, 25, 26, 85, 105, 111, 134
Orange Is the New Black 9, 10, 38
The Originals 105
Orphan Black 9, 11, 14, 30, 31, 34–36, 39–44
Oscar 103, 104
outcasts 110, 115, 123, 124

Padmé Amidala 153, 154, 157, 159, 164, 173–178
Paige Tico 177–179
Pakistan 179, 180
paper bag test 102
paranoia 27, 67
Parent, Gail 3
parody 79, 80, 83, 85
passingness 102
passive 85, 88
patriarchal society 25, 70, 151
patriarchy 9, 12, 20, 23–25, 28, 36, 55, 70, 78, 84, 105, 115, 117–119, 151, 153, 161, 162, 164, 190, 191, 197, 199
Patriot 180, 182, 185
PBS 3
Penny, Laurie 111
people of color 7, 12, 23, 24, 32, 40, 42, 44, 87, 95, 97, 99, 100, 105, 111, 128, 129, 131, 133, 136, 156, 170, 171, 176, 179, 183, 184, 189; *see also* African-American; Afro-Caribbean; Afro-Latino/a; Asian; civil rights; diversity; Latino/a; Mexican; mixed

race; nonwestern models; paper bag test; passingness; prejudice; race flipping; representation; tokenism
Peridot 108, 198
Pink Diamond 192, 196, 198, 200
Pirates of the Caribbean 106
plantation owner 97, 98, 105
political 4, 6, 11, 27, 28, 30, 32, 36, 55, 64, 67, 68, 111, 112, 116, 120, 121, 136, 137, 157, 199
political correctness 54; *see also* labels
Porter, Adina 97, 101
possession 105
postfeminism 6, 153
The Powerpuff Girls 7, 169
pregnancy 20, 59, 69, 72, 88
prince 72
princess 2, 6, 13, 66, 68, 72, 73, 108, 153, 165, 167, 170, 173, 174, 177
The Princess and the Frog 108
privilege 24, 25, 38, 82, 83, 127, 133, 134, 136, 138, 140, 153, 176, 191, 192, 197, 200, 201
producers 2, 12, 31, 32, 35, 42, 43, 44, 52, 101, 105, 110, 112, 169, 183
production 11, 22, 31, 32, 35, 37, 43, 44
property 14, 19, 21, 30, 63, 64, 65, 72, 73
PTSD 57, 79, 80, 89
Pulse shooting 42

Quake 180, 182, 185
queen 66, 68, 71, 99, 100, 153
Queen Ramonda 96, 101
queer 1, 9, 10, 12, 30–34, 37, 38, 41–44, 97, 110, 136, 137–142, 145, 161, 162, 165, 198, 199, 200; artists 44; representation 32; roles 44; theory 146; *see also* LGBTQIA+
queering 7, 31, 38, 41, 43, 136, 137, 142–146, 163, 199, 200

race 7, 10, 12, 14, 24, 32, 39, 54, 85, 102, 103, 111, 113, 115, 128, 130, 136, 137, 141, 143, 144, 155, 172, 177; *see also* African-American; Afro-Caribbean; Afro-Latino/a; Asian; civil rights; Latino/a; mixed race; paper bag test; passingness; people of color; prejudice; privilege; religion; representation; tokenism; white
race flipping 7, 23, 40, 54
racism 1, 9, 10, 12, 24, 81, 95, 98, 105, 106, 121, 128, 129, 131, 132, 185; *see also* backlash; hate crimes; Incels; Mammy; misogyny; plantation owners; segregation; slavery; stereotype; trolls; white supremacists
rape 20, 21, 64, 65, 71, 76- 81, 86, 95, 117, 127, 156, 159, 190
rebellion 24, 27, 28, 120, 159, 170, 175, 177
relationships 8, 11, 13, 25, 33, 54, 58, 69, 70, 95, 96, 98, 138, 163, 176, 189, 191, 193, 198, 200
religion 20, 111, 114, 115, 120, 121, 184; *see also* Christian; Jewish; Muslim; Vikings

representation 20, 21, 31, 32, 36, 42–44, 122, 123, 137, 139, 142, 145, 164, 171
reproduction 35, 136, 142, 143, 144
rescue 2, 3, 4, 11, 51, 62, 63, 70, 71, 80, 84, 87, 93, 95, 119, 135, 145, 163, 165, 171
resistance 11, 24, 26, 27, 28, 30, 42, 44, 151
respect 4, 5, 14, 25, 39, 59, 63, 65, 67, 69–73, 164, 172, 176
Revenge 14
Reverse Fridge 189–201
revisionist history 116, 118
revolution 152, 185
Rey 107, 153, 154, 159, 164, 165, 173–178, 187
Richardson-Sellers, Maisie 105, 108
Ridley, Daisy 104, 153, 173, 177
River Song 144
Roe vs. Wade 11
Rogue One 152
role models 4, 5, 63, 168, 170
romance 1, 8, 9, 12, 58, 80, 93–98, 106, 107, 112, 136, 138, 139, 158, 164
Romans 63, 65, 66, 139
Rose Tico 14, 108, 156, 177–179, 187, 192, 194–197, 199, 201
Rose Tyler 140, 141
Rosenberg, Melissa 76, 77, 80, 81
Runaways 9, 184

Sabine Wren 151, 152, 154, 157, 159–165, 174–177
Sabrina the Teenage Witch 5
sacrifice 54, 57, 86, 95, 99, 106, 140, 141, 159, 178, 193, 197
Sailor Moon 7
Saldana, Zoe 102, 108
San Francisco Pride 41
São Paulo Pride 41
Sara Lance 12, 110, 112–116, 124
Sarkeesian, Anita 77, 82, 85
savior 100, 141, 145
school 19, 35, 52, 56, 106, 130, 167–172, 180, 182, 184
science fiction 2, 4, 5, 7, 9, 12, 14, 23, 30, 31, 38, 41, 42, 96, 102, 110, 127–129, 135, 152, 158, 160
screenwriter 3
Scrofano, Melanie 55, 59
second wave feminism 4, 9, 21, 28, 152
segregation 111, 116, 118
Sense8 9, 11, 14, 30–44
servants 20, 67, 192
Sesame Street 5
sex 6, 9, 13, 21, 30, 41, 57, 59, 67, 82, 88, 96–100, 106, 117
sexism 10, 20, 50, 116, 155; *see also* backlash; Incels; misogyny; prejudice; sexy lamp test; Smurfette Principle; stereotype; toxic males; trolls
sexualization 7, 9, 20, 24, 30, 32, 34, 42, 43, 52, 60, 75, 77, 98, 100, 103, 116, 139, 140, 142, 155, 159, 190
sexy lamp test 13
She-Hulk 51
She-Ra 6, 167
Sheena the Jungle Girl 3
shieldmaiden 64, 71, 72
Shuri 96, 101, 186
sidekick 6, 8, 88, 94, 96, 100, 179, 182
Sidibe, Gabourey 98, 101
Siggy 63, 67–69
Simone, Gail 107, 113, 190
The Simpsons 6
single mother 59
sister 51, 53–58, 76, 79, 82, 85, 88, 96, 105, 171, 178, 179, 200
sisterhood 26, 34, 36, 69, 171, 181, 186
sitcoms 2, 7, 9
slavery 19, 72, 88, 95–100, 103, 105, 106, 132, 165, 176, 177, 199
Sleepy Hollow 100
Smallville 51–53, 112
Smurfette Principle 6, 50, 187
social media 12, 36, 122, 131, 156, 165, 172; *see also* Facebook; Instagram; internet; Twitter; YouTube
Solo 106, 108
son 33, 37, 49, 66–70, 72, 86, 94, 105, 112, 129, 130, 154, 157, 177, 184, 195, 200
Spider-Gwen 179, 180, 182, 186
Spider-Man 108, 179, 180, 182, 184
spy 4, 65, 96, 162
Squirrel Girl 179–186
Star Trek (2009) 102, 108
Star Trek: Discovery 10, 107, 108
Star Trek: The Next Generation 5, 6, 10
Star Trek (TOS) 2, 4, 100
Star Wars 5, 8, 12–14, 95, 102, 104, 151–167, 173–178, 187; *see also* Ahsoka Tano; Amilyn Holdo; Eckstein, Ashley; Hera Syndulla; Jyn Erso; L3-37; Leia Organa; Maz Kanata; Nyong'o, Lupita; Padmé Amidala; Paige Tico; Rey; Ridley, Daisy; *Rogue One*; Rose Tico; Sabine Wren; *Solo*
Star Wars: Forces of Destiny 14, 102, 173–177
Star Wars: Rebels 13, 102, 151–165, 173–177
Star Wars: Return of the Jedi 174, 176, 177
Star Wars: The Clone Wars 8, 13, 152, 154, 162, 173–177
Star Wars: The Empire Strikes Back 159, 174, 177
Star Wars: The Force Awakens 104, 154, 159, 173
Star Wars: The Last Jedi 154, 156, 177, 178
stereotype 40, 94, 96, 98, 103, 106, 138, 144, 145, 153, 167
Steven Universe 13, 14, 107, 108, 189–201
Stockholm syndrome 84
Storm 101, 103, 109
Straczynski, J. Michael 32

strength 4, 5, 7, 8, 10, 51, 52, 58, 73, 78, 81, 83, 84, 96, 114, 144, 145, 158, 170, 178, 185, 189, 194
strong female characters 3, 24, 168
suffering 79, 86, 132, 133, 191, 192–201
Sugar, Rebecca 190, 199
suicide 80, 132
Supergirl 12, 14, 49–55, 59, 112, 170–172
superhero 8, 9, 12, 51–55, 75–77, 79, 83, 86, 101, 105, 112–114, 121, 122, 167–172, 184, 190, 191; *see also The Adventures of Superman*; *Agents of SHIELD*; Amanda Waller; America Chavez; *Ant-Man and the Wasp*; *Arrow*; Avengers; Batgirl; Batman; *The Bionic Woman*; *Birds of Prey*; *Black Lightning*; Black Panther; Bumblebee; Burqa Avenger; Captain America; Captain Marvel; Daredevil; Dark Phoenix; *DC Super Hero Girls*; Dreamgirl; *The Flash*; *Guardians of the Galaxy*; Harley Quinn; Hawkgirl; Inhumans; Iron Man; Ironheart; Katana; Kitty Pryde; *Legends of Tomorrow*; Lena Luthor; *Logan*; Luke Cage; Marvel; Miles Morales; Misty Knight; Ms. Marvel; Night Nurse; Patriot; *The Powerpuff Girls*; Quake; *Runaways*; Sara Lance; She-Hulk; Shuri; *Smallville*; Spider-Gwen; Spider-Man; Squirrel Girl; Storm; Supergirl; Superman; *Thor*; Vixen; Wonder Woman; X-Men; Zari Tomaz; *see also* comic books; costumes; superpowers
Superman 8, 49, 51, 53, 55, 112, 167, 168, 170
superpowers 84, 87, 115, 123, 184
Sutherland, Alyssa 68–70
Sweden 62
symbolism 13, 31, 39, 44, 130, 142, 160, 197

third wave feminism 6, 9, 13, 52, 54, 56, 153, 155
13 Reasons Why 38
Thompson, Tessa 96, 101, 108, 109
Thor 108, 171
time's up 10, 28
tokenism 53, 104, 121
Torres, Gina 101, 102, 106
torture 9, 21, 85, 127, 132, 133, 159, 190
torture porn 127
toxic males 13, 23, 75, 79, 81, 84, 117, 159
Tran, Kelly Marie 177
trans 7, 9–13, 33, 38–43, 55, 102, 103, 140, 151, 155
transmedia 167, 171, 175
trauma 13, 42, 75–80, 83, 85, 86, 88, 99, 127, 132, 164, 193, 195, 198, 201
trickster 105, 123
trolls 12, 13, 167
True Blood 9, 97, 108
Trump, Donald 10, 11, 55, 116, 120, 122, 124, 131, 185
The Twilight Zone 4
Twitter 11, 123, 156, 168, 169

The Umbrella Academy 108
Under the Dome 96
utopian 27, 41, 197–201

Valerian and the City of a Thousand Planets 100, 106, 108
vampire 97, 104, 105
The Vampire Diaries 97, 104
vengeance 70, 82, 85, 95, 99, 106, 161, 190, 195
victim 66, 76, 83, 123, 127, 128, 195, 197
Vikings 14, 62–73, 122
villainess 34, 40, 69, 102, 181
violence 7, 24, 75, 114, 129, 190, 191, 199
Vixen 105, 108, 112, 114, 123
voice 26, 28, 113, 115, 138, 153, 156, 194

Wachowskis 30–44
The Walking Dead 12, 93–97, 109
waves *see* first, fourth, second, third
waveless feminism 155, 163
Weaver, Sigourney 49, 50, 135
werewolf 105
Western 55
Westworld 40, 102, 109
What Comes After 93
white 8–10, 12, 23, 24, 32, 40, 53, 55, 76, 77, 81, 83, 87, 88, 93–106, 111, 113–115, 127–136, 145, 146, 156, 170, 171, 180, 187, 191
White Diamond 198, 200
white savior 98–100
white supremacists 116, 118, 127, 131, 133, 134
widow 67, 129, 161
wife 20–26, 37, 64–71, 76, 87, 100, 112, 118, 129, 132, 154
Will & Grace 7, 10
Wilson, G. Willow 180, 181, 183
Winnick, Katheryn 63, 65, 71, 72, 73
witch 58, 104, 105
womb 194
Women in Refrigerators 113; *see* fridging
Women's March 10, 11, 28
Wonder Woman 1, 5, 14, 52, 119, 167–172, 187
working-class 5, 86, 141
World War II 118
Wright, Letitia 96, 101, 132
A Wrinkle in Time 96, 100, 109
Wynonna Earp 14, 49–59

X-Men (comic books) 120, 180
X-Men (2000) 101
X-Men: Apocalypse 101, 109
Xena: Warrior Princess 6, 7, 9

YouTube 11, 135, 169, 173, 180, 182

Zari Tomaz 110, 114, 115, 117, 119–123
zombie 93, 95